One God

The Histories and Beliefs of Judaism, Christianity, and Islam

William Paul Lazarus

Parson's Porch Books

One God: The Histories and Beliefs of Judaism, Christianity, and Islam
ISBN: Softcover 978-1-955581-60-8
Copyright © 2022 by William Paul Lazarus

Parson's Porch Books is an imprint of Parson's Porch *&* Company (PP*&*C) in Cleveland, Tennessee. PP*&*C is an innovative organization which raises money by publishing books of noted authors, representing all genres. Its face and voice is **David Russell Tullock** (dtullock@parsonsporch.com).

Parson's Porch *&* Company *turns books into bread & milk* by sharing its profits with the poor.

www.parsonsporch.com

One God

The Histories and Beliefs of Judaism,
Christianity, and Islam

Contents

Chapter One

Introduction

High school students around the country used to take a course that introduced them to many of the world's religions. In classes filled with children of many beliefs, teachers would talk about how a particular faith developed and how it spread.

Today, when it seems that the faithful in one religion are inevitably taking potshots at believers in another religion, people may have forgotten how life was in past eras. People of different faiths used to live and work side by side with little concern. At one time, Jews served as advisors and heads of state in Muslim countries. Christians and Jews worked together in Catholic Spain. Christians lived in harmony with Muslims in the Middle East.

Once, Jewish and Christian icons could be found in the Ka'baa, the holiest religious object in Islam, located in Mecca, the holiest city in Islam. Even today, Jerusalem hosts the Dome on the Rock, a sacred Islamic mosque, side by side with the Wailing Wall, the last surviving piece of the great Jewish Temple that once existed there.

Visitors to Jerusalem, the capital of Israel, can see religious Jews, wrapped in prayer shawls, trudging along ancient streets along with Muslims and Christians. Overhead, the cry of the Islamic muezzin, calling the faithful to prayer, rings out along with the tolling bells of Christian churches. The flag of Israel with the Star of David in its center flutters in the same breeze.

Such situations are too rare. Members of the three religions seem to fight more than they pray together. Over time, the three great religions have become separated by seemingly unbridgeable chasms. Actually, they are very much alike.

• They share a common heritage. They each tie their history to a single event and a single person who lived maybe 4,000 years ago.

• They worship the same God.

• They have similar holidays. Easter, for example, the holiest day in the Christian calendar, is tied directly to Passover, the most significant holiday in Judaism.

• They each believe Jerusalem is a sacred city.

There are many more links between the three faiths than differences.

The passing years have clouded how much Judaism, Christianity and Islam have in common. In fact, those comparative religion classes aren't offered any more in public schools. Too many people today have no idea how much these religions share.

Maybe it's time to review the past as a way to create a peaceful path into the future.

How to Use this Book

This book examines the three great religions that believe in the same God. They are among the oldest and most widespread religions on Earth. Jews, Christians and Muslims can be found on almost every continent and in every country.

Each chapter in the *One God* is designed to bring you closer to understanding what these people believe and how they reached this point in time.

This is a book for people who don't know about these three great faiths, but want to learn more. All three of these religions encourage education. They can claim most of the world's greatest scholars. They devoted their lives to helping understand the world. This book continues that honorable process.

All of the topics in these pages, of course, have been extensively researched by many researchers over the centuries. You can find books which devote thousands of pages to tiny aspects of each religion, whole libraries to the founders of each faith. This book gives you an overview. You will find each chapter stands alone. You can pick and choose what you want to know. Then, when you find you need additional information, you'll know what you are looking for.

How the Book is Organized

The book is divided into six parts.

Part I: History is a Happening Thing

This section introduces the origin of religion and explains the rise of a belief in one God. That's when the curtain opens on Abraham, a nomadic tribesman who is credited with fathering the three faiths. Little is known about him, but historians have uncovered lots of information about his time and beliefs.

This section will also explain how all three religions link their history back to Abraham.

Part II: Judaism, Christianity and Islam

This section explains how three different religions were nurtured on Abraham's vision. Each developed in a separate environment, endured hardships and setbacks, then became firmly entrenched in society worldwide.

Chapters 4 and 5 will concentrate on Judaism, the oldest of the three religions. The next two chapters, 6 and 7, will look at Christianity, which developed directly from Judaism. The third section, chapters 8 and 9, discuss Islam, which is younger and was born about 600 years after Christianity.

You will be introduced to beliefs, customs, traditions and rituals that characterize each faith. In many cases, you'll be able to see how one belief influenced another.

Part III: Shared Aspects Among the Faiths

In this section, you'll learn how members of the three religions have developed similar approaches to worship and to expressing their faith. You'll discover their sacred texts that serve as a bedrock to their beliefs, and you will tour their holy cities.

Part IV: Shared Ideas Among the Faiths

In this section, you will read about similar religious ideas and concepts that help link the three religions. They all look to a messenger from God, called a messiah, foresee the day when the world ceases, provide ways to forgive sin and propose ideas of what comes after death.

Part V: Misconceptions

This section presents many misconceptions about the three religions. These misunderstandings have helped drive a wedge between their members.

Part VI: Top 10 Ways These Religions Influenced the World

These three religions have produced some of the most important scholars and scientists who ever lived. Their influence goes far beyond the religious realm, directly creating the modern world.

Translations

Nothing is harder than taking an ancient text and trying to convert it into modern English. It's worse than wrestling pudding. At least, if you do that, everyone agrees that you are talking about pudding. With the ancient documents, particularly those seen as holy, some people even object to the concept of translating.

In chapter 10, we try to explain why it's so hard to translate the Bible and the Koran, the two principal sacred documents of the three faiths. Nevertheless, they are often the only texts that deal with ancient history, and we relied on the best translations we could find. Other writers may translate the words in a different way, but the gist will be the same.

Conventions

Historians today are moving toward marking time by using C.E. (Common Era) and B.C.E. (Before the Common Era.) The old way, B.C., meaning Before Christ, and A.D., Year of Our Lord in Latin, were seen as too religious. With so many scholars from so many different faiths working together, no one wanted to offend anyone else's beliefs.

We don't either and will use B.C.E. and C.E. We don't want to offend anyone. We just are trying to reduce chances of misunderstanding. We are sure our readers will agree.

Feedback

Please let us know what you think about this book. It took a long time to write and produce this book, so we'd love to hear your thoughts. You can write to me at wplazarus@aol.com. I will try to answer all comments.

Chapter Two

Gods

Once upon a time, long before Jesus or most of the religions of today existed, the world was filled with ideas about gods. People worshiped gods who were responsible for fire, birth, agriculture, health and everything else you can think of.

Holy Toledo! How many gods are there?

Some of those deities live on today in the names of planets: Mercury, the planet closest to the sun, was the name of the messenger god to the Romans. Mars was the god of war; Venus, the god of love. Earth is named for a goddess. Jupiter was the chief god of the Romans. Saturn was another god; so were Uranus and Pluto. Neptune, which appears blue in the sky, was named for the god of the ocean.

Days of the week also carry the names. Saturn does double duty: he gets a planet and Saturday. Wednesday is named for Wodin, the chief god of the Scandinavians; Thursday translates into Thor's day, named for the Norse god of thunder and lighting. Friday is named for Frigga, another Norse deity and wife of Odin.

In fact, for most of human history, people worshiped many gods. The idea that there may be only one god, what people who study religion call monotheism, is relatively new. Even today, only about one-third of all humans accept the idea that there is only one god. But, the followers of one god belong to two of the world's largest religions, Christianity and Islam, and developed their faith by following ideas generated by one of the smallest religions, Judaism.

Early Man Found Religion

Regardless of belief, mankind seems to have believed in something as far back as anyone can tell. Religion probably started first as magic. Archeologists found ancient pictures of animals painted on cave walls in France. These pictures show animals being killed. We think the early humans who painted them were trying to magically guarantee a successful hunt. In addition, early graves contain food and weapons to help the dead person survive after death. Also, many early carved images depict pregnant women, possibly more magical efforts to ensure new life.

Early people also had shamans, early religious leaders whose job was to induce the gods to help through magical incantations and symbols.

Eventually, however, people became aware that magic did not necessarily work. Despite the best efforts of shamans and their magic, rivers flooded, the rains didn't come or a beloved relative failed to get well.

As a result, some people concluded that powerful gods ran the earth and that they could only be placated by following rigid rules and prayer. Egyptians, for example, who developed one of the earliest civilizations, began to create rituals to "guarantee" that the Nile River flooded on time every year. They needed the Nile to flood, because it brought rich soil to their farm land. Without it, they would starve.

They started calendars to be sure to know exactly when their gods would send the floods.

Not that far away from Egypt, the Babylonians also built large pyramid-like structures to their gods and invented writing to record the amount of grain and beer worshipers donated to their temples.

Greek Gods Meet Egyptians

The Greeks were great travelers, and many of them visited Egypt and Babylonia. They brought back stories of the gods. They were particularly intrigued by the giant temples and monuments they found. One, the Sphinx, which is a massive carving of a lion with a man's head, ended up in a Greek play. Other ideas about gods began to circulate through the Mediterranean area.

Language and writing were enriched by this interchange. So were ideas about religion and religious views.

One goddess, Isis, moved from Egypt throughout the region. She was still being worshiped when Jesus lived.

Egypt tries one god

The Egyptians developed several important gods, including one named Ptah. He was once the chief deity of a city, but eventually became the main god of the country. The other gods were seen as manifestations of Ptah. As a result, some scholars think that Ptah represented the first monotheism theology. All people had to do was pray to him, regardless of other gods.

Later, after the god Amon had replaced Ptah in the Egyptian belief system, an Egyptian leader, named Amenhotep IV, became tired of having his rule interfered with by priests. So, he changed his name to Ikhnaton, and declared that the god Aton was the only god. This was the first known true monotheism and occurred about 1,300 years before Jesus. His belief was recorded in pictures on temple walls and in the magnificent bust of his beautiful wife, Nefertiti, which is considered the finest statue to survive from ancient Egypt.

Ikhenaton did not rule for very long, and his religion died with him. Only when ancient letters from his reign were dug up in the 1900s did we know how much confusion he caused.

Sigmund Freud, who introduced the science of psychology in the late 1800s, suggested that the priests of Ikhenaton may have taken their dying faith to the slaves, helping develop Judaism. Later scholars don't think that happened. However, Freud's idea reflects the importance of Semites in the creation of monotheism.

Semites: Fathers of Religion

One group of people living in the middle of all these religious ideas were called Semites. That term refers to a group that spoke a similar language. Scholars called them Semites from the biblical account of Noah's flood. In it, Noah escapes the rising water by building a large boat and stuffing it with animals and his family. Everyone in the world drowned, so everyone living now must be related to Noah's family.

One of his sons was called Shem (Sēm). All the people supposedly related to him today are still known as "Semites."

Most non-Egyptian residents of the ancient Near East were Semites, meaning we class their language with early Arabic, Hebrew and Aramaic. Today, Semite means Jewish to most people rather than a general term for a group of people that created a civilization in and around Babylonia. Several times, they invaded Egypt and conquered the land. Other times, they built great empires. The Babylonians, the Assyrians and the Israelites were all Semites.

They are also credited with developing modern monotheism.

Yahweh Steps Down from the Mountain

The first famous Semite who promoted monotheism was a man we know as Abram, who would later have his name changed to Abraham. We don't know exactly when he peered up at the Middle Eastern sky and began asking questions about God and life. One historian, American archaeologist William Albright, suggested that it was about 4,000 years ago. He based that dating on contracts Abram later signed with some neighboring countries like the Hittites and the Philistines. Unfortunately, both groups aren't around any more to check with and neither existed 4,000 years ago. The Philistines probably showed up in Israel about 3,200 years ago. The Hittites, who lived in what is now Turkey, were really important 3,400 years ago.

There's no point quibbling over dates, however. We really don't know a lot about what really happened 4,000 years ago anyway.

We do know only that a group of people, who claimed to be related to Abraham, identified their God as Yahweh. He was a mountain deity who appeared in thunder and lighting. His "still, small voice" was heard by those who believed in "Him" and who listened to "Him."

His commands and directions were eventually written down in books that were collected together in what we call the Bible.

Choosing to Go with Abraham

The children of Abraham believed in Yahweh. But, they weren't true monotheists for centuries. They had other gods. We see that in people's names, which contain the names of other deities. For example, an ancient Israelite prince's name included the name of the Canaanite fertility god, Baal, and so on.

Some of them endure today: Daniel, Nathaniel and Rachel, for example, contain the name of the bull god of the Canaanites, El. Later, followers of Yahweh borrowed that name and gave it to their God.

The multiple gods followed by Abraham's offspring disappeared in the seventh century B.C.E. The followers of Abraham's God, Yahweh, lived then in the small country of Judah and were threatened by the armies of the Babylonians. The Judean priests claimed to have found a book in the sacred temple that reported the history of the people and how God did not accept other gods. The king, Josiah, was so moved that he ordered the other religious symbols stored in the temple to be destroyed.

From that time on, monotheism was the only belief of these people, whom we know today as Jews. Their name was derived from the country, Judah, which was once the name of a mountainous region around their capital city, Jerusalem. The people living there were known as Judahites. When the Judahites became the largest tribe, then the name evolved into the name of the country and their religion, Judaism.

Josiah and His Faith

Josiah really felt that by worshipping one god, he and his people would be protected against the Babylonians. In those days, a people's deity was responsible for protection against other gods. If the enemy conquered, that meant the losers had a weaker god, so they gladly accepted the stronger deity as their own.

As a result, the 10 tribes north of Judah had banded together under the name of Israel. When they were conquered by the Assyrians around 723 B.C.E., they adopted the Assyrian gods and disappeared from history. We know them as the "10 lost tribes."

The priests of Judah had other ideas. They said that, win or lose, Yahweh was God. Moreover, there were no other gods. In a way, they had no choice. If they accepted the existence of other gods, and their country was conquered, their people would believe the other gods were stronger. Eliminating other gods, as Ikhenaton had done in Egypt, erased that threat to their belief.

The priests then instituted what became known as the watchword of the Jewish faith: "Hear, Oh, Israel, the Lord, our God, the Lord is one." Today, Jews recite this statement in every religious service, reaffirming a concept now at least 2,600 years old.

The priests went so far as to ban images of God. Previously, people always made idols to represent their deities. Jews did not. As a result, few Jews ever excelled in art. However, because music was allowed, Jews have given the world many great singers and composers, including Aaron Copland, Leonard Bernstein, George Gershwin, Oscar Hammerstein III and Irving Berlin.

The priests made one other significant upgrade on their belief: they insisted their God was not just responsible for just the Jews, He was universal. Previously, deities were assigned different countries as their "portion." With no other gods, Yahweh was responsible for everyone.

There was even a sacred book written at this time to stress that point.

The prophet Jonah, in the text that bears his name, is ordered by God to go to Nineveh to preach to the people there. Nineveh was the capital of Assyria, so the people Jonah was to talk to were the members of the 10 conquered Israeli tribes now living in their conqueror's land. Jonah doesn't want to go, so God sends a "great fish" to swallow him and deposit him on Assyrian soil.

Jonah reluctantly preaches to the people and, to his amazement, his audience listens.

This is the first recorded incident where God is seen as universal, not limited by any borders or even the condition of His believers.

Find Protection Without Winning

The teaching in the book of Jonah, which is in the Bible, became important when, first, Josiah was killed fighting the Egyptians and, then, the Babylonians conquered tiny Judah. The Jews, like the Israelites in the north, were required to leave their homeland. However, they carried the idea of monotheism with them.

As a result, they were not tempted to follow the Babylonian gods. When the Persians defeated the Babylonians about 60 years later, the Jews were free to return home. They were convinced that God had acted on their behalf. Monotheism was now firmly entrenched.

Jews were the only monotheists then, but they soon had company.

Crossing in a New Direction

By 400 years after the Persians freed the Jews from Babylonian captivity, the Jews were locked in a terrible battle with their new rulers, the Syrians. The Syrians wanted to impose their own faith, but the Jews refused to forget their God.

The two sides fought for 25 years. The war is remembered in the holiday of Hanukkah, which means redemption. Jews recaptured their temple and started the annual celebration for that reason.

Finally, the Syrians left, and Jews established their own independent country. It did not survive long. The Romans took over in 63 B.C.E. Some Jews saw the Roman conquest as a decision by God to punish the Jews for failure to follow His laws. They looked for someone to lead them back into God's good graces.

In time, some people saw Jesus as that person, the "messiah," or anointed king. Born in Galilee, the northern part of the Roman state of Judea, he was crucified on a cross around 30 C.E. That cross became a symbol of a new religion, which took its name from the Greek word for messiah, Christ.

Paul Finds a Way to Link Beliefs

Christians argued that they had replaced the Jews as God's "chosen people." They also were sure the world was coming to an end, and that only people who followed Jesus' teaching would be taken into heaven.

That message was spread by a man we know as Paul. Like Abraham, though, we don't know what he looked like, but he left behind letters written to small congregations around the Roman Empire. These letters were combined with four biographies of Jesus to create another Bible, called the New Testament.

Eventually, Christians combined the Jewish Bible, what they called the Old Testament, with their book to create a single sacred text they called the New Testament. Jews do not recognize the New Testament.

Message Spreads Through the Empire

Paul traveled widely and was able to reach many people. He and his companions spoke at Jewish religious houses, called synagogues, and were able to convince many people to follow Jesus.

He taught monotheism, but said God sent Jesus to teach people the truth. Belief in Jesus would guarantee followers a place in heaven and forgiveness of their sins, he insisted.

Then, in 70 C.E., the Romans fighting Jewish rebels destroyed the Temple, the central religious site of ancient Jews. To many people, this was proof that God had deserted the Jews. Paul was dead then, but his message now took on new urgency. Christianity began to grow. Roman emperors fought against it, but by the fifth century, it had become the only legal religion of the empire.

The second great monotheistic religion was in place.

Islam, the Third

In the desert land southwest of Judah, another religion began to develop in the seventh century C.E.

Muhammad, an illiterate camel herder, listened to the stories of Jewish and Christian travelers. He lived in Mecca, a crossroads city and home to the most sacred object in the region. Called the Ka'baa, it was a stone believed to have come from heaven. Muhammad told relatives that the angel Gabriel visited him and called on him to become a prophet of God. In his language, the word God was pronounced Allah.

Muhammad began to reveal what he had been told. Meccan authorities were not happy with his statements, which undermined their own beliefs in multiple gods. As a result, Muhammad was forced to flee to another city. However, he built up an army big enough to fight back. He conquered Mecca, and his soldiers began to fan out across the Middle East.

They carried their religion, called Islam, which means "submission." Eventually, Muslim armies captured most of the southern part of the old Roman Empire and part of Europe.

The third of the great monotheistic religions had now taken its place under the sun.

All three would develop different rituals, manners of worship and holy texts. But, all link their beliefs back to that lone Semitic shepherd, Abraham.

Chapter Three

Abraham

We do know a little about Abram from some of the later stories written about him. We also have some idea what he might have looked like from various images carved into rocks and left in the ground for us to find. In his day, men wore thick, braided beards, so he would have worn one of those. And, he would have been dressed in a robe. Pants wouldn't come along for another 1,500 or so years.

Most importantly, he would have been a Semite. Abram lived during a great time for his region. A great king Hammurabi had finally ousted Elamites who had conquered the area a few hundred years earlier. Hammurabi, or, as he is also known, Amraphel, founded a new capitol in a city he named Babylon, which means "Gate of God." He then renamed the area Chaldea.

Even then, this area was very old. As best as archeologists and historians can piece it together, the Sumerians, who lived farther to the valley's south, founded the country of Babylonia. No one actually put down a wooden stake and surveyed the land. Boundaries were kind of irregular. Real estate in those days usually only had a definitive border if it were along a river, and most property lines were described as simply "we live over here," and "they live over there."

At the time, the region wasn't crowded. Sumer was the first civilization we know of in the valley. It came into being so long ago we don't know how they got started.

Jewish and Christian accounts specifically give credit to a Sumerian king named Nimrod for creating the city of Babel. According to Sumerian inscriptions, there was indeed a Nimrod, sometimes called Ninus, and was in the business of conquering and naming cities. He was also the builder of Nineveh in Iraq, which means the "habitation of Ninus." Not to mention that the main section of the Nineveh ruins is called Nimrud to this day.

A stone tablet records that King Sargon of Akkad destroyed Babylon about 4,350 years ago, as he conquered Sumer, and from that time forward, Babylon not only got its Akkadian name, but was also under new management.

Then, Hammurabi came along. The king decided to clean up so many years of misrule by organizing Chaldean laws into a written system, also known as the Code of Hammurabi. This was the first time a king had laws written down so all would know them, and local priests and judges could not change the rules at will. From the Code, we get the Judeo-Christian biblical statement "an eye for an eye," without crediting the source. That probably means it had become so much a part of the language by the time it would be written into the Bible that its origins were forgotten.

Writing was nothing new to Hammurabi. The oldest writing in the region was Sumerian, including clay tablets that were at least 1,000 years older than Abram. That language was lost over time, and we still can't translate. However, there are tablets from 4,800 years ago that we can read. Those are in cuneiform -- which looks like a chicken marched across wet clay -- and came from Abram's hometown.

Abram grew up under Hammurabi's laws. He lived in Ur in the southern part of Chaldea. Today, that land is part of Iraq. It was located southeast of Babylon, in what is now Iran. Eventually, Babylon gave its name to the whole area, sort of the way that Rhode Island started out as an island and now is the name for an entire state. Chaldea was located on rich delta land created by the deposits of the two great rivers of the area, Euphrates and the Tigris.

Ur is long gone, but it was quite a place in its time. People left stories about visiting Ur, making it seem like a kind of Las Vegas of the ancient world. Today, it's just rubble, but we can imagine what a thriving city looked like with stone houses, lots of tents, a palace or two for any royalty, a mansion for the governor, stony streets, plenty of roaming dogs and pigs, carts pulled by small, overburdened donkeys, and open-air food markets where a shopper could pick through figs, dates, pomegranates and grains like wheat, barley and rye. There would have been plenty of beer. Not the sudsy drink sold today. Some of the oldest records ever found explain how to brew beer properly. You might not have liked the stuff. It was pungent and acrid, sort of like mead left out for a few days to ferment even more. Some of the beer was thick enough to need a fork.

Here and there would have been impressive temples. One or two would have been shaped like a layered triangle, called a ziggurat, with stones laid on top of each other so that a priest could climb to the top.

Worshipers there prayed to the goddess Sin or the biggest and most powerful god Marduk. There were plenty of gods to go around. The

Chaldeans, like most people in those days, believed that different gods were responsible for various aspects of nature. So, some deity ruled the wind; another one brought rain, which, in a dry country like this, was very important. There were gods of fertility, another to punish people you didn't like and so on. Some of these gods started out in another, nearby culture, like Sumeria and Akkadia, but grew in popularity and were included in the pantheon of the time period. They didn't necessarily look like people. Idol figures sometimes resemble dragons, bulls, lions, and snakes.

Idols were everywhere. You could buy small ones from the idol shops on the street. There were big ones at some city gates, outside richer people's houses, and, of course, at the different temples around town.

Most idols were made of clay, baked and painted or enameled. Having an idol was a reminder of and sign of respect for the god it represented, much like some people have crosses or menorahs on display in their homes or offices today. It was also a public display that showed how the owner of a big idol might be a little bit more religious than the guy who had a smaller idol outside his doorstep. People knew the idol wasn't a god, but figured having the image of a god around couldn't hurt. After all, these deities sometimes did some pretty awful things, like terrible storms, fires or invasions. You wanted to be on their good side.

A Greek visitor much later than Abram lived left this account of what one temple in Babylon looked like.

Below, in the same precinct, there is a second temple, in which is a sitting figure of Marduk, all of gold. Before the figure stands a large golden table, and the throne whereon it sits, and the base on which the throne is placed, are likewise of gold. The Chaldeans told me that all the gold together was eight hundred talents' weight. Outside the temple are two altars, one of solid gold, on which it is only lawful to offer sucklings; the other a common altar, but of great size, on which the full-grown animals are sacrificed. It is also on the great altar that the Chaldeans burn the frankincense, which is offered to the amount of a thousand talents' weight, every year, at the festival of the God. -- *Herodotus History of the Persian War I:183*

Of course, an idol was due the same respect as the god it represented. That meant sacrifices. Babylonia gods demanded and got lots of sacrifices. In fact, those ancient records about beer were actually made by priests keeping track of donations and sacrifices.

Taxes went to the ruler so he'd protect you. But, there were limits to what a human ruler could do. If you wanted rain, better crops, or someone healed, you offered a sacrifice to the god you believed could do it. The bigger the favor, the more expensive or precious the sacrifice. Leaving bread in front of an idol might get you a day's good luck, but saving the family farm from vengeful neighbors might cost you a sheep or goat. Something bigger might cost a child or a slave. Human sacrifice was not common, but not unheard of in old Chaldea.

But, how could a clay god "demand" a sacrifice?

The priests spoke for the gods. They told everyone the rules. How did the priests know? They got the word directly from the gods in divine inspiration or they read holy scrolls and made interpretations. Typically, the priests worked for the king, and the king got his right to rule from the gods. Kings were usually related to the gods somehow, as a son of a god, or as the human manifestation of a god on Earth. This was a pretty cozy situation.

Abram would have known all about the gods. His father, named Terach, made idols, the stone and/or wood representations of the various gods. We don't know that for sure, of course. No one has ever found an idol with any trademark from the manufacturer. Still, that's what we are told.

Under normal conditions, Abram would have stayed in Ur. It was a big, prosperous city even when he was there. It had been bigger and greater hundreds of years earlier when its reputation was pretty wild, but Ur would have more than a country outpost 4,000 years ago.

It wasn't Babylon, of course, the capital a few hundred miles to the northwest. Abram could have dreamed of going there, like young people today dream of living in New York, Los Angeles or some other major city. People did not travel much in those days, but an adventurous young man like Abram would have had no trouble getting wherever he wanted to go. The whole region was linked by canals and waterways. Some provided water to crops; others carried travelers around the bustling metropolis.

If Abram was a homebody and not inclined to float off anywhere, he might have dreamed of taking over his dad's business. Or, he might have wanted to own land and have his own flock of sheep. Maybe, he considered becoming a salesman and sending up deals with companies in Aram -- that's what the people called Syria then -- or in Egypt. He would have spoken Aramaic. That was the language of Aram, which sat in between

Chaldea and the rich and ancient land of Egypt. Everyone who wanted to be a successful businessman then had to learn Aramaic, just as corporate leaders worldwide these days have to learn English.

In some ways, it really doesn't matter what Abram thought, because his future changed right along with his dreams. Urged on by a divine voice, he left Ur. He left his father. He left his idols.

There's a lovely Jewish story that, prior to leaving, he smashed his father's idols. One day, when Abram was left alone to mind the store, he took a hammer and walloped all of the idols except the largest one. He placed the hammer in the hand of that giant idol. When his father returned and asked what happened, Abram said, "The idols got into a fight, and the big one smashed all the other ones."

His father said, "Don't be ridiculous. These idols have no life or power. They can't do anything."

Abram replied, "Then why do you worship them? They have eyes but see not," he told his father. "They have ears and hear not."

With that, he rejected the faith of his father, his grandfather and all the Chaldeans who preceded him.

Instead, he chose to believe in a god who later identified himself as Yahweh and made him an offer: if Abram would leave his home and his family, then God would make him a great nation and bless him. Abram accepted this offer, and the *b'rit* (covenant) between God and his descendents, who became known as Jews, was established. (Genesis 12).

The idea of a *b'rit* is fundamental to Judaism. Jews believe they have a special contract with God, which involves rights and obligations on both sides. In the book of Exodus, God revealed the Torah, and the entire nation responded, "Everything that the Lord has spoken, we will do." According to Jewish tradition, every Jewish soul that would ever be born was present at that moment, and agreed.

By that same tradition, Abram was subjected to ten tests of faith to prove his worthiness for this covenant. Leaving his home was one of these trials. Perhaps symbolizing the new relationship with God, Abram got a new name.

Neither shall thy name any more be called Abram, but thy name shall be Abraham; for a father of many nations have I made thee. -- *Genesis 17:5*

"H" in Hebrew is the symbol of life. Perhaps that's what the additional letter meant. We do not know. Abram actually means "My father is Ram," a reference to a pagan god. The story about the new name is in the Bible, the book that collected all the tales about Abraham and his family, as well as the many people who lived after him. The names Jews and Judaism derive from one of Abraham's grandsons, Judah.

Still, Abraham is called "the first Jew."

However, Abraham was not a Jew. He lived long before there were Jews. Instead, according to Jewish scripture, God spoke to Abraham and promised him that, if he obeyed the will of God, he would become the "father of many nations." Abraham rejected idolatry and obeyed the one God.

However, Abraham did not exactly become the father of nations. Instead, he became the father of Western religions. Three different faiths trace their origins to him.

The smallest and oldest, Judaism, accepted Abraham's vision and followed his God. They produced the earliest literature collected in the Bible and continue to be faithful to the God who first called Abram from his father's shop maybe four millennia ago. They called themselves "the chosen people," a designation that meant not that they were special, but that they were designated by God to carry his message to the rest of the world.

The second religion is called Christianity and is based on a belief that Abraham's God sent his only son to earth as an atoning sacrifice for the sin of disobedience caused by Adam, the first man. His sin was so great that only a great sacrifice would atone for it. The name of God's son is Jesus, and Christians believe he rose from the dead as a promise of eternal life for those who put their faith in him.

Two authors who told the story of Jesus left us genealogies, tracing Jesus back to Abraham. In the opening chapter of Matthew, we read,

The book of the generation of Jesus Christ, the son of David, the son of Abraham. Abraham begat Isaac; and Isaac begat Jacob; and Jacob begat Judas and his brethren. *In verse 16, we reach Jesus:* And Jacob begat Joseph the husband of Mary, of whom was born Jesus, who is called Christ.

Luke, the other author, starts detailing Jesus' family heritage in Chapter 3 of his account and goes back toward Abraham:

And Jesus himself began to be about thirty years of age, being (as was supposed) the son of Joseph, which was the son of Heli, ...which was the son of Jacob, which was the son of Isaac, which was the son of Abraham .."

The evangelist continues on, recounting the generations to Adam.

Christians actually started as Jews who believed in Jesus as an anointed king, a "messiah" who was to rule over the Jews. However, in time, Jews added prayers to their services that the followers of Jesus could not accept. Christian leaders said that Jesus "fulfilled" God's requirements and that, therefore, they assumed the mantle of "the chosen people" from the Jews. That view naturally caused a lot of animosity that continues to this day.

The third major religion, called Islam, was founded around 620 C.E. by a one-time camel herder named Muhammad. He was raised in Mecca to believe in the desert gods, but said the Archangel Gabriel called him to announce a belief in one God whom he called Allah. Muhammad said that Allah is another name for Yahweh, the name the Jews gave God, and that the Arabs are descents of Abraham, too. Unlike the Jews and Christians, who trace their lineage to Isaac, Abraham's son with his wife Sarah (initially spelled Sarai before it, too, was changed). Arabs insist their distant father was Ishmael, Abraham's oldest son. His mother was Hagar, Sarah's handmaiden.

According to the Bible, when Sarah could not conceive, she allowed Hagar to sleep with Abraham so that her husband would have a direct heir.

Now Sarai, Abram's wife, had borne him no children. But she had an Egyptian maidservant named Hagar; 2 so she said to Abram, "The Lord has kept me from having children. Go, sleep with my maidservant; perhaps I can build a family through her. Abram agreed to what Sarai said. So after Abram had been living in Canaan ten years, Sarai his wife took her Egyptian maidservant Hagar and gave her to her husband to be his wife. He slept with Hagar, and she conceived. ...So Hagar bore Abram a son, and Abram gave the name Ishmael to the son she had borne. Abram was eighty-six years old when Hagar bore him Ishmael. -- *Genesis 16*

Sarah wasn't exactly happy with the news and forced Hagar and her baby to run away.

The angel of the Lord found Hagar near a spring in the desert.

And he said, "Hagar, servant of Sarai, where have you come from, and where are you going?"

"I'm running away from my mistress Sarai," she answered.

Then the angel of the Lord told her, "Go back to your mistress and submit to her." The angel added, "I will so increase your descendants that they will be too numerous to count." -- *Genesis 16*

Muhammad thought Jewish residents of his area would accept this new Abrahamic faith, but was rejected. In turn, he founded Islam, which means "submission." His followers are known as Muslims. Within 75 years of his death, Arab armies had conquered much of the Middle East and part of Europe in the name of this new Prophet.

Today, the Muslim faith, along with Christianity and Judaism, touches lives worldwide. Together, about 33 percent of all humanity worship in one of these three faiths.

Since the 7th century, members of the religions have continued to battle for the minds and hearts in often open warfare that has seen crusades, massacres, terrorism and death continue virtually nonstop into our time. Yet, at the core of each religion stands a man named Abraham, a simple Chaldean who was inspired to greatness and still commands our attention despite the passing generations.

Chapter Four

History Takes Some Strange Turns

How do we know what happened when Abraham lived? How about Moses, the leaders of the Jews after they fell into Egyptian captivity? Or, for that matter, how do we know anything about Jesus, Muhammad or what happened 4,000, 3,000, 2000, or 1,000 years ago?

We have a hard enough time figuring out what really happened when President John F. Kennedy was shot in 1963 or where former Teamsters President Jimmy Hoffa is buried. And, we have video cameras, tape recordings and lots of technical equipment to help us.

No one could imagine such devices when Abraham was breathing the air in Chaldea. No one kept notes. If they did, none survived. Most stories were passed along by word of mouth, a notoriously bad way to keep accounts straight. Anyone who has watched a TV crime show knows eyewitness accounts are very inaccurate. Few people could write in those days anyway. Literacy is a modern phenomenon, the result of universal, required schools that didn't show up until the mid-1800s. The first university wasn't founded until the 1100s. When Abraham lived -- or for that matter, Jesus and Muhammad -- the only people who could write were some priests and scholars who read holy books, and scribes who belonged to a distinct class and had special honors because of their unusual ability to record information.

Even if someone felt the urge to take a note, he wouldn't have anything to write it on except the sleeve of his robe, a leaf or a rag. Paper wasn't invented until much later. The Chinese did that, and no one in the Middle East knew the Chinese even existed for centuries. Our friend Herodotus, the "father of history," lived in the fifth century B.C.E., and he was sure people in India walked around with their heads under their arms. Imagine what he must have thought about the Chinese.

Many early people, especially the Egyptians, wrote on papyrus, which is the source of our word "paper," but actually was nothing more than river reeds beaten and dried together. It didn't last long when exposed to the wind and heat of the Middle East. The few written records that have survived typically were buried in ceramic jars.

Writing itself is very old. Written records go back about 6,000 years. They were usually left by priests who recorded how much worshipers donated ("tithed") to the particular temple. Later, we started to find records that businessmen kept. The words were really pictures, which were then combined in different ways to create separate meanings.

That kind of writing was superseded by letters developed by Semites living in Egypt around 1900 B.C.E., the reported time of Abraham. They shared the idea with their relatives. Eventually, it was picked up by Phoenician ship captains. The Phoenicians, who did a lot of sailing and lived in what is now Lebanon, were often hired to carry goods from their country to other lands around the Mediterranean Sea. Naturally, they needed to write down what they put on their ships and how much they received in payment when the goods were delivered.

Writing using the Egyptian pictures (called hieroglyphics) or Mesopotamian cuneiform was cumbersome, so the Phoenicians liked this new approach. Whoever thought of it took a picture, like one of a bull with horns. That became the letter A. You can see by removing the ends of the horns, eliminating dots for eyes and squaring the form how the bull turned into a letter. The word for house, Beth, turned into a B. G comes from the word for camel and so on. The word we use for the group of letters, alphabet, comes from the first two letters of the Greek alphabet: alpha, beta. Each letter became associated with a sound. In no time, this astonishing invention simplified communication and helped spread commerce. Writing was still difficult, particularly when it was supposed to be permanent. After all, kings, who wanted to brag about their successes forever, didn't want artists to reply on papyrus or other flimsy material. They wanted the information to amaze future generations. That required stone. So, they had pillars, called steles, carved with records of their achievements -- real or imaginary -- and added more carvings on tablets, images on walls and statues.

Unlike papyrus, much of that has survived. After all, stone is not affected by sunlight. It doesn't blow apart in the wind. It also can endure when enemy soldiers destroy a town. It doesn't burn. Papyrus doesn't have much of a chance under those dire circumstances. Of course, you can't use stone to line a parakeet's cage and it is a bit heavy to tote around. But, rulers were interested in longevity, not convenience.

Once the carving was done, everyone was interested in what the inscribed images meant. After all, they were all over the place, especially in Egypt and Babylon. Herodotus recorded that one pyramid he visited contained an inscription reporting how many leeks and onions the workers who built the structure ate. That was not true, but the Egyptians festooned their walls with stories of their gods, heroic activities of their pharaohs and more. We find the first references to Semitic people captured in those stylized pictures.

No one could read them, however, until relatively recently. In 1799, French Emperor Napoleon Bonaparte invaded Egypt and brought along some scholars to help explain the many ancient buildings his men found there. Eventually, soldiers building a fort discovered a stone with writing on it.

Dating from 196 B.C.E., the Rosetta Stone, named for the town where it was found, contained two languages in three formats. One was hieroglyphics, then the language of priests, but which by the 18th century, no one could understand. The second was called demonic Greek, which was the common script of Egypt when the stone was inscribed. The third was Greek, which was then the language of the Egyptian pharaohs 2,200 years ago.

The text was prepared by a group of priests to honor their Egyptian pharaoh by listing all of the things that their ruler had done that are good for the priests and the people of Egypt.

By 1822, young French scholar Jean-François Champollion was able to translate the hieroglyphs by figuring out what letters corresponded to the Greek in the Rosetta text. He had to make some educated guesses, but he broke the code. Suddenly, we had a wealth of information that had been locked in stone for centuries.

His efforts encouraged others to begin to search through history. People hadn't really thought about the past. Old structures were simply demolished and the building materials reused. Even famed cities mentioned in the Bible lay buried under mounds of dirt. But, times were changing. The flood of Egyptian artifacts and translations, coupled with increased interest in the real historical nature of sacred texts like the Bible, created real enthusiasm for uncovering the lost past.

The most prominent of early archeologists was Heinrich Schliemann, a German whose father was a pastor in a small church. Born in 1822, he dedicated his life to becoming wealthy. No wine, women or song for this hard-nosed businessman, although he eventually married three times. He figured that knowledge would help him achieve financial success and learned Dutch, English, French, Spanish, Russian, Italian, and Portuguese, among other tongues.

With his language ability, he got a job working in Russia with an import/export firm. As the lone representative of that company in that vast country, he started down the road to wealth. Then, he followed his late brother to the United States as the gold rush began in California and made another fortune by creating a bank in Sacramento to buy and sell gold dust.

Eventually dissatisfied with mere cash, he turned to Homer, the Greek poet, and found inspiration in the stories of the battle of Troy described in the Iliad. So, in 1868, Schliemann went looking for the fabled city. Some scholars had been searching before him, but no one had enough money to really investigate thoroughly. Schliemann did. After some reading, he focused on a small hill in Turkey and hired local residents to burrow their way into the mound. He didn't know anything about surveying the area, preserving artifacts or normal archaeological procedures of today. Actually, no one else did then either.

Eventually, he discovered a treasure trove featuring a copper shield, cauldron, and vase, two golden cups and a silver goblet, seven double-edged daggers, lance-heads, and more. He was sure they came from the palace of Troy's last king, Priam. He smuggled the items from the country. Later, when the treasure was dated, it turned out to be even older than Homer's Troy.

Next, he turned his eye on Mycenaean culture, which is part of Homer's epic and spanned the years 1700-1100 B.C.E. Sure enough, his men uncovered many long-forgotten artifacts in other digs.

By the time he died in 1890, Schliemann had generated a worldwide interest in the ancient world. The search was on for anything and everything that could be found. Old ruins were examined. Even ancient garbage heaps were pored through for clues about long-forgotten people and their lifestyles.

Archeologists began to pierce the dark cloak of time, finding civilizations unmentioned in history books. The Hittites, for example, known only in the Bible turned out to be a mighty people who split the known world with the Egyptians at one time. Who knew?

Archeologists principally focused on the Middle East principally because of its connection to the holy books of the major religions. On Sumerian cuneiform tablets, they discovered a book containing what looks like the beginnings of Jewish, Christian, and Islamic creation stories, and even an account of the great flood and life-saving ark. The Babylonian "Epic of Creation," known as the *Enūma Eliš*, is far older than the Bible. Historians deciphering it were startled to read an account of creation similar to the one in the Bible. The account of how the Babylonian god created the world were spread across six clay tablets. The seventh stone praised the deity's work and greatness.

These texts were first published in Europe and America in 1876 as *The Chaldean Genesis*. The *Gilgamesh*, another epic which contains a story about a worldwide flood, was written on five tablets.

Other archeologists found multiple tablets in the ruins of the library of Ashurbanipal, the king of Assyria. His capital was Nineveh, and he clearly loved knowledge. He gathered documents from around his realm, had his scribes translate them into Assyrian and stored them in a giant building. Although the Assyrians were eventually conquered by the Babylonians, most of the stone documents survived the inevitable destruction. Nineveh is long gone, but the stone tablets live on to tell many tales.

Which came first: the Sumerian/Babylonian accounts or the biblical stories? Determining the age of the documents is not easy. One way is to look at the inscription. Those writings in an alphabet are younger than those that are solely comprised of hieroglyphics or cuneiform, for example. Then, there are names. Different cultures adopt different names. The big clue to the age of Sumerian tablets was that the scribes who made them signed them. Old Sumerian documents feature non-Semitic names, since the Sumerians were not a Semitic people. However, Semitic names were on many of the recopied Sumerian stories. As a result, historians believe these documents were written before Semites under King Sargon took over Babylonia about 4,350 years ago.

We can see that the Bible stories are younger. Apparently, later scribes, aware of the creation stores from ancient Sumeria and Babylon, updated the accounts in what became the Bible.

Not everyone believes that, of course. Many people insist that the Bible (and the Koran, which also has some history in it) was inspired by God. They argue that the writer of Genesis, the first book of the Bible, did not copy older Sumerian stories, but wrote their own versions from a "shared experience" of the events themselves. This would mean that both the Sumerians and the authors of Genesis knew of the same stories, and wrote them at different times and in different places. That doesn't seem likely.

In more recent times, we have been able to more accurately pinpoint dates through the use of a natural element called Carbon 14. Here's how the system works. Everything, including humans, are made of carbon. Carbon atoms are usually comprised of 12 small elements, called neutrons and protons. However, one type of Carbon has 14 of those wee bits. Although much rarer than Carbon 12, Carbon 14 is absorbed naturally by plants and animals in the same way. Fortunately, the amount of Carbon 14 in plants and animals stays constant. That means your body has a certain percentage of Carbon14 atoms in it, and all living plants and animals have the same percentage.

At the same time, Carbon 14 is radioactive and deteriorates at a known rate. About half of the supply in any living creature is gone in 5,700 years. As soon as a living organism dies, however, it stops taking in new carbon. That means no more eating carbon. With death, Carbon 14 starts decaying, but Carbon 12 doesn't.

To figure out time, then, all you need to know is how much Carbon 12 there is, subtract the amount of Carbon 14 from how much there should be, and compare the two numbers. There's a whole mathematical formula for it, but it doesn't matter. It works. As a result, it is possible to determine the age of any formerly living thing fairly precisely up to 50,000 years.

Other chemicals with similar properties have helped us push back that timetable far beyond anything previously imaginable. Potassium 40 is another radioactive element. It has a half-life of 1.3 billion years. Other useful radioisotopes for radioactive dating include Uranium 235 with a half-life of 704 million years; Uranium 238, with a half-life of 4.5 billion years; Thorium 232, which has a half-life of 14 billion years; and Rubidium 87 with a half-life of 49 billion years.

Carbon 14 remains the most popular for our use since we are checking ages on items less than 6,000 years old.

That process worked for bones, wood, cloth or anything made from something that once lived, like papyrus. It was not effective for stones, unless the stones were charred. That black soot on burned stones is carbon. It can be scraped off and dated. Maybe we should thank all those marauders who burned down towns.

All of a sudden, we were able to accurately date a particular inscription or other document. Scientists are aware there is always a danger of contamination in the process. After all, many of those burned stones lay under rubble or dirt for centuries. Fortunately, modern chemists using increasingly sensitive equipment have found a way to isolate out the impure particles. That's why the Shroud of Turin, the famed cloth that supposedly was used to cover the dying Jesus, is now known to have been created around the 1300s C.E. and not when Jesus lived.

There are other ways to date items, too. For example, an artifact found in a particular layer of ground amid other items can be plausibly dated by its location. Debris can be dated, too. People used to write curses against opponents on ceramic jars and throw them to the ground. The broken shards have survived. The names on them can be traced by the style of writing and letters to a particular period in history.

So can the ceramic jars themselves. Each ethnic group produced its own style of containers, which were the principal way to carry and store food and goods. Skilled archeologists merely have to look at a particular jar to know what era it came from and which people created it. Home designs also varied as did the architecture of royal buildings. Even methods of farming shifted from place to place. The clues were everywhere, and all of them could be dated.

Remember those garbage heaps? They are called middens and have turned up a storehouse of information. For example, one collection of villages in ancient Canaan were found to have plenty of animal bones -- dated to at least 3,400 years ago -- but no pig bones. Since Jews are banned from eating pig meat, it is possible these villages represent the first proof of early Jewish settlements or do they belong to a group of people whose disinterest in pork was absorbed into Jewish beliefs. Without further information, no one really knows.

Ancient cities mentioned in the Bible have been dug up, like Jericho, Jerusalem, Megiddo and Bethel. We have found they were rebuilt many times and are able to date each level of construction. Jericho turns out to be perhaps the oldest continually occupied city on earth.

Then, too, there are all those documents and inscriptions. Scholars have devoted their lives to deciphering their meanings, translating strange languages into modern tongues. Historians like Herodotus left us many books.

So did Manetho, a second-century B.C.E. Egyptian who was upset after reading about his country after reading newly translated sacred Jewish books. He thought the Jews maligned his beloved homeland. So, he wrote his own history of Egypt, insisting that Jews were not slaves in Egypt, built no cities nor escaped. His text, titled, *Aegyptiaca*, is a collection of three books detailing the history of ancient Egypt. It was commissioned by Pharaoh Ptolemy II as part of his attempt to combine Egyptian and Hellenistic cultures.

To fulfill his ruler's wish, Manetho used archives held at the temple where he served as priest. His works did not survive, but have been reconstructed by citations appearing in other books, including those by Josephus, the greatest Jewish historian of the first century C.E.

All of this data has been brought to bear on religious stories. For example, consider the story of Joseph. It appears in Genesis, the first book of the Bible. In the account, Joseph is one of 12 children of Jacob, Abraham's grandson. We find the name Jacobel in a letter dated to the 14th century in the Amarna material. That Jacob was writing vainly to his pharaoh for help because marauding tribes were challenging his community.

In the Bible story, Joseph was Jacob's favorite, but he alienated his brothers by relating dreams that show them subservient to him. They took the coat of many colors that Jacob gave him -- based on tatters found in middens, ancient tribes favored specific colors, much like sporting teams today -- and sold Joseph to a caravan of nomads in camels slowly plodding toward Egypt.

Once in Egypt, Joseph worked for a man named Potiphar, but was thrown in jail for allegedly trying to seduce Potiphar's wife. There, he met two former royal officers and correctly foretold their fate based on their dreams. When the pharaoh had a dream he couldn't understand, involving fat and thin cattle, he called for Joseph, who said the cattle represent years and predicted seven years of plenty followed by seven years of hunger.

The pharaoh then selected Joseph to save the country by storing grain. Joseph did, even giving excess supplies to starving people from outside Egypt, including his father and brothers.

Because of his success, Joseph was able to invite his family to Egypt where they settled on rich delta land. That's the way the book of Genesis ends.

By examining artifacts, historians are able to discover a few things about this tale. To begin with, by checking bones, they discovered camels were not tamed until the 1100 B.C.E., long after Joseph must have lived. Camels were part of human diets prior to that time, but not widely tamed for use in caravans. He could not have been sold to the nomads. Money didn't exist then. Money as a legal means to purchase things didn't come into use until the 7th century B.C.E., and then first by the Lydians, who had plenty of gold and silver mines on their land in Greece.

Potiphar appears to be a Persian name, dating to the sixth century B.C.E. when the Persians conquered Egypt. In fact, the entire ceremony that invested Joseph with power after successfully interpreting the pharaoh's dream also exactly parallels the Persian ritual for the same purpose.

Historians found another ancient Egyptian book, one that is earlier than the biblical story. Called *Tale of Two Brothers*, it contains some of the episodes of life in Egypt that echo what happened in the biblical version. Joseph could not have been thrown in jail, because the Egyptians didn't have jails. The court official whose dream Joseph successfully interpreted while in prison carried a title only used during the Persian rule.

Famines were rare in Egypt; only two are known. One occurred in a small town in the seventh century B.C.E. There, the inhabitants stored the grain exactly as Joseph was said to have directed. Moreover, the use of cattle to mean years came into use, according to hieroglyphics, only in the third century B.C.E.

You can see that elements of the account -- and there are more -- are scattered over centuries.

Artifacts, too, have been carefully checked. A German author named Werner Keller wrote a popular book in the 1950s, titled the *Bible as History*, in which he described the discovery of stone knives supposedly used by Joshua, Moses' successor, to circumcise the Jews; wood from Noah's ark found on the designated landing area, Mount Ararat; and an Egyptian canal named for Joseph.

With Carbon 14 dating, archeologists showed that the knives were manufactured about the 9th century C.E., long after Joshua lived; the wood thought to be from the ark also was far more recent; and the canal was built long after Jesus lived, much less Joseph.

The work is continuing. Scholars are not trying to debunk pious stories. Rather, they are trying to create a complete picture of what really happened. Besides, correctly dating an artifact once thought to be associated with Abraham, Moses, Joseph, Jesus or anyone else does not mean the Bible is wrong. It only means that the artifact is not connected to those people in the text. Some other, yet unfound, artifact may be.

Chapter Five

Looking Up Chapter and Verse

Regardless of all the uncovered stones, inscriptions on walls and Carbon 14 dates of ancient trash, the real sources for much of what we know about the origins and history of our three monotheistic religions comes from their holy books.

Such books are not unusual. Every religion has sacred texts. Some are older than the Bible, the basic sources of both Judaism and Christianity. Virtually all are older than the Koran, the youngest of our trio. Each of the books includes historical information as well as philosophical, ethical, moral and social commentary. In some cases, as in the Koran, one person – Muhammad in this case -- provided the textual material. In the Bible, many different people, some called prophets, serve as our guides into the mind of God.

The Bible is the most famous of all religious books and the most widespread. It is the most published book in the world. In fact, the first book ever published in the Western world is the Gutenberg Bible produced in the mid-1400s. The printing press has continued to churn out those pages ever since.

The Bible has been translated into more than 2,300 languages or dialects with more on the drawing board. You can find a copy in the appropriate language in virtually every hotel room around the world, courtesy of the Gideons, a group convinced that the world would be better off if everyone read the Bible. Founded in 1898 by three friends, the Gideons – named for a biblical figure – hands out about 56 million Bibles a year. So, you can take the one in your hotel room and be confident someone will replace it.

The Koran (also spelled Qur'an and a variety of similar ways) is also distributed by a variety of groups in various countries in hopes of easing tensions between the religions. If you read the book, they believe, you are less likely to be misled by what other people claim is in the sacred text.

The texts honored by each religion have their own history. The Jewish and Christian Bibles are inexorably linked, at least from the Christian perspective. They believe the Jewish portion of the Bible, which they call the Old Testament, foreshadows the arrival of Jesus. In their view, the Christian portion, called the New Testament, fulfills the promise of the old.

From the Jewish perspective, however, there is only the one book, and the Christian half has no connection.

To help differentiate between the books, we will use the Christian designation of "old" and "new," just for convenience.

Before we even look at the books, let's consider the name "Bible." What does that mean? It means "books." The same word shows up in bibliotheca, the formal name for a library. Derived from the Latin word for books, biblios, the name was introduced by an early Christian leader, Clement of Rome, in about 90 C.E. He suggested that acceptable books should be used to teach possible converts. The name stuck. In English, the term became Bible.

Why were the books written? That depends which half of the Bible we are talking about. Let's start with the most ancient.

Old Testament

This manuscript contains 39 books. They were written down for several reasons. The first six books were designed to tell the story of the Jewish people and describe God's plan for them. Scholars have dated the final writing from 700 to 400 B.C.E. Later books were added at various times, sometimes to inspire the Jewish people; sometimes to deal with perplexing problems or to counter existing ideas. For example, when some zealous Jews banned intermarriage in the 6th century B.C.E., someone produced the book of Ruth, which showed that one of Ruth's descendents is David, the greatest hero in Jewish history. It's as though someone wanted to trump the intermarriage crowd by throwing down the David card. No one could top David.

Some of the books, like Job, seem to have originated in other cultures and been edited to match up with Jewish ideas.

And some of the books were written after many Jews were forced into Babylonian captivity in 586 B.C.E. Their leaders didn't want their children, caught up in the overwhelming Babylonian culture, to lose sight of their own heritage. Most of the history previously had been memorized. Every time a historian lost a head, an awful lot of the past disappeared, too. Writing the stories down was the best way to preserve it.

Word for Aramaic Word

The Old Testament begins with Genesis and ends with Chronicles II. These book titles are familiar to English readers, but the original texts did not have any names. Jewish scholars designated each book by its first word or the name of the book's principal hero/heroine. For example, Genesis, which is a Greek word meaning "origin" or "beginning," is not the Jewish name of the first book. The first word of the Bible is "b'raisheet," which we translate, "In the beginning." So the name of the book to Jews is "B'raisheet."

In reality, these days, most Jews go along with the accepted Greek names.

All of the Old Testament books were written in two languages: Hebrew and Aramaic. Both are very ancient languages. You can tell because their letters run from right to left, opposite of English. That's because they were first used in inscriptions. Most people are right-handed (about 70 percent of any human population.) A right-handed person who is carving letters into stone must move his hand from right to left to avoid having his other hand, the one holding the chisel, block the letters that are finished. That way, the writer can see where he is in a sentence.

When people start writing on papyrus, the letters reverse so the scribe's hand holding a quill doesn't block the view of what's been written.

It's very logical, and it's another way we are able to date written material.

Aramaic was the language of Aram, as noted earlier, and Abraham's native tongue. Today, very few people speak it, although Aramaic still is used in some prayers in Jewish synagogues. At one time, Hebrew only existed in religious texts, the way Latin once survived only in Catholic masses. No one spoke Hebrew. However, when Israel was founded in 1948 as a homeland for the Jews, its leaders voted to replace English with Hebrew. As a result, Hebrew has become the only "dead" language ever revived.

What's in the Jewish Bible?

Jews divide the Old Testament into three distinct units:

1) The Law or Torah. This contains the first five books, Genesis, Exodus, Leviticus, Numbers and Deuteronomy. The first book covers creation of the world and man through the arrival of Jacob, his 12 sons and families in Egypt. Exodus is the story of Moses who takes the Jews from captivity in

Egypt to freedom in Canaan, which is an old name for modern Israel. Leviticus and Numbers tell stories about what happened to the Jews on their journey with Moses along with the laws that the Jews are to follow after being "chosen" by God to bring His message to the world. Deuteronomy recaps the events and concludes with the death of Moses. It has often been called the "last will and testament" of the great leader.

2) Prophets. This section follows the first five books and includes what many people might think of histories -- the book of Joshua, who led the conquest of Canaan. This book was probably once part of the first five, then separated; Judges, the various tribal leaders who followed Joshua; Samuel, the last prophet who named the first King of Israel; an accounting of the kings of Judah and, after the country split in two in the 10th century B.C.E., Israel. Then, there are books named for individual prophets. Three of these volumes are linked to "major" prophets, a term used for prophets whose writing is extensive – Ezekiel, Jeremiah and Isaiah. The other prophets, like Amos, Nachum and Hosea, are considered "minor." That's because we have little of their writings, not because their words are considered less important.

The works may not be the original sayings of the prophets, which, by the way, doesn't mean that they were busy predicting the future. It actually refers to the fact they were conduits for God's word. Because of extensive investigation, for example, we know Isaiah actually contains works from three different writers. The statements were merged together at some point in the transcribing of the final version.

3) Writings. The last section includes everything from a prophet like Jonah who was swallowed by a "great fish," to Job, Esther, Daniel, Psalms, Proverbs and Song of Songs among others. Early Jewish scholars, called sages, recognized that these books were not necessarily fact, but rather philosophical and ethical volumes designed to guide readers. The book of Esther, for example, deals with a time when the Jews were living in Persia and faced a possible widespread massacre. Only Esther's heroics saved them. The name of God does not appear in the text, and it was the last book accepted into the Jewish Bible because of that. However, the sages thought its message was uplifting and important enough to be included among the sacred texts.

Of course, many more books were written and might have been considered sacred. Many of them have survived and have been included in what we call the Apocrypha. They are not considered holy, but are important to understanding the thoughts of the people during the time they were written.

The various biblical books appear to have been written at various times. Amos, for example, is thought to have lived in the 8th century B.C.E. Many Jews think the first five books were written by Moses, who must have lived anywhere from 1200 to 1400 B.C.E. That doesn't seem likely since internal evidence, such as word choice, reflects a much later time period.

We do know that the first five books were in final form by at least 2,300 years ago. They were already considered sacred by then. Other books obtained that status later. One reason the New Testament authors quoted books from the Writings so often is that those texts had only recently become considered sacred.

We don't know who wrote individual books. In those days, there was no such thing as "pride of authorship" or copyrights. People put famous names on books because they thought the books had a better chance of being read. Since no one published books – the printing press wasn't invented yet – only one copy of any book was likely to be available. So, no one was going to make money selling copies.

There has been speculation that Jeremiah's scribe, Baruch, might have written Deuteronomy. That would have been in the late sixth century B.C.E. We are told in Kings and in Chronicles II that a book had been found in the Jewish temple and that when the text was read to King Josiah, he responded by ordering a complete reformation of the temple and Jewish worship. Josiah was hopeful that the renewed religious spirit would encourage God to protect the Jews from the dangerous Babylonian army that would soon threaten the survival of his country.

Unfortunately, no one bothered to tell the Babylonians about the reformation. Josiah died in battle with the Egyptians in 609 B.C.E., and a later successor, Zedekiah, was captured by the victorious Babylonians, his two sons killed in front of him, then blinded and held captive for the rest of his life. We know that because stone tablets tracking the cost of maintaining the Judean king were found in the rubble created when the Babylonians got their comeuppance from the Persians.

In Jewish tradition, a man named Ezra, who also has a book in the Bible named for him, is responsible for combining the books into a single unit and reading it to the people, possibly in the 5th century B.C.E. Even earlier, in the book of Joshua, named for the successor to Moses, the great leader of the Jews, we are told that the law was read to the tribes.

Other books are credited to David, the second king of Israel or to his successor, Solomon. There's no question that some of the textual material is old enough to have been written during their lifetimes, but most of it is not.

As a result, despite nonstop speculation, we may never know when the books were written or by whom.

Understanding the Bible through JEPD

We are sure of one thing; the first five books of the Bible had multiple stories describing the same event. That was first noticed in the 1700s by Jean Astruc, the doctor to King Louis IV of France. A scholar who studied the Bible, Astruc looked closely at the words and realized that the Jewish Bible uses different names for God, such as Yahweh, Lord, God, Almighty and more. Each required a different word. Astruc wondered what would happen if he separated text using the different names as a key. To his amazement, at least four different strands emerged.

Astruc's insight is called the JEPD theory and is the most widely accepted explanation for the writing of the Old Testament. In Astruc's scheme, J stands for Jehovah; E for Elohim, a Hebrew word for God; P for priestly requirements and lists, such as who begot who and how many bullocks need to be sacrificed on a given day; and D for Deuteronomy, the last of the five holy books and one seemingly independent (and possibly written later) than the other four. Some scholars argue that Deuteronomy was first and the other books were written later to amplify the stories.

Astruc also showed that the J document came from the tribe of Judah, the last of the 12 original tribes to survive. E was produced by the northern tribes, which were led by the tribe of Ephraim. It's just coincidental that the J in Jehovah matches the J in Judah. However, generations of scholars are grateful for the parallel. Imagine how confused everyone would be if the J god went with the E tribe and vice versa.

Careful inspection of the text reveals various accounts in many parts of the text: creation, Noah and his ark, the renaming of Jacob to Israel, the appearance of David and so on. Each was written in a different part of Israel and then combined later. Since the editor didn't know which was correct, he kept both. So, in Chapter 1 of Genesis, man and woman are unnamed and are created at the same time from dirt. In Chapter 2 of the same book, Adam goes to sleep, and his rib is converted into Eve. The flood that Noah endured lasts a week in one story; 40 days in another.

Animals go on the ark seven by seven in one version; two by two in the other.

In some cases, the stories conflict. In the famous account of Abraham's near sacrifice of his son, Isaac, for example, the E god orders the sacrifice, while the J god stops it.

Many explanations have arisen to explain away the discrepancies. The second creation story merely explains the first, Jewish sages have said. However, the texts clearly are different and do not agree.

The important point is not that there are multiple stories, but that understanding how the texts were combined helps us appreciate the complex history of this hallowed book.

In the third century B.C.E., the first five books were translated into Greek. Called the Septuagint – from the Greek word for 70 – the translation helped spread the stories of the Jews throughout the known world.

They became a model for other writers. After the death of Jesus, more books began to appear that dealt with his life and the beginnings of Christianity.

New Testament

This portion of the Bible contains 27 books. Four are mini-biographies of Jesus. Then, there is a book called Acts of the Apostles, which describes events after Jesus died and concentrates largely on the activities of Paul, the first great evangelist of the religion. He toured the Mediterranean region in a tireless effort to set up colonies and to introduce Jesus to distant lands.

Some 13 letters, or Epistles to use the Greek word, attributed to him appear in the next group. That is followed by a prediction of the end of the world, The Revelation of St. John.

We don't know who wrote many of these books either. The first four books, or Gospels, carry a name of their title pages – Matthew, Mark, Luke and John – but actually first appeared without any names on them. The names, which were chosen from among the followers of Jesus, were added around 150 C.E. Luke and Acts is thought to have been written by Clement, a doctor in Rome, and once been combined into a single book.

Paul did write some of the letters attributed to him. Based on computer analysis of word choice and style, scholars think at least six of the 13 epistles in the New Testament are authentic, maybe seven. The rest were produced by people who used Paul's name to get their thoughts accepted by a wider audience. All were extensively edited.

Revelation is attributed to John, a disciple of Jesus, but most scholars believe it was written too late for that to be the case.

Intense study has concluded that Matthew was probably written in Egypt; Luke and Mark in Rome; and John probably in what is now Turkey.

Mark is clearly the oldest book, an idea first suggested in the 1800s, but now universally accepted. That's because 80 percent of Matthew appears in Mark, not the other way around. Mark is also written in rougher language, while Matthew is smoother and written by someone who was better educated.

Three languages were used in the New Testament: Kone, the everyday Greek of the time period; formal Greek, the kind used by sophisticated, educated people; and Aramaic. Scholars have suggested that Matthew was first written in Hebrew, which is why the Roman Catholic Church placed that book ahead of Mark in the table of contents. Others have suggested that the books were initially written in Aramaic and then translated into Greek. No evidence exists for either of those suggestions, and everything that's been turned up points to Greek as the original language.

The books appear to have been written to resolve questions arising long after the death of Jesus. He must have died by at least 33 C.E., while the texts do not appear until after 70 C.E. – some scholars date Mark to the 50s, but there's no evidence to support that. Mark hints at the destruction of the Temple, which occurred that year. That's another reason to think his book is the oldest. None of the other New Testament books comment on the Temple's destruction, which must have been a cataclysmic event in their day. Early followers of Jesus thought the world would end promptly. When it did not cease with his death, they thought he would return to complete the task. However, as years passed, they began to have questions. The texts may have been written to answer those concerns.

Also, the destruction of the Jewish temple in 70 C.E. by Roman troops may have promoted the writing. To many onlookers, the burning of the sacred site represented the departure of the Jewish God from his people. To followers of Jesus, this may have signified the moment they were waiting for – the beginning of the predicted end of the world. Matthew, who has Jesus travel with his family to Egypt, maybe have been writing to encourage Jews who had fled the Roman massacres in Israel and settled in the large Egyptian city of Alexandria. Many would have wanted to return home, which is what Jesus does in Matthew's account.

Matthew and Luke relied on Mark as their source. They also had another document, known as Q (German for "unknown") which provided additional information. However, neither read each other's book, which is why they disagree in many areas.

Matthew and Luke place Jesus' birth in Bethlehem. Mark and John imply he was born in Nazareth; they certainly make no mention of Bethlehem. His mother, Mary, is told by an angel in Luke that she will bear a child of God, but in Mark is puzzled by Jesus' behavior as if divine intervention was unknown. In Luke, a census sends the holy family scurrying to Bethlehem where Jesus is born. In Matthew, however, fear of King Herod's anger forces the same family to flee to the safety of Egypt. Matthew and Luke say Jesus belongs to the line of David; John flatly denies that. Only Luke has any story of Jesus' childhood. Few miracles appear in all four books. John begins Jesus' ministry with the attack on the Temple; the other books end the ministry there. They can't agree when Jesus was crucified or even what happens to him on the cross or afterwards. Mark, for example, has no resurrection account.

The authors relied on word of mouth; documents like the Gospel of Thomas, which was rejected as canonical and survived only by being buried in the desert; Jewish stories; writings in pagan texts about their gods; and many other sources.

By the fourth century, despite the lack of a good publisher (like this company), many books were floating around. No one knew what to believe. Church fathers were upset, as was Emperor Constantine. He figured that one empire deserved one holy book and demanded that all the philosophical debates stop.

Finally, in 382 C.E., Pope Damasus commissioned a young priest named Jerome to revise the Latin versions of the Gospels in existence. He didn't have to look far: Jerome was the pope's private secretary, but he was also a linguist who could speak, write and understand Latin, Greek and Hebrew. Jerome even knew Aramaic and was trained in Latin classics.

He began with the Jewish books first, then dove into the Christian texts. Eventually, his successors produced what became the official Bible. It's not clear if the Jews ever codified their texts. Jewish tradition insists that surviving sages met in the small Israeli town of Jamnia to collect the sacred books after the destruction of the Temple in 70 C.E. However, debates recorded in the Talmud, a collection of rabbinical commentary and stories, show debate raging over which books were truly holy as late as the fifth century C.E. Most books in the Old Testament were considered sacred by that time, but some of the books in the Writings section still hadn't received the stamp of approval.

Jerome changed that with his translations. Suddenly, in the 5th century C.E., as the western Roman empire was being overrun by pagan hordes, the world had a Bible.

The Koran

The process for the Koran was very different. Muhammad did not write anything down on stone, papyrus, paper or anything else, but his revelations were eventually collected and placed in manuscript form. The process must have been complicated. Muhammad is even accused in Muslim tradition of having edited the holy book improperly. Nor is there any record of a Koran existing for at least 20 years after the death of the Prophet. Some historians have conjectured that later writers wrote down material and backdated it.

Devout Muslims, of course, believe that Muhammad dictated every word.

Some historians argue that Ali, Muhammad's son-in-law, and Abu Bakr, Muhammad's military leader, argued over the succession to the prophet. Muhammad could have solved this problem by designating a successor, but never got that message. Ali began amassing the Prophet's revelations for the Koran, but not before several different versions were cobbled together.

Finally, a caliph about 20 years later gathered together all the copies of the Koran, reportedly changed some passages, destroyed the other versions and made six copies of the new edition. He relied on two sources: the written text that had been ordered by Abu Bakr and the various oral texts provided by Muslims who had memorized them during the lifetime of Muhammad. The text has been unchanged since then.

The Koran contains many Biblical characters, but provides alternative versions of familiar stories. Abraham is commanded to sacrifice Ishmael, not Isaac. Haman is believed to be the minister of Pharaoh instead of prime minister of Persia as listed in the book of Esther; and Mary, Jesus' mother, is identified as the sister of Aaron instead of Miriam.

The text is written in poetic style and in rhyme. Muhammad emphasized that the Koran is in Arabic, but limited words in the vocabulary forced him to borrow many foreign terms to express ideas. The combined languages adds a universal element to the revelations.

Today, the Bible and the Koran stand together as monuments of faith, each based on Abraham and his dedication to his new belief, and each trying to provide a path for their followers into the mind of God.

Chapter Six

Follow the Moving Finger

Every morning, Emily Cosgrove, an elementary school teacher in Illinois, picks up her Bible and, like many of you, randomly selects a passage to help guide her through to day. So does Pierre Moule in Paris; Masha Demetrieva in Russia; and Kaori Kyota in Japan. Adil Houriman in Morocco and Samrin Mascarenhas in Bangladesh duplicate that procedure, but with the Koran.

They are among possibly millions of people worldwide who go through the same routine, secure in the conviction that their sacred books contain the wisdom needed to endure the day. Their opinions have some justification. As we have seen, the holy texts provide a wealth of ethical and moral teachings, but may have some limitations with history.

Unfortunately, what they are reading may not be what the books actually say.

Emily -- who, like the others listed, is not a real person, but represents a massive host of people -- has to read her book in English. Pierre's Bible is in French. Masha needs Russian, while Kaori, naturally, looks at her Bible in Japanese. Adil's native language is Moroccan, while Samrin's is Bengali. None of them is reading the same book, nor are they reading what was actually written centuries ago. That's because those languages did not exist when the holy texts were written. They have to be translated.

How accurate are the translations? Not very. They can't be. Let's look at what that limitation means to the understanding of first the Bible, then the Koran.

Translating can be Such Sweet Sorrow

You can read these sentences easily because there are periods, commas, capital letters and other tools to help you. That was not true when the Bible was written.

Ancient Hebrew is simply a steady stream of letters from right to left. There are no capital letters, no commas, periods, exclamation marks or any other kind of grammatical mark. That's true in Greek, too. Hebrew did develop a few final letters to indicate to readers when a word ends -- which is one reason Hebrew sentences sound so similar. However, there are only a handful of final letters. As a result, reading the exact words can be difficult.

As an example, consider this English sentence: Godisnowhere. Does that say "God is now here" or "God is nowhere?" That decision would be up to the translator, who has a 50-50 chance of being right. The Bible is loaded with such problems. If that were the only one, maybe someone would figure out how to solve it. Actually, that's a minor complication. There's a far bigger one: Hebrew has no vowels.

Because Hebrew -- and ancient Greek, too -- are small languages, words often must do double duty. The word for ark, for example, refers to the Ark of the Covenant, Noah's Ark and the cradle that carried baby Moses in the Nile. That means that words that are spelled the same but pronounced differently have different meanings. Translating the correct meaning can only be done with vowels. Hebrew, however, did not add vowels until the ninth century C.E., long after the text had been codified. The result is confusion.

Take a story in Kings, for example. The prophet Elijah has been forced to hide in a cave. He remained there for 40 days. Naturally, he needed food. According to the text, Elijah was fed by "Arabs" or "ravens." Take your choice. Both words are spelled the same; they can only be differentiated by the pronunciation. But, today, we have no idea how the word was actually pronounced then. So, we can never tell which translation is correct. That is one of many instances.

You can see why the lack of vowels can lead to strange translations. Take a word that contains the letters DVD. Does that refer to King DaViD or the word DiViDe? No one knows.

The Bible also uses idioms. Those are phrases that meant something thousands of years ago, but now seem strange. There are many of them in every language. For example, an American might note a heavy storm and say, "It's raining cats and dogs." No one thinks that little furry creatures are falling from the sky. But, someone translating that phrase into English years from now might not know the true meaning and conclude the heavens amazingly dropped kittens and puppies all over the place.

The French have a phrase, "sacre bleu," which they use as an exclamation. It means, literally, "sacred blue." What does that really mean? Blue is a color, isn't it? Yes, but not in this case. Back in the 1700s, King Louis

XIIII, banned profanity in his court. So, courtiers who could not contain themselves swore an oath on the king's dog, Bleu. An idiom was born. Without the explanation, however, any translator would be hard pressed to explain the term and to translate it adequately into another language.

Idioms are very limited to the culture that produces them. That can lead to the following confusion, as occurred in the United Nations in the late 1960s. Hugh Mackintosh Foot, or, as he was also known, Lord Caradon, represented Great Britain from 1964 to 1970. His brother, Baron Foot of Buckland Monachorum, often visited him in New York and spoke at least once to the General Assembly. In the speech, Baron Foot spoke about some action by the UN that he disagreed with. His brother missed the speech, but returned in the afternoon to speak favorably of the same United Nations' activity his brother had disparaged earlier in the day.

A U.N. translator dryly noted, "This was a clear case of one Foot not knowing what the other Foot was doing," playing off the idiom that the "right hand doesn't know what the left hand is doing" when two members of any group work against each other. Half of the General Assembly members erupted in laughter. The other half did not. Only the western portion of delegates understood the idiom; the eastern section did not.

The same reality exists in the Bible. We simply do not know what the idioms mean and, after so many years, can only guess at their proper sense.

At the same time, the Bible uses colloquial terms. These are words that have a meaning at a particular time, but that meaning has changed. We see that all the time in English. Take a word like "celebrate." We all know what that means, right? Have a party, go wild, let it all hang out. Yet, a poem by Walt Whitman, the famed writer who lived in the mid-1800s, described the sad funeral train carrying the body of assassinated President Abraham Lincoln back for burial in Springfield, Illinois. Whitman depicted mourners meeting at intersections to watch the train pass. He said they were "celebrating." He meant something completely different than what we mean when we use the word. That's because, in his day, "celebrate" means what "sadly commemorate" means today.

The list of such meaning changes is virtually endless. The word "family" 600 years ago meant everyone connected to a person -- including the butcher, baker and candlestick maker who worked for the lord of a castle. Today, we limit it to close relatives.

Take a more dramatic change. The word "gay" today means someone who is a homosexual. Increasingly, these days, it refers only to males. However, prior to the 1960s, the word meant "happy." It was used in a variety of songs. The Flintstone's television cartoon show's theme song promised viewers that they would have a "gay, old time." Songwriter Cole Porter in the 1930s wrote about "gay Paree." And so on. But, what did the word mean when it first was used in Southern France in the 1600s? It meant "homosexual." It abruptly shifted meanings in the 1700s and did not revert back until the Gay Rights movement of the late 1960s.

Our vocabulary changes like that constantly. Look at William Shakespeare, considered the greatest of all English writers. He lived from 1564 to 1616. We cannot read his works today without translations because new words have replaced words he used in his day, and meanings have shifted dramatically. That's true of any language. Many of the words of French author Victor Hugo or Russian novelist Leo Tolstoy, both of whom lived in the 1800s, no longer have the same meaning.

Think how many word meanings have changed in the Bible, which contains writing as much as 3,200 years old. Unfortunately, we do not necessarily know what the words meant originally and can only estimate what they mean now.

Then, too, there are strange sentences in the Bible which defy understanding. Take the story of the prophet Samuel and the first king of Israel, Saul. Samuel is able to locate Saul and anoint him king because the new monarch was the tallest man in the crowd. Then, we are told that Saul ruled for one year and 21 years. Why didn't the Bible say 22 years, which would make more sense? That's because we can translate these sentences. The Bible clearly says, "Saul was one year old when he began to rule." That would seem to eliminate the possibility that he was the tallest man in the crowd. Obviously, there is some confusion in copying the words.

The same kind of problem crops up in The Lord's Prayer. The prayer starts with "Our Father, who art in heaven ..." and closes with "and deliver us from evil." Actually, the text reads "deliver us from the evil one." Today, with the lessening emphasis on the presence of a devil, the idea of asking God to rescue us from such an entity seems archaic. So, the word is dropped.

There are many other similar circumstances. For example, the 23rd Psalm, "The Lord is my shepherd, I shall not want" does not really say that, despite its familiar words.

Translators had to find ways to reproduce the words in a way that sounded good to the ears of their countrymen. That meant taking liberties to capture the sense of the passage, while not necessarily repeating it word-for-word. That approach, while necessary, can lead to confusion. In Matthew, for example, Jesus rides in Jerusalem astride two animals. That's because Matthew, relying on the Greek translation of the old Hebrew texts, read that the messiah would appear on the back of an ass. That line is followed by the "foal of a horse." He thought that meant two animals. Actually, in Hebrew poetry, the second line duplicates the first line using different words. Matthew tripped over a translation.

Scholars are well aware of this problem. In the 11th century, a great French scholar named Rabbi Solomon Isaac (better known today by his initials, RASHI) wrote a beloved commentary on the Torah. His thoughts are still read today in synagogues around the world. Repeatedly, RASHI was forced to write "Hebrew unintelligible" as he tried to make sense of the Bible. And that was 1,000 years ago.

To make matters worse, we don't have any original texts to compare the current Bibles to. The oldest Hebrew versions go back to about 200 B.C.E. The oldest New Testament texts date from around 200 C.E. That's because people in ancient times had no ability to make multiple copies. So, if a text wore out, they simply copied the old one, discarded it and kept the new one.

Eventually, Jews started a custom of retaining older texts, arguing that the name of God should not be discarded, and any book containing that name must be retained. As a result, there are regular burial ceremonies for religious books and artifacts. Archeologists years from now may be baffled by the finds.

Going Back to Basics

The lack of original texts means, of course, we do not know what the original writers of sacred texts actually wrote. This can cause even more confusion in translation. In fact, the Bible that people read today is not the same one read 100 years ago for that reason.

The situation arose because a German biblical scholar named Dr. Constantine Von Tischendorf went looking for original texts of the New Testament. "I resolved, in 1839, to devote myself to the textual study of the New Testament, and attempted, by making use of all the acquisitions of the last three centuries, to reconstruct, if possible, the exact text, as it came from the pen of the sacred writers," he wrote in an 1866 report on his efforts.

He felt that only the earliest texts could possibly resolve arguments over the authenticity of the existing documents upon which so many people placed their faith. He also recognized why the need was so great.

"We should also here add that from the very earliest age of the Christian era, the Greek text had been translated into different languages -- Latin, Syriac, Egyptian, etc. Ancient manuscripts of these versions were also brought to light, and it was impossible not to see what variation of readings there had been in the sacred text. The quotations made by the Fathers, from as early as the second century, also confirmed in another way the fact of these variations. It has thus been placed beyond doubt that the original text of the Apostles' writings, copied, recopied, and multiplied during fifteen centuries, whether in Greek or Latin, or in other languages, had in many passages undergone such serious modifications of meaning as to leave us in painful uncertainty as to what the Apostles had actually written."

His goal was to recover the original text or to get as close as possible. That way, he felt he could undermine arguments that the Bible was inaccurate. In his day, a scholarly school had arisen in Germany that was claiming just that. Some of the historians went so far as to argue Jesus had never existed. Believers like von Tischendorf were incensed and looking for evidence to provide counterarguments.

To accomplish that, he journeyed to old monasteries in the hopes their libraries would contain some of the ancient, if forgotten, manuscripts. His travels finally took him to the Sinai Peninsula between Egypt and Israel. There, near a mountain named for the summit where Moses received the Ten Commandments, von Tischendorf made an incredible discovery.

"It was at the foot of Mount Sinai, in the Convent of St. Catherine, that I discovered the pearl of all my researches. In visiting the library of the monastery, in the month of May 1844, I perceived in the middle of the great hall a large and wide basket full of old parchments; and the librarian, who was a man of information, told me that two heaps of papers like these, moldered by time, had been already committed to the flames. What was my surprise to find amid this heap of papers a considerable number of sheets of a copy of the Old Testament in Greek, which seemed to me to be one of the most ancient that I had ever seen. The authorities of the convent allowed me to possess myself of a third of these parchments, or about forty-three sheets, all the more readily as they were destined for the fire."

These texts were copies of Old Testament books. He rescued them from the furnace.

On a subsequent visit, in 1859, von Tischendorf stumbled over more ancient documents. Eventually, he carefully unrolled a copy of the gospel of Mark, the oldest ever found. It was a copy dating from the 3rd century C.E. Not permitted to take the text with him, von Tischendorf transcribed it, making from memory the thousands of changes that had crept into the manuscript with the passage of years. He also noted that Mark contained no resurrection account. He knew that the versions in Matthew and Luke were based on Mark's book, but the omission did not bother him. He was sure space limitations or even time had prevented the copyist from faithfully recording that portion of the text.

Eventually, he went to the Vatican. There, hidden away for 1,500 years, he found another copy of the manuscript he had first read at St. Catherine's. There was no resurrection account in this version of Mark either. For the first time, von Tischendorf realized that the resurrection story was a later addition to the text. As a result, new editions of the Bible in the 1800s eliminated the resurrection story in the first book of the New Testament. The other accounts in Matthew and Luke remained. So did the thousands of changes, what historian Paul Johnson called "pious editing," that had been added to the texts over the years.

The Dead Sea Scrolls Arrive

Our understanding of the holy texts received an enormous boost in 1947. Then, young Bedouin shepherds claim they were walking near the Dead Sea in Israel and tossed rocks into caves built into the steep marl walls. The caves are high up and look like black, unblinking eyes staring back. There's no easy way to access them. No one ever put in staircases. The young men may have been challenging each other to tests of accuracy. Today, some historians think the story of the boys throwing rocks is not true. It really doesn't matter. A rock supposedly hit something. The boys heard a crash. Using a rope ladder, they went to investigate.

They found huge ceramic jars containing old manuscripts. Some on papyrus dissolved instantly when exposed to air, but those written on prepared animal skin (velum) survived. The Arabs knew the value of old manuscripts. Pieces were torn off and sold in open marketplaces. Eventually, the various shreds came to the attention of scholars interested in ancient documents. The scraps were traced back to the caves, and a thorough investigation began. In time, more than 900 scrolls were recovered from various caves. All had been placed in storage centuries ago, possibly because of the Jewish prohibition against destroying the name of God. Or, as some historians speculate, they represented either the library of residents in the nearby city of Qumran or had been brought there for safe keeping around 70 C.E. as Roman troops threatened the Temple in Jerusalem and its sacred archives.

Qumran, some suggest, was an isolated site where people who thought themselves holy, called Essenes, had separated from the rest of the Jewish society. A more recent claim is that Qumran actually held a crude plant for manufacturing ceramic jars and was not a religious colony. We may never know the correct answer.

The documents are more important anyway, and they definitely were stored in the caves near Qumran. Every book of the Old Testament is represented, except Esther, which was a much later addition to the canon. In addition, there were many other books that we do not think of as sacred today, but obviously had that connotation then. In some cases, they are the only copies ever found of texts later quoted by authors of that era.

We learned several important lessons from the Dead Sea Scrolls:

1. The texts date from about 200 B.C.E. to 70 C.E. That places them a lot closer to the original writing. The oldest complete Hebrew Bible prior to the Dead Sea Scrolls was written about 1000 C.E.

2. The texts were obviously thought of as sacred. That helps us believe the original wording was retained for many years until these copies were made. Still, there are multiple versions of almost every book. So, we still don't know what the original manuscripts contained.

3. Some books were not considered as important. There are many copies of three books now in the Torah, Genesis, Exodus and Deuteronomy, but only a couple copies of the two other books in the Torah, Leviticus and Numbers.

4. Some of the material in the New Testament was influenced by the Dead Sea Scrolls. For example, the Essenes are awaiting the return of a Teacher of Righteousness, a man persecuted and either killed or excelled at least 90 years before Jesus lived. No one argues that the Teacher of Righteousness was Jesus, only that the idea of a returning leader preceded Christianity.

In addition, the "dark and light" ideas that fill the Essene manuals are reflected in John.

How Do They Help Us Translate the Bible?

The Dead Sea Scrolls may have been the greatest archeological find of the 20th century if not in all of religious history. Artifacts from thousands of years ago are rare. Many simply were worn away through use, discarded and destroyed. Others may have been buried in areas where water or weather eventually ruined them. Some were reused.

That's especially true for buildings. We have lost many important structures. The Ark of the Covenant, the sacred carrying case of the engraved stones Moses brought down from Mt. Sinai, has vanished. Even Indiana Jones would have trouble finding it, despite the movie. The first and second Temples, the holiest shrines in Jerusalem, are gone. All that remains of the Second Temple is a retaining wall known as the Wailing Wall. The massive stones once used to build the Temple, the ritualistic utensils and the priestly robes have disappeared. The list could go on.

The Dead Sea Scrolls help bridge some of that empty space. Because so many books are included -- books written in the same limited vocabulary that appears in the Bible -- we can isolate idioms, colloquial terms and strange writing. Then, by comparing the documents, we can get a better sense of what the author may have meant. That has led to new translations, relying on the old texts.

The work continues. Most of the Dead Sea Scrolls were translated and published in the 1950s. The rest, a mixture of fragmentary letters and words torn from scrolls and seriously damaged texts, have required decades to decipher. Contrary to claims that a conspiracy was limiting release of the material, the remaining texts were simply slow in appearing due to the magnitude of the problems and the desire of long-time scholars to pass along their projects to their protégés. Today, very little of the Dead Sea Scrolls is not in public domain.

While not all of it is historically significant, much helps us appreciate and understand the Bible better than before.

The Koran's Advantage

If Emily, our schoolteacher from Illinois, joined Adil and Samrin and picked up the Koran, she can be sure that what she is reading as close to the original as possible. The book is newer than the Bible, and there is only one accepted version.

However, any translation of the Koran must endure the same problems that afflict biblical translations. Arabic, too, is an old language, and related to Hebrew. It also has no vowels. Two words, as in the Old Testament, can look identical, even though they are pronounced completely different.

The problem is complicated by changes in the modern Muslim world. Although the Koran is in Arabic, today about 20 percent of the population uses Arabic. As a result, like the Latin of the first Bible prepared by Jerome in the 4th century C.E., the Arabic language is slowly being reserved for religious documents. That means more difficulty in understanding the nuances, metaphors and idioms expressed in the text.

As a result, most Muslim scholars today believe the Koran cannot be correctly translated. That leads to immense misunderstandings as journalists and writers try to communicate the words of the Koran into a language non-Muslims can understand. It's no wonder the Western world is puzzled by behaviors that seem alien compared with what they are told is in the Koran.

The reality is that the Koran, like the Bible, is hard to translate. The language is archaic. The structure reflects 7th century Arabia, not modern ideas. Add in the cultural biases, and the book becomes a minefield for any intrepid interpreter.

That doesn't mean people haven't tried. The first attempt to translate the Koran came in 1143, when a monk traveling with the Crusaders decided to replicate the words. He used Latin, which was still understood by the leaders of the Crusade who were seeking to recapture Jerusalem and the Holy Land from the Muslims and succeeded for a brief period.

Then, in the 1800s, scholars from various Western countries attempted again. Napoleon's invasion of Egypt spurred not only a desire to find artifacts that would clarify the Bible, but heightened interest in the dominant religion of the region. Their books have gained limited support and little encouragement from the Muslim world.

"Muslim scholars believe that any translation cannot be more than an approximate interpretation, intended only as a tool for the study and understanding of the original Arabic text," one scholar noted.

Many of the translations include artificial additions that reflect the view of the writers and are not in the text. For example, the Koran says, "Guide us to the straight path, the path of those whom You have favored, not of those who have incurred Your wrath, nor of those who have gone astray." One popular translation renders those words this way: "Guide us to the Straight Way, the way of those on whom You have bestowed Your Grace, not (the way) of those who have earned Your anger (such as the Jews), nor of those who went astray (such as the Christians)."

To heighten the tension, during the Crusades and the brief establishment of a medieval Christian state in Israel, Muslim scholars re-interpreted the Koran to remove any idea that Muhammad may have been influenced by the Bible or Jewish commentaries, even though he often quotes them. Today, those interpretations remain the standard of teachings of the Koran, adding to the barbed fence between Muslim and non-Muslim worlds.

To aggravate the problems, the Koran has achieved status akin to the Bible. Like many modern readers of the Bible, Muslim believers now claim that the Koran reflects the unchangeable views of God. That has led to further estrangements both within Muslim society and without. For example, Muhammad was enlightened for his era regarding the treatment of women. Interpreted in modern times, however, women become completely subjugated. For example, Muslim courts have ruled, based on the Koran, females can only inherit half as much as males.

The end result is the same as in the Western World: a poorly understood document from another era remains the guide for people living in a different time and place, and under totally different conditions.

Emily, Kaori, Pierre, Masha and Adil may continue to seek daily counsel from their sacred texts, but they read from translations that not only cannot capture the actual meanings of the words, but which may actually continue to divide them by far more than the oceans that exist between them now.

Abraham, who spoke only one of the languages in the holy books that he engendered, would have been equally lost.

Chapter Seven

Jumping Jehoshaphat...He Was a King, Too?

Archaeological findings and the religious texts serve as a backdrop to understanding the origins and history of the three great monotheistic religions. We will start with Judaism, the oldest of the trio, to see how the faith developed and how the history of the Jewish people affected the religion.

The Jews Appear

Abraham would have been amazed by what his vision led to. In his day, he would have seen temples in Babylon, but all of them would have been devoted to gods whose names are now mere shadows in history books. He would have known rituals, but nothing like the waving of palm branches during the Jewish fall harvest holiday or annual fasts. He would have been baffled by prayer shawls and skull caps that adorn observant Jews, had no idea what a Bible is or understood a word of Hebrew.

The laws and customs that comprise Judaism today did not exist then. They developed over centuries, finally becoming recognizable about the 6th century B.C.E. Then, after the destruction of the Temple in 70 C.E., the religion transformed itself again.

Initially, the people who became Jews were called Hebrews. The Bible uses that term throughout the book of Genesis. We are not sure what Hebrew means. It is thought to translate "from across the river," a reference to people who crossed the Euphrates River, which waters the land around Babylon. Abraham would have had to ford the Euphrates and its sister waterway, the Tigris, en route to Aram.

On the other hand, the word "Hebrew" is very close linguistically to Habiru, the name for the marauding tribes poor Jacobel complained about in Chapter 2. Based on letters written by Jerusalem officials to their Egyptian overlords, the Habiru appear to be a serious problem, attacking without warning. There also seem to be a lot of them, as though Habiru referred to any group of raiders outside a tribal structure. As a result, it's hard to associate the Hebrews with the Habiru because the Bible indicates that there are few Hebrews. There's Abraham; his two sons, Isaac and Ishmael; Isaac's twin sons, Jacob and Esau; and Jacob's 12 sons. That doesn't seem like a large enough crew to be attacking Jerusalem and other settled communities.

All we know then is that some residents of the land of Canaan were known as Hebrews. They claim to be descendents of Abraham, his son Isaac, and his grandson Jacob. They worshiped a god named Yahweh, which is essentially four vowels. At one time, no one but the High Priest was allowed to pronounce the name, and then only one day in the year. We can date some documents by whether the name appears in them or not. Older documents used the name. Because symbols and other names were used to represent God's name in holy texts, we ended up with "Jehovah" in English. That was just an effort by translators to make sense of symbols used to represent God. Remember the translating problems discussed earlier? This is another example.

We have less trouble with the name Israel, which was Jacob's other name. It is supposed to mean "he who strives with God." The reference is to a story in Genesis where Jacob wrestled all night with an angel of God. The story reflects an ancient belief that spirits took human form at night. We don't know if the translation of that name is accurate either. We do know that the suffix "el" on the name Israel is a reference to the Canaanite bull god of that name, but came to mean God in general. That same name lingers on in such names today as Daniel, Rachel and Nathaniel.

All we can say is that, for some reason, a small band of shepherds, who may or may not have also been Hebrews, identified themselves with the name Israel.

Abraham would have lived in the southern part of what is now Israel, an arid, desolate region called the Negev. That's a Hebrew word for "dry." Stories about him visiting other cities seem to have been a method for later writers to link their glorified patriarch with important shrines around the country. Only nomads and armies traveled far in Abraham's time.

Moreover, historical documents show that Abraham's life and activities were not given any special significance until around the 8th century B.C.E. There are several possible reasons for that rise in emphasis. In the first place, the country had been badly split by a civil war that began in the ninth century B.C.E. When the northern tribes were conquered by the Assyrians and disappeared in the eighth century B.C.E., becoming the "10 lost tribes," the remaining Jews may have wanted to retain claim to the territory now under enemy control. Abraham would be a perfect tool for that. His visits maintained a tie with sites now lost to the survivors.

61

Then, too, human sacrifice was fading as a way of placating gods. The Greeks ended that practice in the 8th century B.C.E. at about the same time the ritual seemed to have lost support throughout the Middle East. Abraham may have been used to change attitudes toward that traditional (and sinister) behavior. Widely circulated stories about Abraham at this time probably included one that suggested he sacrificed his son, Isaac, to God. That was updated then in what became the biblical text . In it, Abraham takes his son to the top of a mountain to be sacrificed, stopping only at God's order and substituting a ram. That event, known in Hebrew as the *Akidah* ("the binding"), remains a highly valued Jewish, Christian and Muslim motif demonstrating blind obedience to God's will.

However, some scholars note that after the sacrifice was halted, Isaac somehow vanished from the biblical account. Instead, the text relates that Abraham rode off "with his young men," the same individuals who accompanied him to the site. Isaac earned no mention. Moreover, the stories about Isaac that pick up soon after in Genesis duplicated what happened to Abraham, as if the biblical authors had no source for Isaac's activities. In addition, a statue has been found dedicated to the great Isaac, indicating that Abraham's son was worshiped as a god. Could Isaac have been sacrificed, then turned into a resurrection god, a being worshiped in early religions prior to the advent of Judaism? The speculation has led some scholars to suggest that the original story has Abraham sacrificing Isaac, and, when social mores changed, the account was altered. Once again, Abraham may have fulfilled a significant role far removed from his days as a nomadic herdsman in the wilderness.

Abraham would have also been important when the Torah was written down around the 5th century B.C.E., creating the unifying person who held together all of the diverse groups of Jews – by then, widely scattered – in his paternal embrace.

Today, all we can say is that the name Abraham is attested to in historical records. None of those people bearing the familiar name, however, are the biblical patriarch.

Once Abraham died, the Bible shifted its focus to Jacob's family. The principal in this account was Joseph, Jacob's second-youngest son, who rose to be second in command in Egypt. We have no corroborating accounts from Egyptian historians. As we saw in Chapter 2, some of the biblical stories were based on later events. More importantly, the Egyptians detested and feared the Semites. They were not likely to let a Semite like Joseph become one of their primary rulers. Their dislike was understandable. At one point, Semitic raiders, known to the Egyptians as Hyksos ("foreign conquerors"), overthrew the native pharaoh and ruled the country between about 1750 and 1550 B.C.E.

Given the native Egyptians' animosity toward Semites, some scholars have proposed that Joseph could have reached power during the time of the Hyksos. One archaeologist suggested that a tomb containing a mummy with its arms in an unusual pose might have been Joseph. Conclusive evidence, however, has not been found.

As noted in Chapter 2, Joseph reached his high office by interpreting a dream to predict a terrible seven-year famine throughout the land. As lyricist Timothy Rice recorded in a 1960s musical about Joseph, the dream that Pharaoh saw in his "pajamas was a long-range forecast for the farmers." The Bible reports that when famine struck the region, Jacob and his sons were forced to seek food in Egypt where Joseph was overseeing food storage and distribution.

The purpose of the story may be to explain how the Jews ended up in Egypt. Many Jewish customs and rituals, as we will see later, seem to have an Egyptian tinge. In the Bible, Jacob and his family are invited to join Joseph in that country. Historically, Egypt was the dominant nation in the region. Many of its ideas would have naturally filtered into surrounding cultures, especially when carried along by powerful armies. No one had to live in Egypt to learn them.

Moses, Receiver of God's Laws

Once the Jews are settled in Goshen, a wealthy, well-watered delta region created by the Nile at its entrance to the Mediterranean Sea, things started to go wrong. Genesis ends with the deaths of Jacob and Joseph. Exodus, the second book of the Bible, begins with a report that a Pharaoh arose "who knew not" Joseph. He enslaved the Hebrews, who had grown numerous and were frightening their neighbors with fears of a revolt. They were then set to build the cities of Pithom and Raamses.

Those cities did exist. Moreover, they were originally controlled by the Hyksos, the Semitic conquerors of Egypt, then renamed when the Egyptians ousted the invaders in the 14th century B.C.E. One reason that the Exodus is dated to the time of Raamses II is because of the name of one of the cities the slaves supposedly built. Goshen actually had been a stronghold of the Hyksos. However, we know that the Egyptians did not use slaves to erect such important projects. Reluctant people inclined to sabotage don't make the best construction workers. Major projects, like cities and pyramids, were handled by Egyptians in a kind of government relief program for farmers waiting for their fields to dry out from the annual floods.

Recent digs in Egypt turned up a city that housed the construction workers in Giza, where most of the pyramids are located. Based on an analysis of the garbage, the residents were well fed. Slaves, of course, were not. There were lots of meat bones, an unusual and protein-rich diet for people usually limited to vegetables, but who would need the extra calories for all the hard labor.

The Bible says the Jews were slaves for 400 years before a great leader arose to rescue them. His name was Moses. That name is not Hebrew for "lifted from the water," as the Bible says, but rather is a perfectly good Egyptian name. We see it in Raa<u>mses</u>, the supposed Pharaoh of the era, and in Thut<u>mose</u>, a great Pharaoh of another era. It means "son of." Raamses means "son of Ra," the Egypt word for spirit. Thutmose means "son of Thoth," the god of wisdom.

The Bible relates that Moses came from the tribe of Levi, and he had a brother, Aaron, and a sister, Miriam. Even his parents are named. In the account, Moses faced death simply by being born. To reduce the population, the Pharaoh ordered the two midwives who worked with Jewish mothers to toss all male babies into the Nile River. Moses' parents save him by creating a basket and sending it floating away, hoping someone will rescue the baby. A princess in the court found the basket, pretended Moses was her own child and hired Moses' mother as his nursemaid.

The story is probably not true. Two midwives would not be enough to provide services for a population threatening to overrun natives. In addition, the harsh edict did not curtail the number of male Israelites who show up later. In fact, the decree is not mentioned again after Moses is rescued, further emphasizing its legendary status.

Besides, the child-in-a-basket tale parallels ones known from older mythologies. Legendary Babylonian ruler Sargon was also sent floating in a basket, for example. So was Osiris, the Egyptian god of the underworld. Many great heroes went through such trials, including Cyrus the Great of Persia, who was supposedly abandoned as an infant and almost killed, and Alexander the Great of Macedonia. The theme reflects the belief that leaders prove they have their god's protection and support by miraculously surviving harrowing events as infants.

Raised in the palace, Moses did not know he was the son of a slave until he killed a vicious overseer and was forced to flee after discovering the truth of his parentage. In the desert land of Midian, he meets his future wife, gets sage advice from his father-in-law and has a face-to-face meeting with God before a burning bush that is on fire yet remains unscathed by the flames. He is told to return to Egypt and, with his brother's help, confronts the Pharaoh and demands the slaves be set free.

The story may have been partially culled from an ancient Egyptian novel featuring a man named Sinuhe, who was an important figure in the Egyptian palace, committed a crime, fled and then pined to return. Scholars have noted the parallels, although the moral tone is completely different. Moreover, Sinuhe wanted to rejoin the court and died happy when he did. Moses, on the other hand, continues to leave the land of the pyramids in his dust.

Armed with a staff that reverted to a snake upon command and performed miracles, Moses succeeded in freeing the Israeli slaves with the help of God, who sent 10 consecutive plagues. The last one, death of the first born, required the Israelites to smear lamb's blood on their homes so the Angel of Death would not visit them. Deeply hurt by the slaughter, including the death of his son, Pharaoh let the Israelites begin their long-awaited exodus from Egypt. They hastily packed up and streamed out of Egypt, behind Moses. Led by fire at night and a whirlwind by day, they crossed the Sea of Reeds (not the Red Sea as early translations said) when Moses parted the water, only to let the waters wash over the hapless Egyptian soldiers trying to recapture the fleeing slaves.

The song that Miriam reportedly sang as the Israelites rejoiced on the opposite bank of the waterway is extremely ancient and is still repeated in synagogues around the world. Its age adds authenticity to the account.

Unfortunately, little else does. The Suez Canal, connecting the Red Sea to the Mediterranean, was once the Sea of Reeds. It was a shallow marsh that a man could walk through. When the canal was built, archeologists carefully examined the dredged up lake bottom to see if any remnants of armor or chariots from Pharaoh's army survived the watery grave. Nothing was found. Nor does Egyptian history discuss anything like an escape of slaves or the drowning of an army. Of course, the Egyptians preferred to record victories and great successes. Maybe they skipped over this embarrassing episode.

Some historians argue that the Exodus is really the re-telling of the expulsion of the Hyksos around 1550 B.C.E. That definitely happened. However, the Hyksos conquered Egypt around 1740 B.C.E. because they had chariots and their enemies did not. According to the Bible, in contrast, only a few Hebrews slipped into Egypt. Then, too, the Hyksos were leaders, heads of government with the latest technology. The fleeing Jews demonstrated no such materials or leadership abilities.

Finally, moving the Exodus back to 1550 B.C.E. creates chronology problems that are irreconcilable, not to mention problems with the canonical reports. One televised account listed a series of natural events to account for the plague. Natural events, however, do not spare certain people – but in the Bible, Jews are protected. Moreover, if the Exodus was the result of natural coincidences, such as an eruption of gas which turned the Nile blood red with iron particles, where is God in the equation?

More commonly, placing this event in historic context has centered on Raamses the Great, whose name is attached to one of the cities slaves supposedly built. Born around 1302 B.C.E., he followed his father, Seti, to the throne and ruled for nearly 70 years until his death around 1213 B.C.E. In the 4th century C.E., Christian historian Eusebius insisted that Raamses was the pharaoh of the Exodus. If so, then there was no time for the slaves to get established in Israel. That's because of the stele left by Merneptah, Raamses' son and successor, reported that "Israel is no more" less than 100 years later. For the pharaoh to have that inscribed, a people known by the name Israel must have been established in Canaan. That could not have happened in the time sequence described in the Bible, unless more than one ethnic group used the name Israel.

In the biblical account, Moses led the Jews to the Promised Land and through 40 years of wandering in the Sinai desert. Despite repeated archaeological efforts, no evidence of a large group of people surviving in that barren land has ever been found, although sites from far earlier dates have been located. Moses also received God's rules of behavior, called the 10 Commandments, on Mt. Sinai, a mountain so designed that the Israelites could camp around it, but not see Moses because of clouds. No such mountain exists anywhere in the world. The 10 Commandments themselves are transcribed in two forms in the Bible, each reflecting a different era.

Moses died overlooking the Holy Land after turning over his leadership to Joshua. His obituary is recorded at the end of Deuteronomy, the last book of the Torah.

How Did the Jews Settle Israel?

A one-time spy, Joshua then led the Israelites in their conquest of Canaan, a land described as flowing with "milk and honey." He parted the water of the Jordan River so the people could pass through dry shod, directed attacks on major cities and then distributed the captured land among the existing 12 tribes.

Archaeological efforts to pinpoint the cities and match the dates of their demise have not created a pattern appropriate with successful armed conquest. Jericho, whose walls supposedly fell down when Joshua marched around it with his troops, and then they blew their rams' horns, apparently didn't have walls when Joshua must have come through. Ai, another city he supposedly destroyed, was already in ruins for the entire second millennium. Ai actually means ruins.

The stories in Joshua create some historical conflicts, too. He marched around Jericho for seven days. There's no mention of the Sabbath, the required day of rest, in the biblical account in the book that bears his name. Even more troubling is the complete lack of any evidence of a foreign invasion by masses of Israelites. Artifacts, such as ceramic jars and clothing, which typify various cultures, remain the same for centuries. Today, historians believe the Israelites either gradually filtered into the land and adopted the customs or were there all along and simply absorbed a new religious belief.

In another theory, a few enslaved Israelites fled Egypt, then joined their brethren still living in Canaan.

Once again, all that we have is speculation.

To compound matters, there are no other known Joshuas in Jewish history until the 6th century B.C.E. when a priest named Joshua helps lead the exiled Jews back to Israel from Babylonian captivity. Normally, many children would be named after a great leader. The whole situation is highlighted by the biblical admission in Judges, the book following Joshua, that the Jews did not control much of the land supposedly won for them by Joshua.

As a result, some scholars suggest that the biblical events of the 1100-1200 B.C.E. time period represent an attempt by later writers to give the priest from the 6th century a greater pedigree by amplifying the deeds of a minor figure from the past. No one will ever know.

All we can say is that after Joshua, whatever rules were imposed by Moses and his successors, abruptly disappeared. The Jews have to be reintroduced to various laws and holidays centuries later.

Monotheism finally takes a bow

At this stage, the people we will eventually call Jews are not monotheists. They may believe that their God is supreme, but they recognize the existence of other gods and definitely worship them. Some scholars have said they got the name Yahweh from the sound wind makes when it whips across the tops of mountains. After all, Yahweh was depicted as a mountain god. A god named Yahweh is also listed in the Babylonian pantheon and may have originally appeared (there's some debate) as Yaw also in ancient Ugaritic texts.

Prophets railed against Israelites who worshiped the Canaanite fertility god Baal or other deities. In those days, people accepted whichever god seemed strong. Conquerors had no trouble imposing their religious beliefs. After all, the winners' god definitely had to be stronger than the god of the losing side.

Besides, no one wanted to be wrong. Why not keep placating all gods, just in case one of them actually had some power? As a result, Jeremiah in the sixth century B.C.E. will argue that God is punishing the Jews for maintaining the snake god of Moses and other idols in the Temple.

After the Exodus, the Israelites lived in Canaan and adopted the gods of other residents there, including deities like Moloch who demanded human sacrifice. Their leaders in those confusing days were called Judges, individuals who arose when trouble threatened and would save their people. One of them was Samson, who, like a sun god, lost his power when his hair (rays of the sun) were shorn by a devious mistress. Another was Gideon, who may have been a real king and whose name was borrowed by the earnest folks passing out Bibles worldwide.

Most of the Judges are only names that echo through history, but not in archeological evidence. The most significant may have been a woman named Deborah, whose blessing of the tribes is considered one of the oldest pieces of text in the holy manuscript. Given the usually subservient role of women in her day, her status as a leader was also a sign of an enlightened people.

The Judges were followed by a long line of kings. Saul, David and Solomon head the list. The finding of a 10th century B.C.E. artifact with the phrase "kingdom of David" on it has helped historians demonstrate that David was a real person, even if archaeology has shown that Jerusalem apparently was a minor community in his day, not the major metropolis implied by the biblical accounts. Other kings include Rehoboam, Jeroboam – now names for large containers of wine – Ahab, Omri and Jehoshaphat, a king of Judah who ruled in the middle of the 9th century B.C.E. There's a valley in Israel that bears the same name, which may be the source for the "jumping Jehoshaphat" exclamation. Then, again, the alliteration does have an appealing sound. It's unlikely the king ever did any leaping.

The monarchs initially ruled a united kingdom. However, under Rehoboam, Solomon's son, the country split into two unequal halves. The land north of Jerusalem became known as Israel. The southern land containing Jerusalem took the name Judah, the most powerful of the surviving tribes.

The halves battled for decades. Then, after the Assyrians conquered the north, little Judah, now basically only Jerusalem, limped along until the Babylonians showed up in 597 B.C.E. to complete the job.

Abraham's dream seemed to be dead. The northern tribes had assimilated, adopting Assyrian gods who must have seemed stronger than their own. Today, scientists using markers in chromosomes have traced the last descendents of those Israelites to a tribe living in South Africa.

The Jews in the south had tried to keep the Israelites in the fold. The biblical book of Jonah, written around the time when Israel was conquered, describes God's demand that Jonah preach in Nineveh, the capital of the Assyria. His target was not the Assyrians, but rather the Israelites who had been forced into exile and had begun to forget God. Job did not want to go, but ended up being swallowed by a "great fish" and coughed up on the Assyrian shore. To his amazement, people listened to him. The book represents the first time that Jewish writers argued that God was universal and not limited to tribal boundaries.

That step forward in religious thinking would help Abraham's children continue to maintain his vision in the troubled years ahead.

Chapter Eight

Oy, Vey, It's a Long Road to Walk

Abraham probably thought he had bought himself a pack of trouble when he loaded up his ox cart and headed east from Ur into the unknown wilderness. Actually, he had it easy compared to his descendents, who have become the punching bags for most every western country and ethnic group for the past 2,400 years. Yet, they have endured, continuing to recite prayers dating back as much as two millennia and reading from holy texts that are far older than that.

What Has Happened to the Jews Across the Centuries?

The civil war in the 9th century B.C.E. between the northern and southern tribes started the problem. The northern tribes built their own sacred temple, followed their own version of the religion and, generally, ignored the voices of haranguing prophets. They were persistently told that if they continued to ignore God, they would face dire consequences, which finally took place around 722 B.C.E. when the vicious Assyrians show up.

The southern tribes got the same harrowing message. They ignored it, too. The Bible picked up on that theme by praising those who followed divine law and blistering those who wandered into idolatry. For example, Manassas, a very successful king who ruled for around 50 years, was criticized severely for defying the priests, while Josiah, the man who reformed the religion, was praised for his outstanding effort. Ironically, archaeology has shown that Manassas ruled during a time of peace and prosperity, while Josiah's short reign was marked by immense social upheaval and destruction.

Once Josiah cleared out the old idols in the Temple, however, Judaism can truly be said to have started. Suddenly, only God was acceptable. Monotheism had become Jewish property. Never again, would they turn to another deity. As noted in Chapter 3, the Babylonians were not impressed with this new conviction and overran Jerusalem. The prophet Jeremiah assured his people that God would not forget them.

Sure enough, about 60 years later, the Persians conquered the Babylonians. They also inherited a lot of ethnic people, like the Jews, who had been transplanted from their native soil and moved to Babylon. Unlike the northern tribes, who disappeared from history, the southern survivors had not been captive for enough time to assimilate completely into the Babylonian culture. Jewish priests had done a masterful job of arguing that God was punishing them for not following his laws concisely. Jews also were prepared to believe God had journeyed with them because their God was not confined to the small land of Judah. In the past, gods had been assigned people to lord over. The Bible tells us in Genesis that the Jews had been assigned to him. However, the book of Jonah, mentioned in Chapter 4, had made it clear that God traveled with His people. They didn't need images. They didn't need anything. God was recognized as universal.

Of course, some Jews joined with their conquerors and moved to other gods. But, enough remained faithful that the religion endured. They began to write down their history so their traditions would not die out. Eventually, those writings would be collected into the Bible.

The Jews were also lucky – or maybe it was divine will. The Persians were followers of an unusual god. Unlike the Babylonians, who still had idols and multiple deities, the Persians believed in a supreme god, Ahura Mazda, who was locked in a fierce struggle with an evil god, Ahriman. A prophet named Zoroaster (also known as Zarasuthra) had said Ahura Mazda had come to him in a vision and declared that he was the true god. Zoroaster said that anyone who believed and supported Ahura Mazda would help the deity defeat the villainous Ahriman.

However, Zoroaster touted a new concept called "free will" – the right for anyone to choose which god to support. Of course, people who went with Ahura Mazda and the "truth" were rewarded with paradise after death. Those who went with Ahriman and the "lie" were consigned to eternal punishment. Yes, that's the origin of ideas about heaven and hell.

The family of Cyrus the Great had adopted the Zoroastrian faith. They were from Mede, a country neighboring Persia and ethnically linked, but had rebelled against their cousins. They couldn't ask their familiar gods to aid them, so selected another god, Ahura Mazda, who just might be stronger. In doing so, they also accepted free will.

When Cyrus the Great overran Babylonia and absorbed that country into his empire, he did not impose his religious beliefs as previous conquerors invariably did. Instead, he offered his new subjects the opportunity to choose the "truth" of Zoroastrianism or the "lie" of their own faith. That quirk of fate meant that Jews could practice their own faith. They were even permitted to return to conquered Judea. Some made the long trek, duplicating Abraham's journey perhaps 1,500 years earlier.

They were led by the priest Joshua and by Zerubbabel, a descendant of David. The Davidic dynasty had led the southern tribes for almost 500 years, one of the longest reigns by one family in history. As a result, many Jews thought only a man who was related to that fabled king could possibly be their leader.

At the same time, guided by prophets, Jews began to see themselves as a nation of priests, instructed by God to carry His message to the world. They created laws to isolate themselves from others, banning intermarriage, for example. They wanted to remain "pure," avoiding violating rules that could lead to more punishment. One terrible invasion was enough. That meant they must live in the Holy Land. Jews who chose not to were (and are) said to be living in "diaspora" from the Greek "to sow" or "to scatter." The message is that they have chosen temporary quarters elsewhere and would eventually join other Jews in Israel.

Once the Jews were back in Israel, they wanted to build God a suitable home. That effort caused conflicts with the neighboring Samarians. These were the people forcibly settled in what had been Israel while the former residents had been shipped off to Assyria. The Jews planned to build a temple, and the Samarians insisted the building was to be a fortress against the dominant Persians. Cyrus – and his later successor, Darius – had to step in to stop the fighting and let the construction begin.

What is the Temple?

The Temple that eventually was constructed was more than a large building. It was the house of God. For years, Jews had carried around an Ark, a gold-plated box that served to house a stone. Some scholars think it was the stone tablet bearing the 10 Commandments. Others are sure it was just a stone, possibly a meteorite, which to ancient people would have seemed to have come directly from a deity in heaven. Meteorites were turned into holy artifacts as late as the Middle Ages in France.

In early years, Jews worshiped stones. In fact, the Middle East is littered with old stone altars. The Bible, too, contains evidence in that belief. Joshua sets up stones to "listen" to him read the law and "bear" witness. Psalms talk about the "stone that bore you" in reference to the old idea that God, as a stone, gave birth to his people. Even today, the song "Rock of Ages" reminds us of that nearly forgotten concept.

The Bible has stories about how the Ark and its sacred stone were carried into battle. It was captured once, but the Philistines who seized it suffered so many misfortunes, they demanded that the Jews take it back.

The Temple in Jerusalem built by the former exiles was not the first one in Jewish history. In the book of Samuel, we are told that David started to erect a home for God in Jerusalem, but was told to desist because his hands were bloody from wars. His son, Solomon, completed the task with cedars from Lebanon. The design as given in the Bible resembles Egyptian architecture. The Babylonians weren't fond of large buildings that could house troops, even if it was home to a deity. They destroyed what has become known as the First Temple.

The building served as a solid symbol of God's presence among the Jews and was the central cultic site. All animal sacrifices were conducted there; the high priest lived there; and many Jews regularly made pilgrimages to the site for specified annual holidays. In many ways, the Bible seems to focus on the building, as though it was the culmination of Jewish religious beliefs.

No evidence of the First Temple has survived, nor are there any accounts of anyone visiting it. However, Jeremiah clearly acknowledged one existed in the 7th century B.C.E. and, of course, the Bible described it. Some historians argue it was built later than David and backdated to connect it to the most significant Jewish king. That's possible, but it's more likely the structure did exist if, for no other reason, than what happened when the Jews returned from Babylonian captivity.

When Jews trooped into Jerusalem around 530 B.C.E., they expected that God would restore their independence so they could worship Him without Persian overseers hovering around. That didn't happen, so the prophet Ezekiel suggested that God was waiting for them to build a new Temple. They created one on the site of the old structure, but, lacking funds and manpower, could not make it as massive or as ornate as the initial version. Nevertheless, over time, it became the center of the religion again. Herod the Great in the first century C.E. initiated a huge rebuilding process that was barely completed when the Romans destroyed it.

The Temple then will provide another link to the success of Christianity, which we will discuss later.

The Jews had their Temple and their Torah, which was in its final form sometime in the fourth century B.C.E. Credit is given to Ezra, a man who accompanied the Jews from Babylon and wrote an account of his experiences. In a canonical book that bears his name, he is described reading the Law to the people.

What is the Talmud?

Of course, not everyone understood what the words meant. Translation from Hebrew to any language – in this case, Babylonian or Persian – was a problem already. Occasionally, the text was clear – "Remember the Sabbath and keep it holy." That sounds obvious enough. Or "Do not seethe the kid in the mother's milk." That seems to prohibit boiling some goat meat in milk. But, was that all these sentences meant? How could someone "honor" the Sabbath, which, according to the Jewish calendar, which is based on the moon, extends from sundown Friday to sundown Saturday? What was wrong with boiling meat?

Everyone had some ideas. People began to discuss these commands and try to understand them. Since the requirements were God's law, failure to obey could be catastrophic. Soon, scholars known as "sages" began to study the texts and issue rulings to help guide the people. For example, "honor the Sabbath," they decided, meant the people should pray all day, rest and do no work. Rest meant not doing anything that might force someone else to work. As a result, even today, very Orthodox Jews cook during the day on Fridays so they do not have to work in the kitchen on Saturday. They won't even turn lights on, because that means someone at the electric company has to work. They walk to synagogue rather than use a car.

The boiled meat led to all sorts of what are called "kosher" laws. Kosher means "ritually prepared" and is indicated with a "U" on food labels. Preparation of foods that obtain that rating must be overseen by a rabbi to be sure none of the detailed kosher laws are broken. Jews are banned from mixing milk and meat at any meal and must wait hours between eating one or the other. In families with only one set of dishes, plates and utensils have to be washed at a high temperature to prevent contamination. In addition, because sages reasoned that the mother goat would be hurt by seeing her young chopped up and boiled, they instituted the first known laws against animal cruelty.

The biblical prohibition has actually been linked to a Canaanite ritual that involved boiling meat in milk and offering it to a god. Many of the food prohibitions, such as not eating an animal that lacks a cloven hoof (a pig, for example) and avoid shellfish and other scavengers, may also have been the result of efforts to prevent Jews from participating in cultural rites linked to other gods. The end result of the rules is that Jews typically enjoyed a healthier diet than their pagan counterparts, but the connection between food and health was not made definite until more recent times.

For years, people memorized the various decisions that carefully controlled their lives. In time, sages realized that every time one of them died, enormous amounts of information vanished, too. So, they wrote down the commentaries, discussions and rulings in what became known as the Mishnahh ("repetition.") Included in the text were stories about the patriarchs, like Abraham destroying the idols, as well as commentaries on holy books and debates. One version was created in Babylon, where some Jews remained. A second version appeared in Israel. This is the "oral" law, which sages insist was handed down to Moses on Mt. Sinai along with the 10 Commandments.

After the Mishnah was produced, sages tried to stop all the bantering, but scholars are hard to keep quiet. In time, another book appeared, called the Gemara ("tradition" in Aramaic; "completion" in Hebrew) and written in Aramaic. It provides commentary on the Mishnah. In the third century C.E., the two were combined into what we call the Talmud.

Some Jews did not like the use of the oral law, preferring to limit their beliefs to what was written in the holy texts. The oral law would eventually become an area of contention between two large Jewish political/religious groups at the time of Jesus. The Pharisees supported the oral law; the Sadducees rejected it.

In time, the Talmud was almost equal to the Bible in importance to Jews. In the Middle Ages, the Talmud was actually burned by Christians who thought it was the Jewish holy text.

Beware of Greeks

The Persians ruled the Middle East until they made two large mistakes. First under Darius, then duplicated by his successor, Xerxes, they decided to invade Greece. The wars led to the burning of Athens, but not victories. Worse, they left the Greeks aching for revenge. In the fourth century B.C.E., a Macedonian named Alexander took over for his murdered father, Philip, and conquered Greece. He then set his sights on the Persian Empire, which had grown soft and weak.

In an incredible, swift campaign, Alexander the Great succeeded in overthrowing the Persians. He established a Greek empire that stretched from Greece and Egypt to India. The Jews were part of it. They have a story about Alexander coming to Jerusalem to acknowledge the Jewish God, but histories of that time period reveal that Alexander hurried south to Egypt and there was initiated into their religious cults.

Despite showing disinterest, he probably knew about the Jewish beliefs. The Greeks were enchanted to find a culture as old and literate as their own. The Torah was translated into Greek, sharing the knowledge Jews had accumulated. Moses was given a special place in the Greek pantheon of intellects. On the other hand, Jews were not impressed. They saw themselves as confronting an enticing philosophy that threatened to lure young Jews away from their faith.

They were appalled that the Greek athletes performed without clothes on. Some Jewish men who wanted to compete with their Greek counterparts underwent an operation to restore a foreskin lost during circumcision. The Greek gods were also enticing. The Greeks had holy texts, the *Iliad* and the *Odyssey* ascribed to Homer, and they had a great hero in Alexander, whose victories heightened the culture's allure.

More religious books poured from Jewish authors, many of which ended up among the Dead Sea Scrolls. Some predicted dreadful calamities as the Jews began to move away from their old faith.

What are the Noahide Laws?

The confrontation with Hellenism, as Greek culture was called, also created an opportunity. Just as Jews were drawn to Greek ideas, so young Greeks found Jewish morals and ethics very intriguing. The Greek gods were not exactly the paragons of virtue. Zeus, the chief god, was busy seducing every female in sight and hiding his behavior from his wife, Hera. Apollo, the handsome god of wisdom, was no slacker in the skirt-chasing profession. Venus, the goddess of love, cheerfully and frequently cuckolded her husband, Vulcan, the limping god of fire who gave his name to volcanoes. Straight-laced Jews were appalled. So were many Greeks, who wanted their children to develop better ideas of morality.

To make it easier for Greeks – and others – to become part of the Chosen People, sages combed the holy texts to uncover a variety of ways someone could become Jewish without undergoing circumcision. That last, painful, requirement deterred many would-be converts. The sages adduced seven basic standards, which were called Noahide laws and named for Noah, the righteous man whom God selected to resuscitate mankind after the great

76

flood. However, since Noah lived before Abraham, he couldn't be Jewish. God rewarded him anyway. So, sages asked: What did it mean to be righteous?

Here are their answers:

1. Prohibition of slavery

2. Prohibition of blasphemy drawn from the Second Commandment prohibition against the taking of the Lord's name in vain.

3. Prohibition of murder. That's another of the 10 Commandments.

4. Prohibition of theft. Another rule borrowed from 10 Commandments.

5. Prohibition of illicit relations, educed from the Commandment banning "coveting" of a neighbor's wife and property.

6. Prohibition of eating live meat. This is from the kosher laws. People used to dine on meat cut from a living animal. Humane rules created by the Jews banned that behavior.

7. Failure to establish courts of justice. Both Noah and Moses are credited with setting up judicial systems.

Each of these laws featured multiple other regulations to ensure exact compliance.

These laws brought many people within the Jewish fold. Ancient synagogues uncovered by archeologists often contained plaques listing Jews who were members and those who were admitted under the Noahide laws. Often, there were more non-Jews than Jews on the list. As a result, by the time the Romans destroyed the Second Temple in 70 C.E., scholars have estimated that 10 percent of the entire Roman Empire was either Jewish or what was known as God-fearers. That's one reason why Christianity found a welcome audience. It did not require circumcision to be fully accepted, unlike Judaism. That's also why Christian missionaries, like Paul, found informed audiences on their travels.

The sages' effort to make Judaism more accessible ironically opened the door to Christians, who, despite their shared origins, would devote more energy than any other conqueror to trying to destroy the ancient faith.

Hammer in the Horning, Hammer in the Evening

When Alexander died in the fourth century B.C.E., the situation for the Jews did not improve compared with the Persians. The empire eventually divided into three parts led by different generals from Alexander's successful army. The Egyptians under Ptolemy argued over Israel with the Syrians led by Seleucus. Sometimes, the Jews fell under one country's control, then the other. Finally, late in the second century B.C.E., the Syrians won.

The Syrian leader, Antiochus IV, decided to attack Egypt, but was stopped cold by Roman legates who had signed a mutual defense treaty with the Egyptians. Humiliated, Antiochus, who styled himself "the Great," returned to his capital via Jerusalem, ransacking the Temple treasury along the way. He also appointed a converted Jew named Jason as governor to force the Jews to change their beliefs. They were to sacrifice pigs on holy altars to the Syrian king, not eat kosher food and not follow normal Jewish ritualistic behaviors like circumcision.

Jews responded in two ways: First, they took out their reed pens. The canonical books of Daniel and Esther were produced to "show" that God would take care of them. Although set in Persian times, they depicted heroes arising to destroy an overpowering enemy. In his book, Daniel refused to obey the three new requirements. He grew fatter by eating only small amounts of food and survived a visit to a lion's den by not worshiping Antiochus as god. Even a fiery furnace could not singe him or his friends.

Nebuchadnezzar ordered the furnace heated seven times hotter than usual and commanded his strongest soldiers to tie up the three men. The soldiers then dragged Hananiah, Mishael and Azariah to the furnace. As the three bound prisoners fell into the blazing furnace, the soldiers who had pushed them in were overcome with the intense heat and keeled over dead.

"Look!" the king ordered pointing to the furnace. "I see four men walking around in the fire, unbound and unharmed, and the fourth looks like a son of the gods!"

Nebuchadnezzar went as near to the fire as the heat allowed and shouted, "Shadrach, Meshach and Abednego, servants of the Most High God, come out! Come here!"

At his summons the three young men came out of the fire and everyone crowded around them. People were amazed to find that the fire hadn't seemed to have done them any harm. Not a hair of their head was scorched, their clothing showed no signs of damage and there wasn't even the smell of smoke about them.

Esther rescued her people, too.

The pen, however, was not mightier than the sword in this situation. The second option was war. Led by the Hasmonean family, which were nicknamed the Maccabees ("hammer"), the Jews fought a guerilla-type from about 167 to 142 B.C.E. When they recaptured the Temple in 165 B.C.E., they commemorated the feat with a celebration. That became Hanukkah ("rededication"), a holiday still maintained today. In fact, its proximity to Christmas makes Hanukkah possibly the best known of Jewish holidays, even though it is of minor importance. Nevertheless, the war represents the first known battle for religious freedom.

Eventually, dynastic battles back in Syria prompted a later king to withdraw the troops. The pro-Greek Jews, without an army, were unable to hold off the religious Jews. The Jewish state was restored in 142 B.C.E. To Jews, the promise made long ago to Abraham had finally been fulfilled.

Chapter Eight

A Little Humor Helps

By the time the Jews finally re-established an independent country in the second century B.C.E., they had to believe that God had kept His word to Abraham and protected them. However, fractures in the faith began showing up almost immediately. Some Orthodox Jews, the ones eventually known as Essenes, objected to how the Jewish monarchs were running the country. King John Hyrcanus, for example, took money from the Temple, continued to serve as high priest instead of choosing someone from the appropriate priestly family, and, horrors, actually produced coins with his face on them – in direct violation of their interpretation of the Commandment banning graven images. Moreover, he was not related to David and, in their view, shouldn't have been king anyway.

Their animosity was so intense that the two books describing the details of the Maccabees-led war never made it into the Bible and are part of the Apocrypha.

Eventually, the Essenes pulled out their tent pegs and refused even to worship at the Temple, sure that God would again punish the other Jews for the failure to follow His laws.

Others coalesced into political parties. Sadducees (a name possibly derived from Zadok, a Biblical priest) supported Hyrcanus and would become the conservative voice of the country. In time, only Sadducees could be high priests. The Pharisees ("separate") became the opposition party. They would be more open to working with people and have widespread support. Overall, there were an estimated 24 political-religious parties. Pharisees, Sadducees and Essenes were the largest, although none was believed to have more than 5,000 members.

The fourth significant party consisted of the Zealots. They were the most violent. Josephus, the Jewish historian of the era and the reason we know so much about the first century C.E., blamed them for all the bloody fights between Jews and Romans. They firmly believed in military maneuvers to combat intruders, rather than waiting for God to send his angels, and fought a guerrilla war against the Romans for decades.

Hyrcanus was the most successful of all Jewish kings in this brief era of Jewish freedom, but his policies foreshadowed serious problems ahead. He ordered the forced conversion of Edomites and maintained a defense treaty with Rome. Both decisions would haunt the Jews. Herod the Great, the hated king around the time Jesus was born, was half Edomite; the treaty with Rome eventually led to the loss of Jewish independence.

That took place in 63 B.C.E. Two Jewish leaders – one was Herod's father, Antipas – were fighting with a third ruler for control of the country. Antipas remembered the old treaty with the Romans and evoked it. By then, the Romans were hungry for more land. They welcomed the invitation, gobbled up the country and renamed it Judea. Pompey the Great, the leading Roman general of the day, even had the audacity to march into the secret room in the back of the Temple, called the Holy of Holies, to see what God looked like. He expected to find an idol. Instead, the room was empty.

However, his curiosity caused Jews to blame all Romans for violating their religious rules. After all, only the High Priest was allowed in that special room, and only one day a year to pronounce God's secret name. As a consequence, for the next 175 years, the Jews would fight three wars against the Romans and constantly battle with these impious overlords.

In 39 B.C.E., the Romans named Herod as king of the Jews. He tried to placate his stiff-necked people by building lots of magnificent buildings and upgrading the Temple. His efforts failed to please anyone. As a result, to be sure he was mourned after dying, Herod placed the country's leading sages under armed guards in Jericho with orders for them to be killed when he died. That way, he was convinced his people would definitely shed tears when the Angel of Death dropped by his bedroom. The guards, however, did not comply, and Herod died unlamented.

For most Jews, however, whether Herod lived or died meant little. They remained servants to Rome. That's where their tax dollars went. Most were scraping out a living as subsistence farmers or fishermen in territories governed by one of Herod's three sons. Eventually, even the Romans got disgusted with one of Herod's sons and deposed him. As a replacement, they assigned governors to rule the portion of Judea that contained Jerusalem. The man who held that post the longest was Pontius Pilate, more famous for his role in the arrest, trial and crucifixion of Jesus than anything else he did as a governor.

The Jews kept waiting for someone to sweep away the Romans and restore the independent Jewish state. This person would be an anointed king, just like Saul, David and Solomon in days of old. Anointing only meant that a priest blessed oil and then transferred the blessing via the now-holy olive oil onto the head of a selected individual. It's an Egyptian custom borrowed by the Jews. All biblical kings were anointed. The name for an anointed king in Hebrew is "meshiach." In Greek, that becomes "messiah."

The Jews weren't sure if the messiah would be a military man, like David, or a prayerful man, like Joseph. They didn't know if he would be related to David. Some prophets said yes; others said no. They couldn't even agree if the messiah would be Jewish. For example, Cyrus the Great, the Persian leader who allowed the captive Jews to return home, is identified as a messiah in the Bible.

Naturally, lots of people claimed that elusive title in the first century C.E. The most famous outside of Jesus was Simon bar Kosiba. He didn't like the messiah idea and preferred to be known as *nasi* ("prince"). He also took the name Bar Kochba ("son of the star") to emphasize his status. One of the great sages of the day, Akiba, called him the messiah. As Kosiba launched a bold attempt to take back the land of Israel from Rome. The war started when Emperor Hadrian, once a friend of the Jews, announced a plan in 132 C.E. "to transform Jerusalem into a pagan city-state on the Greek *polis* model with a shrine to Jupiter on the site of the Jewish Temple."

After initial success, the might of Rome proved too overwhelming. Around 135 C.E., Kosiba was killed, and Jews were banned from living in Jerusalem.

Other messiahs have shown up from time to time since then. One of the more prominent was David Alroy, the subject of a book by 12th century traveler, Benjamin of Tudela. Alroy was described as a Jewish scholar also versed in alchemy and magic. When taken prisoner, he miraculously escaped and supposedly fled across the Gozan River on his turban. Thieves took advantage of his claims to insist Jews wait on their rooftops for golden chariots to whisk them off to Jerusalem. As they vainly watched the night sky, their homes were looted.

Another tried to convert the Catholic pope to Judaism; a second claimed he was leading an army behind Arab lines and tried to con money from world leaders before being unmasked.

Such people are a minor sideshow to the misfortunes that befell the Jews. Once Christianity achieved prominence in the fourth century C.E., Jews found themselves increasingly harassed and persecuted.

Anti-Semitism Appears

The Romans didn't have any problems with the Jews. They teased them about taking a day off every week and didn't understand their dietary restrictions. But, they actually catered to such religious convictions. Food normally distributed to the poor on Saturdays, went to impoverished Jews on Sunday. Roman emperors were clearly aware of Jewish laws. One, Augustus, made a crack about Herod's tendency to kill his kin by saying it was better to be Herod's pig than one of his relatives.

Pilate was even recalled after Jews complained that he was deliberately violating their beliefs.

Jews were briefly banned in Rome after riots there around 40 C.E., but evidence shows they returned soon after. That's about the only indication that the Romans bothered with the Jews. Even when Emperor Caligula ordered his statue placed in the temple, to the outrage of the Jews, the Roman regional officer in Judea delayed long enough to avoid offending the Jewish residents, even at the risk of his own life. His decision was vindicated when the emperor was assassinated. The demand for a statue died with him.

After multiple revolts, however, Jews were given "enemy status" – *dediticci* in Latin. That still didn't mean the Romans wanted to or tried to kill them all, only those fighting a guerilla war against them in Israel. Genocide would have to wait until World War II. The Romans simply wanted tribute to continue to flow into their treasury. Revolts interfered.

The generally benign view changed with the advent of Christianity. In an effort to hold back views they felt were contrary to the fledgling church, leaders of the new faith developed rules to control and eliminate what they saw as heresies. They were particularly upset that Jews did not accept Jesus. Many did, of course, but others refused to abandon their religious views or turned to Bar Kosiba in the second century as the "true" messiah.

As a result, Jewish persecution began. Ironically, the church leaders turned to laws Jews themselves had first issued in the fifth century B.C.E., the ones barring intermarriage and some business transactions, and turned them against the Jews. Gradually, Jews were cut off from society. As Christianity spread, Jews became more isolated. They often were shunted into ghettos or faced murderous attacks, called pogroms, targeted only because of their religion.

Christians developed "passion plays," which even today depict Jews as the villains who killed God.

Denied the ability to work at many jobs in a Christian society, Jews were regularly hired to fill positions no one else would take, like tax collecting and money lending. That didn't endear them to anyone. In many centuries, Jews would be invited into a European country to help develop the commercial part of society. Because they were outside the church, they were not prohibited from charging interest on loans. Christians were, but who was going to loan money for free? However, once the businesses were established, Jews often would be ordered out, and their goods and money confiscated.

In 1492, when Christopher Columbus braved the unknowns of the Atlantic Ocean and headed west from Spain, Jews were being evicted from a country they had helped boost to enormous intellectual and economic heights. Many Spanish Jews died as a result. Some eventually ended up in South America and, from there, came to New Amsterdam (now New York) to help colonize the New World.

From the rise of Christianity into the 1800s, Jews faced ordeals of unspeakable horror. There would be forced conversions. Their holy books were tried, convicted of heresy and burned. Rabbis would be forced to debate Christian theologians. If they lost, everyone in town was forcibly converted to Christianity. If they won, the Christians would riot and kill the Jews. When the Black Death struck Europe, Jews were killed on the basis that they had poisoned wells. When Crusaders headed to the Holy Land, they often massacred Jews en route on the theory that if the brave knights were away fighting infidels that the Jews might do something nefarious in the rearguard.

The extended persecutions led to major societal changes among Jews. In some ways, the pain and agony gave birth to aspects of the Jewish character that changed the world.

Jewish Emphasis on Education

Isolated, separated from society, Jews turned to their holy books. Tevya, in the musical *Fiddler on the Roof,* wishes he were rich so he could "study the holy books with the learned men seven hours every day... That would be the sweetest thing of all." The emphasis on education and acquiring knowledge to understand God's commands meant Jews became very scholarly.

While the Roman Catholic Church told their smartest members, priests, not to marry, the children of rabbis became prize catches, no matter what they looked like.

As a result, Jews continue to populate the academic world in numbers far beyond their meager numbers in the world. Jews today comprise approximately 0.25 percent of the world's population and 2 percent of the U.S. population. Yet, as of 2021, at least Jews and persons of half-Jewish ancestry account for 20 percent of all individual Nobel Prize winners worldwide. In the same time period, more than 36 percent of American winners have been Jewish.

The largest percentage has been in economics where 51 percent of the winners from this country have been Jewish.

Jews are not necessarily smarter, but powerless and unable to muster up an army to defend themselves, they relied on intelligence to survive. They rewarded those who were smarter among them and, as a result, created an ethnic trait that has remade the world in many ways.

The three major thinkers who had the greatest impact worldwide in the last 150 years were all Jewish: Albert Einstein in science and math; Sigmund Freud in medicine and psychology; and Karl Marx in social behavior and government. None of them were particularly religious, but all of them are products of a culture that stressed learning.

Language

For centuries, Jews had adopted the language of whatever land they now called home. The Bible was written principally in Hebrew, but the language of the day was typically Russian or Polish, spoken in the Eastern European homes to the vast majority of Jews.

In an effort to communicate without interference from authorities, Jews developed secret languages. In Spain, the language was called Ladino. In Germany and later Russia, the language was Yiddish. Both shared a common trait. They sounded like the native tongue, but the words were written with Hebrew letters. As a result, even if some administrator could read Hebrew, he would find himself trying to translate an unfamiliar word.

Ladino barely survived the eviction of Jews from Spain, but Yiddish thrived on stage and in the media even in this country. Eventually, the words slid gracefully into English, enriching the language. Familiar terms like shlep, nosh, kibitz, oy, vey and more all were born in Yiddish.

Today, the language is reportedly being revived. Yet, Philip Roth's book, *Portnoy's Complaint*, published in 1969, may have been the last major American novel in this country to feature many Yiddish words. Historians are scrambling these days to record the last speakers of Yiddish and to preserve old newspapers.

However, language lives on in our everyday words, a constant reminder of how the *tsuris* ("sorrow") of yesterday can evolve into the *naches* ("joy) of today.

Humor

Ethnic humor is not distinctive. All cultures have certain traits we associate with their comical way of appreciating the world. Jews, however, stand out. Locked in ghettos and forgotten, they developed new ways of laughing at the world. In many ways, laughter was their only weapon.

The Old Testament contains particularly sardonic examples. In Esther, for example, the king asks Haman, his evil prime minister, how someone should be properly honored. Thinking he is the person to be praised, Haman suggests that a dignitary lead the individual through the city on a horse, shouting the reason for the king's benevolence. The king agrees and orders Haman to lead Mordecai, Esther's uncle and Haman's bitter enemy, around on the horse. In Judges, we are told a king was killed by a Jewish assassin, but the king's guards did not respond because they confused the smell caused by the wound with the usual odor from the king's toilet. Jewish humor is invariably dark, vivid and pointed.

The Jews developed types of characters to poke fun at: the schlemiel trips and falls while carrying a tray of food; the schlimazel is the one the food lands on. A shnorer is someone who is always begging for money. And, so on.

In one classic joke, a wealthy man declines to give his usual gift to a shnorer. The shnorer complains. The wealthy man explains that times are hard and money tight.

The aggressive shnorer replies, "You have troubles, so I should suffer?"

These stereotypes are familiar to us because Jews carried them onto the American stage and into movies.

Entertainment became a key aspect of Jewish life. In Russian shtetls, the small villages living isolated on the steppes, the Purim holiday became a time when Christians could be lampooned. Jews developed skits – short plays – that are now a mainstay in entertainment. They came up with the comic emcee, the comedian who misspoke constantly, the nutty professor and more. Their modern counterparts, including Jack Benny, Milton Berle, George Burns, Jerry Lewis, the Marx Brothers, Henny Youngman, Rodney Dangerfield and many more, became the leading comic lights of the last 100 years.

Jewish humor remains distinctive, carrying on a tradition more than a thousand years old.

The American Dream

Perhaps the greatest gift Jews gave their new land was the ideas encapsulated in the American Dream: the right to be left alone, the ability to achieve success on one's own merit, and the chance to own a house and to raise a family without government interference. All of those hopes developed in ghettos, where Jews were hounded by authorities and dragooned into the military, not allowed to buy homes or to live in peace, limited by their religion in choices of jobs and careers, scorned and abused by people of different faiths.

Welcomed to America by the Statue of Liberty, which bears a poem written by a Jewish poet, the immigrants from abroad found a way to express themselves in literature and the movies. Jews did not create the movies, but they dominated the early years. Jews like Harry Cohn, the Warner Brothers, Sam Goldwyn and Louis Meyer completely transformed a bedraggled art form, once shown as a signal for patrons to leave a live performance, into the most significant cultural powerhouse of our time. The awards they invented to add importance to this scorned medium, the Oscars, have become one of the most appreciated prizes in any field.

In keeping with the desire to boost education, the movie moguls reproduced great literature on screen in hopes of educating the masses. As a result, some of this country's greatest writers, artists, designers and musicians worked for the movies.

Hollywood was a dream, but it was also the image of what Jews wished the world was like. The idea of a little man standing up and succeeding against all odds, a standard theme of American life, was born in the desperation of Abraham's distant relatives, slowly being grinded by the huge millstones of military and government might. In time, Americans accepted that vision as their own.

Many Sects

Under pressure from persecution, Jews often looked to assimilate -- appear to be like their neighbors, but retain their separate beliefs. Conversion to Christianity was labeled the "ticket to civilization," but few Jews wanted to go that far. Instead, they wanted to eliminate the skull cap and prayer shawls, perhaps even the kosher laws, which had created such a wall between themselves and their neighbors.

The first attempt was called the Reform Movement. Starting in the 1700s, it grew out of the obvious realization that a Jewish settler in Minnesota could hardly be expected to keep kosher when the only rabbi and kosher butcher was 1,000 miles away in New York. Reform Jews took off their skull caps, stayed dressed in typical clothing for Sabbath services, worked on Saturdays anyway and, generally, blended into the predominant Christian landscape. In the 1800s, some rabbis thought the Reform Jews had become too secular and pushed back the pendulum to find a middle ground. Skull caps and prayer shawls must be worn in synagogues, but not all day as the Orthodox insisted. Services were largely in Hebrew, rather than the vernacular tongue: not as much Hebrew as the Orthodox, but more than the Reform.

Later, a fourth group, called Reconstruction, found a niche between Conservative and Orthodox. There are other, much smaller groups. Most are ultra-orthodox.

The sects have not mingled easily. Several years ago, Orthodox Jews burned down a Reform school in Israel and have harassed Jews who do not follow their views. In their mind, other Jews do not belong to the religion and, in fact, may invoke God's anger at their impiety, as happened with the Babylonian, Persian and Roman conquests. They actually have an example much closer to current time.

European Agony

The success Jews enjoyed in America was not reflected worldwide. In Russia, they were targets of severe anti-Semitism, a term created in the 1800s to describe the hatred of Jews simply because of their religion. Isolated and friendless, they suffered in silence.

One small band in Russia took advantage of a brief thaw in cultural bias to create the Yiddish Theater, which eventually migrated to England and the United States. The actors left behind a real drama.

After World War I, Germany was rocked with soaring inflation and the rise of various political parties eager to blame anyone and everything but themselves for their country's defeat. One, the National Socialist Party, was led by a former corporal and mediocre painter named Adolf Hitler. The Austrian had been temporarily blinded in the war and moved to Vienna, but returned to Germany as a captivating speaker who condemned Jews as the cause of Germany's problems.

A failed coupe left him briefly in prison, where Hitler dictated his thoughts on what the future of Germany could be if people he labeled inferior could be eliminated. In Hitler's mind, everyone without "pure" German blood, what he called Aryan, as well as anyone who opposed his ideas, was worthy of being liquidated.

Although the Nazi Party never captured an election, Hitler eventually gained enough power to be named head of the government in 1932. Within a few months, he had managed to close down the German parliament and begun a dictatorship. He would start World War II in 1939 by clandestinely raiding a radio station in Germany and blaming the Poles. In "retaliation," Hitler sent troops across the border, triggering the intervention by France and Germany. The United States would not march into battle until the Japanese, allies of the Germans, deviously bombed the U.S. naval base in Pearl Harbor, Hawaii, while supposedly in the midst of peace negotiations.

Meanwhile, inside Germany and captured Poland, German troops were building, then manning, camps opened to detain enemies of the newly named Third Reich, including intellectuals, political leaders and non-Aryans.

At the same time, virulent laws forced many Jews to leave their jobs. Lucky ones managed to escape the country. Most did not. Eventually, they ended up in the concentration camps, too. There, German scientists experimented with ways to kill many of them as quickly as possible. Poison gas was the fastest, they found. Soon, thousands were being shipped into camps on open train cars, systematically dehumanized and then slaughtered. The horror was so unbelievable that people in other countries initially could not believe the reports smuggled from Germany.

Films, reports and eyewitness accounts published in trials after the war opened everyone's eyes to the reality of mass executions.

An estimated 11.5 million people died in the camps. Almost 6 million were Jews. An untold number more were hounded to death working in slave labor or in retaliation for underground activities against the Nazis.

By the time the war ended in 1945, the Jewish population in Europe had been decimated. The event, called the Holocaust, raised emotional, philosophical and humanitarian questions still festering to this day.

The Blue and White Banner

Many Jews wanted to go to Palestine, the name given to what had been Israel. Instead, a large number of concentration camp survivors were shunted into holding camps on Cyprus. The truth was that no one knew what to do with them. England, which controlled the Holy Land, did not want to upset the Arab countries by letting more Jews into Palestine. They had started trickling into the Holy Land in the late 1800s following the founding of an organization trying to turn Abraham's old pastures into a Jewish homeland. The Zionists had been quietly buying up land, replacing Arab nomadic territory with Jewish settlements.

Amid the growing tension between the long-time Arab herdsmen and the newly arrived Jewish settlers, England found its troops there the target of militia from both sides. Eventually, the beleaguered country, battered physically and financially by World War II, dumped the issue on the United States.

In fall 1947, in perhaps the most dramatic single political event in the history of the United Nations, the General Assembly overwhelmingly voted to divide Palestine into two units: Jordan, to house Arabs, and Israel, to serve as a Jewish homeland. The decision would take effect in April 1948. For the first time since 63 B.C.E., the Jews had regained control of the Holy Land.

The Jews had to beat back Arab armies determined to destroy this new country. At the same time, they had to reverse the age-old thinking of Jews as meek patsies who could be bullied around. Instead, the Jews won and, today, boast one of the most powerful armies in the world.

In some ways, Jews have returned to the position that the Bible accords Abraham: a powerful leader, with rich cropland, with the strength, courage and a belief in God strong enough to withstand any challenge.

Chapter Nine

A Little Egypt in the Mix

The various cultures that trampled Jews over the years left plenty of skid marks. Their religion was something like a sponge, quickly absorbing a new idea and then transforming it to meet the needs of believers. Judaism developed some original concepts – the kosher rules, for example – but much of what people think today was created by this ancient faith has its roots somewhere else.

Holidays

Planting and Harvesting

Spring planting and fall harvest holidays are normal for many religions. People once lived by the rhythm of the changing seasons. Nothing was more important than food in the days before corporate farms and high-speed transportation. One bad harvest could lead to starvation, as happened in Europe in the Middle Ages. The Irish nearly vanished when their vital potato crop was hit by a blight in the 1830s. Holidays built around planting and sowing took on special significance in ancient times. Jews celebrated Shavuot in the spring to mark planting, even attaching the arrival of the Torah to it to give the celebration extra meaning.

The fall holiday, Sukkoth, required Jews to live in small huts for seven days with samples of grains being collected. The huts may have had nothing to do with reaping. Instead, Jewish sages insisted those makeshift shelters actually reflected the temporary, movable housing the Jews used in their exodus from Egypt. Others have suggested the huts replicated shelters that Jewish shepherds used while tending the sheep before Egypt came into the picture.

A third scenario comes from even further back. To prove a young man was an adult, many ancient people used to set up small huts some distance from a village. The youngster would have to live there and fend for himself for a designated time. Once the interval passed, the boy was now a man and welcomed on that basis back into his tribe. The Sukkoth huts could have been residue from a very misty past. Their links to the fall holiday would have come later.

Passover

The traditional explanation for this spring holiday is that the Jews celebrated their Exodus from Egypt with a festival. Because they had no time to bake, bread used during the 7-day celebration is unleavened. Called matzoh, it's turned into cereal, toast and every other part of a meal. Certain foods, such as potatoes, are banned because the fleeing Jews would have had no time to dig them up. The fact potatoes are not native to Egypt and were unavailable then doesn't matter. In fact, all foods requiring long preparation or cultivating – regardless of origin – are not considered kosher for Pesach (Hebrew for Passover.)

Jews annually host a big meal at Passover, reading the story of the Exodus, drinking four symbolic cups of wine and saying prayers. This dinner, called a Seder, later was linked to the Christian Last Supper as well as medieval myths that Jews killed young children to get blood to bake into matzoh. Kosher laws ban the use of blood, but that hardly mattered when the "blood libel" motivated mobs.

Actually, Passover is probably the oldest, continually celebrated holiday on earth and precedes any Exodus by thousands of years. Shepherds used to sacrifice a lamb to their deities every spring. The blood of the lamb shows up in the Passover story as being smeared on Jewish doors as protection against the avenging Angel of Death. The annual lamb roast was combined with an otherwise unknown holiday for dry bread and given a whole new meaning around the 8th century B.C.E.

Christianity added to the interpretation by seeing Jesus as the "lamb of God" and likened his death in the spring to the sacrifice of the Paschal lamb.

Purim

This early spring holiday is linked to the canonical book of Esther. In it, Esther rescues the Jewish people after the evil Persian prime minister Haman gets the king to approve an edict allowing the Persian troops to kill them all. Esther convinces the king to arm the Jews, who then defeat the Persian army. Haman and his sons are then hanged on gallows meant for the Jews.

The entire episode never happened, but the holiday associated with the account has turned into a pretty riotous occasion with people dressing up in costume, saucy plays and loud noise makers to drown out the sound of Haman's name when the story is read in the synagogue.

Purim means "lots," as in "odds," rather than a place to park cars. However, the holiday is a pagan event that was branded with a new meaning later on. Jewish children liked the festival so much that Jewish leaders figured they were better off adopting the holiday and creating some kind of Jewish tie rather than trying to fight it.

No one has any idea anymore why the holiday was held in the first place.

Sabbath

No holiday is more identified with the Jews than the day of rest. To the Greeks and Romans, the Sabbath was proof that Jews were crazy. Who took a day off? And every week yet? They probably shuddered to think slaves might pick up that routine.

Yet, the day is honored with its own commandment – "Remember the Sabbath and keep it holy." It's been linked to creation: In Genesis, God rested on the seventh day after creation. In Deuteronomy 5, however, the Sabbath is tied to the Exodus. Having two irreconcilable explanations implies that Sabbath existed before anyone knew why.

It did. In Babylonian records, we find several similar words. All of them, including Sabbath, are derived from the Babylonian word meaning to "cease." In the Babylonian account, the gods destroyed mankind and then "ceased" working on the seventh day. Also, in Babylonia, the last day of the week was dedicated to Sin, the moon goddess whose name lives on in the word Sinai. It was not a pleasant day. Jews probably reversed the idea to give it a nicer meaning. After all, living in Babylon, they would see the day commemorated no matter what they did.

That approach was hardly original. The Babylonians borrowed the special day concept from an earlier culture. Christians did the same thing with Samhain, an ancient Celtic holiday to mark the beginning of winter. The Church relabeled it All Saints Day, hoping to give a positive slant to a holiday replete with masks and witchcraft. The old idea, however, has proven too strong, although the original reason for Halloween has long since faded from memory.

Jewish liturgy today welcomes the weekly return of the "Sabbath Queen," a possible remembrance of the old goddess. Sin readily lives on in monthly Jewish prayers to the new moon.

Rituals

Circumcision

At one time, circumcision was the one aspect of Judaism by which Jewish males were immediately identifiable. The removal of the foreskin on the tip of the penis began in Egypt or even earlier, possibly to reduce pleasure in sexual relations. Some societies considered sex evil. It may also have developed to replace human sacrifice. This way, only an unnecessary portion of the body was dedicated to a deity, not the whole person. That's why females were circumcised as well, losing their clitoris in what today is considered mutilation, but is still practiced in some Muslim sects.

In the Bible, God orders Abraham to initiate the procedure. Moses is almost ambushed by God for not circumcising his son. His wife, Zipporah, rescues him with an abrupt operation. (Exodus 4:25) Moses apparently did not require circumcision while the Jews wandered about the desert for 40 years, but Joshua re-instituted the practice. (Joshua 5:2-10)

Greeks and Romans disagreed completely with the procedure. The Romans actually passed several laws banning circumcision, although they did not require Jews to stop.

The Christians objected, too. At the Council of Jerusalem (Acts 15), they joined the Romans in prohibiting the ritual. Paul, the leading missionary, actually separated groups into circumcised and uncircumcised. He told parents not to circumcise their kids (Acts 21:25) and warned his assistant, Timothy, about the "circumcision group." (Titus:1:10-16)

The practice became very widespread in this country about 1870. It was seen as a way to prevent masturbation, then considered a horrible activity with dire consequences for practitioners.

Americans carried the surgical procedure with them around the world. For example, Koreans began to circumcise their children after being introduced to American culture during the Korean Conflict.

The practice peaked in 1971 after a series of medical reports found no medical evidence to support the operation. The American Academy of

Pediatrics issued a report that year rejecting circumcision. The number of procedures has declined slowly ever since.

Jews have paid no mind to such statements. In Jewish circles, a circumcision is a joyous event, a "bris," and usually conducted by someone trained for the procedure, called a "moyel." It also remains the one sure link between Jews of every generation back to the hallowed names like Abraham, Isaac and Jacob.

Bar Mitzvah

The one rite of passage familiar to non-Jews has to be this one, which marks the moment when a Jewish child becomes accepted as an adult in the religious community. Most people think it's an ancient custom, but it's surprisingly new.

Christians had developed confirmation as a way to mark entry into adulthood. Jews had no similar event. A boy turned into a man when he was capable of reading the Torah. That could be any time. Religion was man's work; women need not concern themselves.

To counter Christianity, in the 12th century C.E., Jewish leaders developed a new ritual called bar mitzvah ("son of a good deed"). In it, the Jewish boy read from the Torah and led the service, then got oodles of fountain pens as gifts. In the early 1900s, a rabbi with only daughters came up with a bat mitzvah ("daughter of a good deed") and guided his girls through the unusual event. By the 1960s, bat mitzvahs and bar mitzvahs had become standards in the Jewish community. Today, they can be lavish with huge dances and endless presents. The "good deed" these days may refer to property given as a gift.

Wedding

In a religious Jewish ceremony these days, a bride and groom first sign a "get," which is a legal document attesting to the marriage. Then, they gather under a canopy, called a chuppah, to recite their vows. As a final ritual, the groom breaks a glass. The ceremony can be very brief or, with a long-winded rabbi, go on for a while.

The chuppah is a remnant from the ancient days when the bridal couple – in what usually was an arranged marriage – met in the groom's room or tent. In fact, there were two ceremonies, one for betrothal, followed as long as a year later by the wedding. Talk about long engagements. At the conclusion of the betrothal period, the community escorted the bride to a room, called the chuppah, and the bride and groom consummated the marriage.

These days, the chuppah is just a canopy, and the honeymoon is a private occasion without onlookers to verify the virginity of the bride or that the groom was virile.

The broken glass has been linked to the memory of the destroyed Temple or a reminder that a little sadness accompanies even the greatest happiness. The glass originally was thrown against a wall, as though at a drunken party. In Germany, at one time, the glass was broken on a stone set against the north wall of the synagogue. Supposedly, evil spirits would be scared away by the noise. The breaking of the glass could even represent the end of a wife's virginity.

Or, as one wit noted, it's the last time the groom gets to put his foot down.

The truth is that no one knows how the idea originated, but it's likely to have something to do with the evil spirits. They were always spoilsports, and people continually came up with dramatic plans like this to counter them.

A *get*, on the other hand, has been very important for millennia. It was a legal contract focusing on divorce. Should the groom die before the nuptials, his fiance actually was banned under Jewish law from getting married again. The *get* also was necessary for any divorce to be official.

Another important aspect of a Jewish wedding is the *ketubah*. It, too, is a legal document, but it is designed to shield the bride by spelling out her legal rights. The document has turned into a source of art. Since Jews are banned from making graven images, artists among them have decorated everything from legal documents to ornaments.

Symbols

Menorah

This seven-pronged candelabra has served as a symbol of Judaism for centuries. Its existence is attested in ancient documents and inscriptions. According to the Bible, Solomon's Temple featured 10 golden menorahs: five along the northern wall and five along the southern wall. Another menorah sat in the courtyard. They vanished when the Babylonians razed the Temple.

The Second Temple had only one menorah, which Syrian king Antiochus appropriated in the second century. When Jewish troops retook the Temple from the Syrians in 165 B.C.E., they added a menorah to replace the stolen one. The familiar story that the resulting celebration of Hanukkah was seven days long because, miraculously, the holy oil found in the Temple burned far longer than expected comes from the Talmud and sounds more like an explanation after the fact. Hanukkah simply replaced Sukkoth, the seven-day harvest holiday, because fighting prevented the usual fall celebration.

The holiday was extended to eight days after the Temple was destroyed by the Roman armies led by Titus. Sages felt Jews wouldn't be able to figure out when a holiday fell because the official calendar in the Temple was gone. So, they added a day to every holiday to guarantee proper observance.

Titus recorded the image of the menorah on the arch he built in Rome to commemorate his victory over the Jews and the destruction of the Temple in 70 C.E. His design, however, does not match the biblical description. Titus' menorah features an octagonal base. The Bible says the menorah stood on three legs, shaped, perhaps, like lion's paws. The artist who incised the menorah into stone may not have seen it. We can't check. The artifacts taken from the Temple are thought to have been carried off when the Vandals sacked Rome in the first part of the fifth century C.E. They may have sunk in the trip across the Mediterranean to Africa.

Jewish scholars who have looked at the menorah and its seven candleholders have suggested its design was derived from a type of plant. More likely, it's an astrological device representing the five visible planets, sun and moon. That would also explain the persistent use of the number seven throughout the Bible, something vegetation would not do.

Ark

Every synagogue comes with a large container to hold the sacred Torah. It is called an ark, reflecting the wooden box that once carried God around. The word only appears three times in the Bible: the great ship of Noah in the flood; the basket that carried baby Moses in the Nile; and the container holding the stone representing God.

The ark is of Egyptian origin. They, too, carried around gods in similar containers.

Mezuzah

These little containers are placed on the entrances to every Jewish home. They contain a small prayer called the *Shema*: "Hear, Oh, Israel, the Lord our God, the Lord is one." This is called the "watchword" of the Jewish faith and is part of a longer prayer in the Bible. That prayer adds that "these words which I command this day shall be in thy heart ... and the doorposts of thy house." So, observant Jews place the prayer in boxes and nail it by the door.

Over the years, mezuzahs have become works of art in themselves.

Orthodox Jews also wear tefillin, which are small boxes containing the same prayer. They dangle between the eyes and on the left arm, to fulfill the prayer's request that the *Shema* be kept in the "forefront of thy eyes" and near the heart. The left arm is closest to the heart.

Jewish Star

The six-sided Jewish star has a convoluted background. Although called the Star of David, it's unlikely that king ever saw it. Still, it does appear in ornamentation on walls dating as far back as the sixth century B.C.E. It actually became prominent in the Middle Ages as various rulers searched for ways to identify Jews among their people. England's Edward I forced Jews in the 13th century "to wear a piece of yellow taffeta shaped like the Ten Commandments. French Jews of the 14th century were required to wear circular yellow badges, and Pope Paul IV in the 16th century had Jewish men wear yellow hats and women yellow kerchiefs," according to a historical report.

The six-pointed star was simply another image to be worn by Jews.

Eventually, the stars, known in Hebrew as the *Magen David*, became inexorably attached to Jews. In the 1890s, Theodore Herzl, the founder of Zionism, naturally used the star on the masthead of his journal *Die Welt*. That's also why the Nazis required all German Jews to wear the star. Today, the star is in the center of the Israeli flag.

In a book tracing the history of this symbol, Rabbi Gunther Plaut concluded, "The Magen David had made its way through uncharted and sometimes murky waters; it had been used for noble as well as evil purposes. It had emerged alone among many symbols, a star of hope that had survived the night. "

Prayer Shawl/Skull cap

Orthodox Jews are quickly identified by their skull caps (called "yarmulkes" or "kepot") and the prayer shawls worn under their clothing. Only the fringes usually poke out.

Skull caps are reminders of days when people put on hats to go into a holy place or building. Now, the opposite is true. They may also be linked to the power invested in hair. Orthodox women shave their heads to eliminate hair, which could lure men away from religious studies. They wear wigs instead.

Prayer shawls help fulfill a biblical requirement of clothing having fringes on them. Since clothing in more recent times doesn't come with that frizzy styling, the shawl contains fringes and fulfills the law. No one knows anymore why the Bible contains such a demand.

Religious Leaders

Jews have never been particularly organized. Priest ran things in the early years, but kings were independent. And, prophets often stood up to both kings and the leaders of the religion. Multiple religious/political parties guaranteed diversity of opinions.

Moses set up a council to help him. Later Jews imitated that approach with a body of 70 individuals called a Sanhedrin. Mention of that august body is included in the New Testament and the Talmud. It featured the High Priest, who was in charge of the Temple, but did not run the Sanhedrin. Instead, one of the scholars, called sages, headed that formal debating society.

They would argue picayune points of religious sanctity and issue rulings. For example, Shamai, a leader of the conservative wing of the Pharisees, suggested that all Hanukkah candles should be lit the first day, decreasing one each day until none was left. Hillel, the leader of the Pharisee's liberal section, disagreed. He suggested that one candle be added each day until all seven were burning on the last day. Hillel won the debate, and Jews since then have lit an additional candle each night through the eight days of the holiday.

In small communities throughout Judea, Jews did not have time to make regular visits to Jerusalem to discover the latest teachings. So, they would send a learned citizen, usually someone no longer capable of fishing or farming, to gather the news and report to the residents. If literate, he might even write down some of the holy texts as they were recited to pilgrims or during Temple activities. Some of those records survive and are called "targums." They are not necessarily accurate copies of the Torah.

After the Temple was destroyed and the sages either killed or scattered, the only religious leaders left were these old men from the villages. They were called teachers. In Hebrew, that's "rabbi." Today, rabbis remain the heads of synagogues, still instructing and carrying information to their congregants. They are not like priests or imams, having no perceived connection to God. Rather, they work under contracts with the synagogue board as any other employee. They direct services, provide words of wisdom learned through years of study and conduct ritualistic activities.

They are often aided by a cantor, a person who sings the prayers and words from the Bible. Early notes show up in the biblical text. Jews may not have invented them, but they quickly incorporated music into the liturgy. The ban against graven images shunted many talented artists into music, and noted Jewish composers and singers dot history, including George Gershwin, Irving Berlin, Richard Rodgers, Aaron Copland, Richard Tucker, Bette Midler, Barbra Streisand, Paula Abdul, Mel Torme, K.D. Lang, David Lee Roth, Paul Simon and Art Garfunkel, to name a few more recent examples.

The revelation accorded Abraham grew into a religion formed around Moses and the exodus from Egypt. It focused on the building of God's Temple in Jerusalem and a priestly people carrying the divine message to the world. With the destruction of both Temples, the religion coalesced around its rabbis, creating rituals and a culture that continues to present a simple message first proclaimed probably 4,000 years ago: there is one God.

Chapter Ten

Christians Take a Bow

Abraham enters the picture as a full-fledged adult. Any stories of his childhood never survived. Jesus, in contrast, arrives as a squalling baby, asleep in a manger. His entire life is played out in the pages of the New Testament. As with the Old Testament, multiple versions of many stories appear in the sacred text, giving us a distinct view of how Jesus was seen by different people in the first century C.E.

For example, there are two birth stories. In one, Jesus' parents trek to Bethlehem to comply with the demands of a Roman census. There, he is born in a stable with shepherds to welcome him. He then is taken to the Temple for the traditional baby-naming ceremony and bris. In another, he is born in Bethlehem with three kings guided by a star bringing him gifts. Then, he is rushed off to Egypt because King Herod is imitating the Egyptian pharaoh of old and trying to kill all the newborn males. In the other two biblical texts, Mark and John, no birth stories are told, and Jesus is presumed to have been born in the obscure village of Nazareth.

In another example, the first three Gospels "(good news") insist Jesus comes from the line of David, while in the fourth, John, a townsperson asks how Jesus could be the messiah if he is not related to David. John also says Jesus is about 50; the other three think he is about 30. The age is significant: In Jewish teaching, a man doesn't become wise enough to really understand the Bible until he turns 30.

Still, it is possible to develop a basic understanding of the life of this extraordinary individual, who is believed to be God incarnate by close to 2.4 billion people. Briefly, Jesus grew up in Galilee, which lies to the north of Jerusalem. There, he began to preach, speaking out for social justice and expressing love for all mankind. He called on his followers to prepare for the coming end of the world. Some thought he was the promised messiah, although the texts are unclear whether Jesus himself claimed that role. Eventually, his preaching began to irritate community leaders and the Romans.

Jesus was arrested and tried. He was convicted for treason against the Romans. Since the Roman emperor was a god, no one else could claim that status or challenge him. The Romans then crucified Jesus, an excruciating death consisting of nailing a victim to a cross and leaving him there to die.

He was buried, but, according to his followers, arose in three days to reappear to his disciples. They believed he had conquered death and, if they followed his teachings and believed in him, they, too, could be saved from death.

Like Abraham, we do not know what Jesus looked like. However, we can guess. He would have been short – diets in those days had little protein, limiting growth. He would have been dressed in a fringed robe and, as any Jew of his day, worn a skull cap. He would have had a dark beard and long hair, since barbers were unknown.

Many attempts have been made to construct an image of Jesus, using the descriptions available to us of other Semites living in that era. Since we have yet to uncover a portrait – and probably never will given the Jewish ban on graven images – every generation has created its own vision of Jesus. Some have been borrowed from other cultures. The Romans had a "good shepherd," whose benign gaze and long hair has given rise to similar images of Jesus. A statue of the Egyptian goddess Isis with her son Horus was once mistaken for Madonna and Child and widely imitated.

We will also probably never know exactly when Jesus died. The conflict in biblical dates has created problems in developing a chronology for Jesus. As historians found when trying to estimate when Abraham and his descendents actually lived, the problems of locating Jesus in known history are severe.

Events provided by the Evangelists in the New Testament confuse matters more. Luke wrote about a census, which forced the Holy Family from their hometown in Nazareth to Bethlehem. That census was real; it took place in 6 C.E. The census is recorded in the writings of Jewish historian Josephus and on the tomb of the Roman legate who directed it, Quirinius. The detested event was ordered after the Romans ousted one of Herod's sons from control of Judea. But, Nazareth was located in Galilee, the new name for old Samaria. It wasn't part of the census.

Adding to the confusion, no one was ordered to leave his home and journey back to the town of birth, as Luke reported. After all, the Romans wanted to know how much a man owned where he lived, not where he was born. Moreover, as we saw, the countryside was torn by constant guerilla fighting in those years. Putting thousands of people on the road back to their hometown would have simply aggravated the situation.

Matthew's version of the birth also runs into a time roadblock. As you might recall, he said Herod tried to kill all the infant Jewish boys because he heard a story that a new king was born. Herod died about 4 B.C.E., but that was 10 years before Luke's census. To compound the problem, Josephus does not tell us about any attempted murder of newborns, although he detested Herod. Instead, he reserved the "murder of innocents" tag that Matthew used to describe Herod's planned murder of the sages in Jericho to create sorrow for his own death.

As a final complication, there's that 20-year difference in Jesus' age between the four Gospels.

The best historians can do is look at the lives of two known historical figures in the texts: Pontius Pilate, the Roman governor who presided over Jesus' trial; and John the Baptist, a visionary who baptized believers in the Jordan River in preparation for the end of the world.

Pilate was in office, according to Josephus, from 26 to 36 C.E. The fifth governor ("procurator" in Roman terms) of Judea, he was forced out early in 36 when multiple complaints about his behavior convinced the Roman Emperor Tiberius to act. That meant that for Pilate to preside over Jesus' trial, Jesus must have lived between 26 and 36.

John the Baptist, who was also mentioned in Josephus, appeared in 28. Luke said that Jesus and John were cousins, and that John was older and active before Jesus began to preach. All the texts agree that John baptized Jesus in the Jordan River, although they say that John knew that Jesus was more important.

John preached extensively, had many followers – some who thought he was the messiah – and was beheaded by Herod Antipas by no later than 35. Although the exact obituary doesn't exist, Josephus said that Antipas, another of Herod's sons, lost a war against his ex-father-in-law in 35. That loss was considered punishment by the local residents because Herod Antipas had slain John the Baptist, Josephus wrote. John, therefore, must have died shortly before the war ended, or no one would have made a connection between the loss and John's death.

According to the Gospels, John died before Jesus. That means Jesus must have died between 34-36 C.E. John the Baptist must have died by 35. That leaves only 35 as the year when Jesus died. There simply isn't any other time available, because Pilate couldn't have presided over a trial in spring 36; he was out of office by then. However, 35 does not match up with other clues in the text, including the names of the high priests of the time period and the day when Passover falls. Nor would there have been enough time for Jesus to have circulated around the area, preaching his message and attracting followers.

As a result, historians have concluded the exact date of Jesus' crucifixion cannot be determined. So the usual date assigned for the tragic event is 33 C.E. That's a compromise between those who think the date was closer to 30 and those who prefer 35.

We would be helped by archeological data or more accounts left by other historians. Unfortunately, little has survived.

Known comments about Jesus in extant Roman literature:

Cornelius Tacitus (55-120 C.E.)

Consequently, to get rid of the report, Nero fastened the guilt and inflicted the most exquisite tortures on a class hated for their abominations, called Christians by the populace. Christus, from whom the name had its origin, suffered under the extreme penalty during the reign of Tiberius at the hands of one of our procurators, Pontius Pilatus, and a most mischievous superstition, thus checked for the moment, again broke out not only in Judea, the first source of the evil, but even in Rome, where all things hideous and shameful from every part of the world find their center and become popular. Accordingly, an arrest was first made of all who pleaded guilty; then, upon their information, an immense multitude was convicted, not so much of the crime of firing the city, as of hatred against mankind. Mockery of every sort was added to their deaths. Covered with the skins of beasts, they were torn by dogs and perished, or were nailed to crosses, or were doomed to the flames and burnt, to serve as a nightly illumination, when daylight had expired. Nero offered his gardens for the spectacle, and was exhibiting a show in the circus, while he mingled with the people in the dress of a charioteer or stood aloft on a car. Hence, even for criminals who deserved extreme and exemplary punishment, there arose a feeling of compassion; for it was not, as it seemed, for the public good, but to glut one man's cruelty, that they were being destroyed.

That would seem to be a big help, but for the date of the commentary. Writing as late as he was, Tacitus could have gotten any information about Christians from members of the religion, rather than from actual historical documents. His phrasing, "suffered under," which is clearly Christian, seems to indicate that. Moreover, early Church fathers did not cite his comment nor does the reference to Christians show up in Tacitus' writing until a translation was issued hundreds of years later.

Actually, no reference to Jesus by a non-Christian author is cited by Church fathers until the 4th century.

Lucian, a second-century Greek satiris:

The Christians, you know, worship a man to this day – the distinguished personage who introduced their novel rites, and was crucified on that account... You see, these misguided creatures start with the general conviction that they are immortal for all time, which explains the contempt of death and voluntary self-devotion which are so common among them; and then it was impressed on them by their original lawgiver that they are all brothers, from the moment that they are converted, and deny the gods of Greece, and worship the crucified sage, and live after his laws. All this they take quite on faith, with the result that they despise all worldly goods alike, regarding them merely as common property.

Lucian also reported that the Christians had "sacred writings" which were frequently read. When something affected them, "they spare no trouble, no expense."

His text, again, is so late that he must have gotten his information from practicing Christians.

• Pliny the Younger, Roman governor of Bithynia in Asia Minor around 112 C.E.

In a letter to Emperor Trajan asking for advice for dealing with Christians, he states:

(Christians) were in the habit of meeting on a certain fixed day before it was light, when they sang in alternate verses a hymn to Christ, as to a god, and bound themselves by a solemn oath, not to any wicked deeds, but never to commit any fraud, theft or adultery, never to falsify their word, nor deny a trust when they should be called upon to deliver it up; after which it was their custom to separate, and then reassemble to partake of food – but food of an ordinary and innocent kind.

Emperor Trajan, in reply to Pliny:

The method you have pursued, my dear Pliny, in sifting the cases of those denounced to you as Christians is extremely proper. It is not possible to lay down any general rule which can be applied as the fixed standard in all cases of this nature. No search should be made for these people; when they are denounced and found guilty they must be punished; with the restriction, however, that when the party denies himself to be a Christian, and shall give proof that he is not (that is, by adoring our gods) he shall be pardoned on the ground of repentance, even though he may have formerly incurred suspicion. Information without the accuser's name subscribed must not be admitted in evidence against anyone, as it is introducing a very dangerous precedent, and by no means agreeable to the spirit of the age.

The exchange only proves that the Christians were involved in regular worship services at this time and had drawn the attention of Roman officials. It doesn't help us pinpoint any facts about Jesus. Recently, several historians argued the letters may be forgeries anyway.

Emperor Hadrian (117-138 C.E.), in a letter to Minucius Fundanus, the Asian proconsul:

I do not wish, therefore, that the matter should be passed by without examination, so that these men may neither be harassed, nor opportunity of malicious proceedings be offered to informers. If, therefore, the provincials can clearly evince their charges against the Christians, so as to answer before the tribunal, let them pursue this course only, but not by mere petitions, and mere outcries against the Christians. For it is far more proper, if anyone would bring an accusation, that you should examine it.

Hadrian further explained that, if Christians were found guilty, they should be judged "according to the heinousness of the crime." If the accusers are only slandering the believers, he added, then those who inaccurately made the charges are to be punished.

Gaius Suetonius Tranquillas, chief secretary of Emperor Hadrian.

There are two references, appearing in his books from 117-138 C.E. In his account of Emperor Claudius' reign, Suetonius wrote, "Claudius banished from Rome all Jews who were continually making disturbances at the instigation of one Chrestus." Then, on the reign of Nero: "Nero likewise inflicted punishment on the Christians, a sect of men who held a new and maleficent superstition."

Again, the information is scant. Is Chrestus a misunderstanding for Christ or refer to another person altogether? After all, Chrestus was a term often applied to pagan gods. Besides, "Jews" actually may be "God-fearers," people who mixed Jewish beliefs with pagan beliefs and who were not typically of Jewish descent.

Timing is significant, too. Suetonius, a prominent historian in his day, was referring to a time period close to when the false messiah Theudas was crucified. The passage may be a nod to Theudas' followers in Rome, who rioted in protest to his death at Roman hands.

The text also seems to imply that Chrestus was in Rome, spearheading the uprising. Christians claim that the passage refers to Jesus, and unrest began after Paul brought news of him to Rome, and that Suetonius was only mistaken about Jesus himself being in Rome. Regardless, the information is too limited and too removed from Jesus' time to be of any historical help.

There are simply no other non-Christian works to turn to outside the New Testament. As you can see, few of the comments contain even a shard of information about the historical Jesus. They simply verify that Christianity existed by the time of the writing.

Josephus' history of the Jewish war that ended with the destruction of the Temple does contain a paragraph that many believers point to as exact proof of Jesus' existence.

At about this time lived Jesus, a wise man, if indeed one might call him a man. For he was one who accomplished surprising feats and was a teacher of such people as are eager for novelties. He won over many of the Jews and many of the Greeks. He was the messiah. When Pilate, upon an indictment brought by the principal men among us, condemned him to the cross, those who loved him from the first did not cease to be attached to him. On the third day he appeared to them restored to life, for the holy prophets had foretold this and myriad other marvels concerning him. And the tribe of Christians, so called after him, has to this day still not disappeared. -- *(17:3:3)*

Few, if any, historians think Josephus actually wrote those words. Just for starters, Josephus died around 93 C.E., before the word "Christian" was used in common vernacular for the small Jewish sect. Moreover, the first time in history that this particular passage is mentioned occurred around 320, when Bishop Eusebius, the first Christian historian, refers to it. At least 16 church fathers are known to have written about Josephus without mentioning this paragraph. They would not have ignored it or complained, as they did, that Josephus overlooked Jesus, if that paragraph existed.

One other line in Josephus, "James, the brother of Jesus, the so-called messiah," (20:9:1) once widely accepted as valid, has also been questioned. Robert Eisenman, a professor of religion at the University of California, suggested that someone added "brother of the messiah" as a margin note. Someone else, who was more skeptical, added "so-called." The marginalia was then included in the text by scribes lovingly copying every word, Eisenman proposed. It is not known when the other passage was added in. Such alterations are known to have happened elsewhere.

Regardless, all the lines tell us – even if Josephus wrote them – that Jesus lived and was thought of as the messiah. It provides no additional information. It certainly doesn't define the term "messiah," which in Jesus' day meant an anointed king, like David, who would rid the land of Romans and return Israel to Jewish control. Jesus, a man who spoke of peace and love, did not fit that description anyway.

Josephus wrote a later book in response to attacks on the historical claims of Jews. In it, he retold the history of Judaism, beginning with creation. The text, too, also dealt with the calamitous first century events and, once again, does not mention Jesus.

Some historians claim that Josephus knew more about Jesus and early Christianity, but didn't want to offend the Romans. Besides being an attempt to read Josephus' mind, that theory ignores the fact he wrote extensively about other would-be messiahs, lambasting their pretensions and accusing them of fostering unrest.

Two other non-biblical Christian documents can be dated to the first century C.E. and concern themselves with Jesus: The Gospel of Thomas and the Didache. The recently found Gospel of Judas may have been written in the first century, too, but the current copy is thought to be older.

Before Gospel texts were written, there were likely to be small collections of the sayings of Jesus floating around Judea. The Gospel of Thomas, found in 1945, fits that description, although only a handful of the quotes it ascribes to Jesus made their way into the New Testament. Also, some of the quotes attributed to Jesus were edited after they were chosen for a particular Gospel. It's possible that Matthew, Mark, Luke and (maybe) John never saw the Gospel of Thomas, but did have a collection of quotes akin to it.

One historian has suggested that John was written to counter Thomas, who did not see Jesus as the son of God existing before all time. That's why, in this view, John starts his text with "In the beginning, there was the word," and also tells the story of a "doubting Thomas," who had to be shown that Jesus had truly been resurrected, an idea not included in the Gospel of Thomas.

The Didache, which began as a sectarian Jewish document, was probably written during the turmoil of the Jewish-Roman war from 66 to 73 C.E. The original version contained moral teachings and predictions of the destruction of the current world order. Christians later revised it, adding a story of Jesus and rules of worship for early Christian communities. That was completed no earlier than about 95 C.E. From about 100 to 130, the Didache was used by a church in Syria as its principal religious book.

Like Mark, the oldest Gospel text, the Jesus story in the Didache makes no mention of a virgin birth. There are no miracles. Jesus is called the "son" of God, but only figuratively. In Jewish thinking, everyone is a son of God anyway. There's no account of the crucifixion of Jesus, although the Didache does mention a cross in the sky as a sign of Jesus. The twelve apostles are referred to as representing the 12 tribes of Israel. If nothing else, the Didache only helps us understand how the mythology about Jesus developed; it doesn't help us place Jesus on a calendar.

In the end, we must rely on the Gospels, which were written starting around 71 C.E. There are plenty of people who think Mark is earlier, but, as with the story of Joseph in the Old Testament, word choice and other factors help isolate the date.

Historians have carefully examined all four canonical Gospels and narrowed down some aspects of them. As noted in Chapter 3, Mark was probably written in Rome. Matthew, who has Jesus and the Holy Family rush off to Egypt, may have been written there. He could have been trying to encourage Jews who fled to Egypt during the war against the Romans that, if they followed Jesus, that they, too, could return to their homeland. In many instances, he describes Jesus outdoing Moses: For example, Moses turns the Nile into blood; Jesus turns water in wine, which is far more useful.

Luke is thought to have been written in Rome, while John is believed to have been written in Turkey, then part of the Roman Empire.

110

Searching for Information

We know some of their sources: older sacred texts, word of mouth and written reports.

Sacred Texts

There was no Bible in Jesus' day. The Old and New Testaments would not teach their present forms until centuries later. However, there were recognized holy books available, most of which would become part of the Old Testament. The Dead Sea Scrolls reveal there were multiple "holy" texts and many versions even of what became biblical books, as well as then-sacred books that lost their aura with time. The Gospel writers did not know Hebrew, the principal language of the holy texts, so they relied on the Septuagint, the Greek translation of the first five books of the Old Testament completed in the third century B.C.E. The scholars finished Genesis, Exodus, Leviticus, Numbers and Deuteronomy first. Later books were translated with varying skill across the next 200 years. As a result, errors in the Septuagint were repeated in the Gospels.

Word of Mouth

In an illiterate society, stories were memorized and passed along. However, as we saw with the Old Testament, this is a poor way to retain facts, even though some people were trained to remember and repeat the stories. Embellishments were common. Still, people in those days were better attuned to this method, since they couldn't rely on any media. Gospels writers certainly would have heard stories about Jesus and incorporated them into the text.

Despite claims to the contrary, it's highly unlikely they had any witnesses to talk to. The Jews had risen up in a war against the Romans that began in 66 C.E. It ended with Jerusalem and the Temple in ruins, and more than 1 million dead. Countless others were sold as slaves. The early church was based in Jerusalem; anyone who knew Jesus was there, too. Few, if any, would have survived.

Writings

Finally, sages regularly discussed the holy writings as townspeople listened and recorded what they heard or copied portions of the text itself. These copies, mentioned earlier, are called targums. While often inaccurate, they do provide one additional source of information.

Gospel writers also drew on available biographies of famous people and other works to develop the biography of Jesus, in the same way the Old Testament writers drew on various sources for their accounts of Joseph, Moses and Abraham.

No one was trying to hide or fabricate the truth. Instead, they were hoping to create a clearer picture by drawing on material most people would have understood.

The new converts tell the stories; and since the faith necessarily grows exponentially, most of the people telling the stories were not eyewitnesses and indeed had never laid eyes on an eyewitness or even on anyone else who had ... I should stress that Christians would not have to be deceitful or malicious to invent a story about Jesus, about something he said or did...They were instead meant to convince people that Jesus was the miracle-working Son of God whose death brought salvation to the world, and to edify and instruct those who believed. ... -- Ehrman, pgs 51-52

Chapter Eleven

Finding Jesus

As we saw with the Old Testament accounts, little history was available to verify details in the texts. As a result, modern scholars are split into two camps: minimalists, who believe the Bible has virtually no history in it; and literalists, who believe the Bible has extensive history, some of which has not yet been verified but will when archaeology finds the missing evidence.

Both sides agree, based on current research, the Bible stories prior to David are likely to be mythology. However, as the clock ticks down to the date when the text was written down, the history becomes increasingly accurate. Of course, religious views tend to color the writing, but the basic information is correct.

Is the same true in the New Testament? This is a trickier subject. Jesus plays such a prominent role in people's lives worldwide that historians have actually shied away from the discussion. No one wants to hurt someone else's belief.

Nevertheless, over the past 300 years, detailed investigations have been made of New Testament accounts. The search has not undermined the philosophical base of Christianity, but rather the history in its pages. The two aspects must be separated. History is objective, requiring data and evidence. Belief does not need that. Belief reflects the inner being.

The Roman Catholic Church has accepted the judgment of history. Pope John Paul II told followers that the Bible reflects "the belief of the authors." The same message is in the Catholic Encyclopedia.

Actually, the lack of information about Jesus and the time he lived was not realized for centuries. Until the 1700s, the Gospels had served as the lone source, the bedrock of Christian belief in the divinity of Jesus. He walks through its pages as a real, albeit saintly, person. Challenges to the historical nature of the text were not acceptable. At one point, the Church limited reading the Bible to priests in hopes of reducing questions and private interpretations.

A person who bravely challenged the Church and actually published some contrary research might as well make reservations to be personally charbroiled.

However, as society changed, more scholars began to examine the holy texts. In the aftermath of the Renaissance, an era of soaring art, music and philosophy, historians began to look at all religious manuscripts from a more rational perspective. We call the era the "Age of Reason."

The wave of intense study came as the Catholic Church was losing control of Europe. The struggle was not just over men's hearts and souls, but also over the question: what is truth? Stories from the Christian past were suddenly exposed as legends.

Lorenzo Valla (1407-1457) opened the door by proving the *Donation of Constantine*, a document in which Constantine "deeded" the Church huge tracts of land in Italy, was a forgery. He based it on the textual grammar, which was not in use when Constantine was alive. Valla, a meticulous researcher, then said the "*Apostles' Creed*" could not have been written by the 12 Apostles. Ironically, the Church had hired Valla to verify the documents, but was now embarrassed. Convicted of heresy, he was spared by his royal patron in what was really just a skirmish in the war between absolute monarchs and the universal church.

By the early 1600s, Dutch Jesuit Herbert Rosweyde (1569-1629) had erased the legend of St. George, a move that "horrified the devout in England." Jean Mabillion (1632-1707) had to be defended by Pope Clement XI when his studies undermined the believed history of the saints in Rome. Saints have been vanishing ever since, including Christopher in the 20th century.

Biblical criticism (meant in the positive way of "examining" rather than "demeaning") began in earnest when a mathematician named Hermann Samuel Reimarus (1694-1768) got into the act. He claimed that Jesus' failed predictions of the end of the world, which would begin with his death, convinced his followers to steal his body and create a new biography structured around aspects of Jewish messianic beliefs. Reimarus argued that the Christian faith is not based on anything Jesus actually said or did, but rather on interpretations wrought by those misguided expectations.

A university lecturer at Wittenberg and a teacher of oriental languages at the Johannes Gymnasium in Hamburg, Reimarus began his serious religious writing at the age of 60 after rejecting convoluted philosophical thought for mathematics.

Based on his study of animal behavior and reasoning, he concluded that Christianity's value lay in moral lessons. He studied the Bible, eventually spurning the claim that it was the revealed word of God. He called the stories "forgeries," created by the Apostles and thought that the theology masked a simple, human Jesus.

That line of reasoning led him into a search for a historical Jesus, whom, he eventually concluded, was a Jewish apocalyptic preacher who realized at his death that he had failed.

You can imagine what would have happened had he published such controversial findings even in that enlightened age. The Inquisition was still in business. He would have made a perfect customer. As a result, the professor was not so bold as to issue his works while living. Like the astronomer Copernicus, who waited until he was dying to release his report that, contrary to the Bible, the Earth orbits the sun, Reimarus was dead when his controversial essays appeared. A librarian and colleague, G.E. Lessing pretended he had discovered the papers hidden among the contents of a library and published them.

Known today as the Wolfenbuttel Fragments, the essays were titled *Apology or Defense for Reasonable Worshipers of God*, and initiated a burst of historical research and creative views about Jesus that is still ongoing.

The next intensive search for Jesus was initiated in the mid-1830s by David Friedrich Strauss, who produced a two-volume book, covering a jaw-dropping 1,400 pages, and entitled *Life of Jesus*. The book was wildly controversial. One reviewer called it "the most pestilential book ever vomited out of the jaws of hell." Still, the book went through several editions and was translated into English a decade later.

Strauss dismissed the biblical stories about Jesus as mythology, shrugging off prevalent theories of his day. He insisted the Gospel authors drew on known accounts in holy books of the day to develop stories about Jesus. For example, the miracle of feeding the multitude, one of only two miracles in all four Gospels, Strauss argued, was drawn from Exodus 16.13–36, where God fed the people of Israel in the wilderness with manna. Strauss said the Gospels were not trying to capture an event on a particular day, but rather to claim that Jesus is "the bread of life" who feeds his followers with "spiritual food" daily.

He carried that reasoning through his book, arguing that the Gospel stories are based on Jewish ideas of what a messiah should be to support the claim that Jesus was that long-awaited dignitary.

Strauss, a German who served as vicar of a county church before becoming a professor of theology, was only 27 when he published *Life of Jesus*. It promptly cost him his career. Dismissed from his position at Tübingen, he found an appointment at Zurich, only to be sent packing before he gave his first lecture. He never taught again. He did write other books, including a popular version of his most famous work, married an opera star, tried to get elected to office and finally died in 1874. At his own request, he was buried without Christian rituals.

His courage, however, helped establish that the accepted Jesus of history was not necessarily the Jesus of the Bible. With that, the search for the real Jesus spread through European intellectual centers. Everyone in academe pored over clues and released their results in a rain of philosophical and historical musings. The results splashed on to heads of the unsuspecting population like blessed oil. Some of it helped narrow the focus of the search.

For example, Karl Lachmann, another German scholar, gave a historical underpinning to the Gospels. He concluded that, contrary to past belief, Mark was the source of Matthew and Luke, not the other way around. The Roman Catholic Church placed Matthew first in its canon by claiming Matthew was first written in Hebrew then translated into Greek. Research inspired by Lachmann convincingly demonstrated that almost 80 percent of Mark appears in Matthew, not the reverse. Mark is now almost universally accepted as the oldest of the four canonized Gospels.

Lachmann also claimed that a third, unknown document, labeled "Q," was used by Matthew and Luke in addition to Mark to compose their accounts. That, too, is now the accepted theory. However, it destroyed claims that Matthew and Luke were eyewitnesses, since they were writing far too late to have been alive when Jesus hiked the Holy Land.

By the turn of the century, theories about Jesus reached a logical conclusion. Several scholars argued Jesus never existed, or that he was a victim of a pagan ritual in which one person was selected to bear the sins of a community, then sacrificed.

He was certainly no longer particularly unusual. One 1875 study by Kersey Graves found 16 other crucified saviors scattered through history:

1. Chrishna (India): he was sent by God to atone for sins, crucified, worshiped by followers as God, wore a halo, symbolized by a cross, performed miracles, was the subject of an inspired book, born of a virgin,

visited by shepherds as an infant, baptized, helped followers catch fish, taught with parables, born on Dec. 25, crucified between two thieves, dead at age 33, rose from the dead, ascended into heaven, said he would return.

2. Sakia (Hindu): His symbol was a cross. He died as atonement, was known as the Savior and Light of the World, had a virgin mother called Queen of Heaven, was tempted by the devil, healed the sick and performed miracles, and preached commandments.

3. Thamuz (Syria): He was called Risen Lord, Savior, was crucified to atone for sins and rose from the dead. His sacred city was Bethlehem. An ancient shrine was "active there well into biblical times." -- *Baigent, pg. 79*

4. Wittoba (Telingonese): He was crucified for man's sins; icon was a cross.

5. Iao (Nepal): He was called Savior, crucified, thought as God incarnate.

6. Hesus (Druid): He was crucified with a lamb

7. Quetzalcoatl (Mexico): He was crucified between two thieves as atonement, rose in three days, had a virgin mother, endured 40 days of fasting and temptation, anointed, forgave sins, baptized

8. Quirinus (Rome): He was titled the Savior, born of a virgin, crucified, rose from the dead, ascended into heaven

9. Prometheus (Greece): He was crucified; there was an earthquake at death. He was called Lord and Savior, and rose from the dead

10. Thulis (Egypt): He was crucified, rose from the dead; and his death was considered a benefit to mankind

11. Indra (Tibet): He was known as God and Savior, nailed to cross, born of a virgin, died to atone for sins, rose from the dead, walked on water, knew the future, believed to be eternal

12. Alcetos (Greece): She was crucified for man's sins and was part of holy trinity.

13. Atys (Phrygia): He was believed to be the messiah, was crucified to atone for sins and rose from the dead

14. Crite (Chaldea): He was called Redeemer, Son of God and atoning offering of God, and was crucified.

15. Bali (Orissa): He was believed to be Son of God, crucified as atonement, and was part of holy trinity.

16. Mithra (Persia): He was crucified to atone for sin and born on December 25. His ritual included a communion-like ritual accompanied with the words: "He who shall not eat of my body nor drink of my blood so that he may be one with me and I with him, shall not be saved." -- *Baigent, pg. 79*

Such reports naturally forced devout Christians to look at Jesus from a different perspective. The historical Jesus began to vanish. He was no longer lost as much as he simply faded into a very busy drop cloth of history.

Adolph von Harnack, best known for his extensive study of dogma, began the process of reorienting the search by ignoring the historical aspect to focus on the teaching. He claimed Jesus was an enlightened ethical teacher whose importance lay in his view of God, man and love. His actual birth and death did not really matter. In short, there was no reason to look at the man when philosophy was where attention really belonged.

His approach smacked into Albert Schweitzer's *Quest for the Historical Jesus* (1906), which still may be the most important text in this field. His study of 30,000 extant biographies of Jesus showed that the authors were more influenced by their beliefs than by any historical interest. As such, he said, the Gospels could not serve as valid historical sources. Nothing is more discouraging than examining the Bible from a historical perspective, he noted.

A devout believer and renowned scholar, Schweitzer made a serious search for the historical Jesus by examining the New Testament and concluded that if all the mythology were removed from the texts, nothing would be left.

He specifically rejected miracles.

We are not able to reconstruct the process by which a series of miracle stories arose, or a series of historical occurrences were transformed into miracle stories. What has been gained is only that the exclusion of miracles from our view of history has been universally recognized as a principle of criticism, so that miracle no longer concerns the historian either positively or negatively.

That finding didn't deter him from devoting his life to humanitarian efforts based on his view of what Jesus expected of him. In essence, having dismissed any plausible historical elements, Schweitzer, like Harnack, concentrated on philosophy.

That view remains prominent today. Dr. James Charlesworth, a leading religious scholar and Methodist minister, told participants at a 1990s Stetson (Fla.) University seminar on the historical Jesus that they should focus on the philosophical statements attributed to Jesus and not base their faith on history. They will only be "disappointed," he told the 400 or so ministers at the annual Pastoral College.

Schweitzer was followed by Rudolf Bultmann, who dominated New Testament scholarship for 50 years. He accepted that the Gospels were pure myth. He argued that the first-century Palestinian Jews held a mythical view of the universe. Their belief that a Son of God can come down to earth, absolve sins by his death, defeat satanic powers, rise from the dead, and return to heaven was plausible to them, but, he said, is unbelievable for modern humans.

He decided that Gospel writers relied on the memory of the early Christian communities to develop their texts, and believed that any authentic sayings of Jesus, if any endured, were modified to fit emerging thinking while others were simply created.

"I do indeed think that we can now know almost nothing concerning the life and personality of Jesus, since the early Christian sources show no interest in either, are moreover fragmentary and often legendary; and other sources about Jesus do not exist," he wrote in a book published in the 1920s.

Other devout Christians were not willing to forget the historical individual. Confronted with astronomical observations that refuted biblical teaching as well as by the introduction of Charles Darwin's theory of evolution, religious organizations in and outside churches began to look for a way to respond. Many felt the historical truth about Jesus was just below the surface and began spending a great deal of money to dig it up. The field of Biblical Archeology was born in the 1920s, building on the archeological excitement generated by the discovery of Troy and the Micean culture in the mid-1800s. Led by the American, William Albright, archeologists fanned out across the Middle East, intent on finding even a sliver of proof of any biblical claims. The field died in the 1970s when the turned-up evidence repeatedly contradicted the Bible.

Meanwhile, orthodox Christians took on liberals in the courts. The best-known case took place in 1925 and involved John Scopes, a Tennessee high school biology teacher who had violated a Tennessee law prohibiting the teaching of evolution. The trial pitted William Jennings Bryan, a political and religious leader from Nebraska, against Chicago attorney and agnostic Clarence Darrow. Not allowed to present witnesses to support the science behind evolution, Darrow put Bryan on the stand as a biblical expert. By the time Darrow had finished, claims of biblical inerrancy were in shreds, along with Bryan's reputation.

These days, the question of whether the Bible reflects historical accuracy no longer seems to matter. Believers and nonbelievers alike recognize that the authors were not historians, but rather believers inspired by something greater than themselves to report what they felt. Their lack of historical expertise has been emphasized by the Jesus Seminar – a group of religious scholars who, despite intense criticism from conservative Christian groups, have been meeting for several decades to attempt to squeeze out any information they can about the historical Jesus.

Although the Seminar rejected much of the history and many of the quotes ascribed to Jesus as being authentic, they came up with this list of what they believe are the true teachings of Jesus:

• God loves you and is with you

• Love one another

• Immense value of each person

• Good news: kingdom of God has come to earth

• Reality of judgment to heaven or hell

• God forgives those who ask.

John Dominic Crossan, a leader of the Seminar, placed the discussion in perspective:

It's clear that the passages show that Jesus was seen by his followers in many different ways. That strikes me as imminently reasonable and imminently historical. He will have been seen or interpreted differently by different people. Some will have seen him as a prophet. Others as a holy man. Others as John the Baptist returning from the dead. Or a wide variety of possibilities. But, how he saw himself is really a mystery to us, because that is hidden from us. It is impossible to disentangle in the New Testament accounts what the later church believed Jesus to be, or the later church believed Jesus thought himself to be, from what the historical Jesus actually thought himself to be. I don't see any way to ... distinguish very clearly and securely what exactly is the historical core and how it then gradually develops in the history of the church. That is lost to us. And I don't know how anybody can know what Jesus thought about himself.

Somehow, the concepts expressed by Jesus began to spread around the Mediterranean. Along with those views came questions about the man who said them. This is the same process that was initiated with Abraham and with every biblical patriarch.

Chapter Twelve

Say Goodbye to the World

For the first few years after the death of Jesus, few people knew about him. One renowned Jewish philosopher in Egypt, Philo, a man desperate for a messiah to rescue the Jews, never commented on Jesus in his extensive writings. As we saw, no other historian or writer did either. As Christians note today, it's remarkable that a man who attracted so little attention in his day has become the center of the world's largest religion. They see God's hand in that situation.

The earliest followers of Jesus may have been called Nazarenes, supposedly because they followed Jesus of Nazareth. Historians have noted the dual versions of where Jesus was born and realize that the Gospel authors use Nazarite, Nazarene and Nazareth interchangeably, as if they may be unsure of the exact meanings.

They suspect that the authors knew Jesus came from Galilee, but wanted to include Bethlehem, David's hometown, to cement the match with the old king. Moreover, they may not have known what Nazarite meant.

The term comes from the Old Testament and was used in connection with two important figures: Samson and Samuel. We met both of them earlier. Samson was a judge who helped the Jews fight off the Philistines. He was very strong and did not cut his hair. After being shorn through trickery, he was imprisoned. But, when his hair grew back, he regained his strength and killed many Philistines by destroying their temple. He died along with his captors.

Samuel was a judge and a prophet, linking the two worlds together. Born to a long-barren woman, he was dedicated to God as a child. As a result, he, too, did not cut his hair. The Israelites asked him to name a king. He chose Saul first, and then David. Later, when Saul was having troubles with the Philistines, he directed a witch to bring back Samuel from the dead. The grumpy prophet complained about his sleep being interrupted, then bore bad news for Saul, who was later killed in battle.

The tie between the two men was the hair: Nazarenes did not shave, cut their toenails or do anything to tamper with God's creation. A sect, called Nazarenes, developed around this concept of holy men completely absorbed in God.

Historians believe Jesus might have been a member of that group because no trace of historic Nazareth has ever been found. A city in Israel today that bears that name may or may not be the same one. Josephus does not mention Nazareth, although he was the general of the Galilean army in the fight against the Romans and listed all the communities in that country that he must defend. It's possible that Nazareth was a tiny suburb of a larger city, but evidence of its presence until several hundred years after Jesus died is scant.

Equally, if the city existed, but was so small as to evade both archaeological digs and historic citation, why would Jesus have identified himself with the community? Wouldn't he have chosen a larger city, such as Sepphoris, the capital of Galilee or Capernaum, home of his principal disciple, Peter? There's no real answer, of course. The only plausible explanation is that the Gospel authors saw Nazarite, Nazareth and Nazarene as similar and tried to find an explanation for them.

Making things more confusing, the Nazarenes lived in Jerusalem and continued to be faithful Jews. Later, they would be called Ebionites ("poor ones"), a derisive reference to their communal living and the sharing of their skimpy possessions.

Ebionites disliked the apostle Paul, the first great Christian evangelist, and insisted he was not Jewish. They claimed the apostle had distorted their beliefs and corrupted the views. In the surviving Heresies by Epiphanius, the Ebionites testified that "Paul had no Pharisaic background or training; he was the son of Gentiles, converted to Judaism in Tarsus, came to Jerusalem when an adult, and attached himself to the High Priest as a henchman. Disappointed in his hopes of advancement, he broke with the High Priest and sought fame by founding a new religion."

One historian called them the "first heresy."

The Nazarenes, who are also labeled Jewish-Christians by modern historians, viewed themselves as a reform movement within Judaism. They saw Jesus as a prophet and sage, akin to Hillel or Gamaliel, but not as a deity. They organized a synagogue, and worshiped and brought animals for ritual sacrifice at the Temple. They observed the Jewish holy days, circumcised their male children, followed Kosher dietary laws, and practiced the teachings of Jesus as they interpreted them to be.

Residents only of Jerusalem, they probably did not survive the civil war against the Romans or the destruction of the city in 70. Josephus describes a desperate group of Jews who made a suicidal charge against the Roman soldiers as the Temple burned. Some historians believe that group to be the Nazarenes.

They truly believed Jesus had correctly warned them about an onrushing end of the world. We have to understand this concept to appreciate why Jesus and his views initially attracted any support.

Wave Goodbye

The idea the world was about to end has enjoyed a lot of support throughout history, predating Jesus, but was very current in his day as it is in modern times. Scholars have created words to describe writings dealing with this phenomenon: eschatology and apocalysm. The words are used synonymously, but do have slightly different meanings: *eschatology*, from the Greek for "end" or "final," is the scientific term of the study of the end of the world; *apocalysm*, from the Greek word for "revelation," refers to the religious aspect, less an emphasis on individual events and more on God's saving power. Both ideas show up in apocalyptic literature, a style of writing which describes the world's end and became popular around 160 B.C.E. as Jews struggled to understand the ghastly murders associated with the war between Hellenistic Jews and their religious counterparts.

Jewish prophets did not originate the end of the world concept; they simply tied it to a divine being who would initiate the process.

The idea grew up, in fact, that Yahweh would fulfill his covenant not simply by making Israel supreme above nations, but by bringing about the actual end of the world through some kind of cosmic catastrophe. Then would come a great judgment, in which Yahweh himself would condemn sinners to destruction and reward the righteous — by which was meant the righteous Israelis. These Israelites would then, at last, become supreme rulers of all nations. As God's 'saints,' they would command the whole earth, or the new earth that had been fashioned. -- Humphrey, pg. 32

The prophets did not have to search for the end of the world idea; it had long been a popular motif in the culture of many cultures, even though it runs contrary to biblical teachings.

In the biblical story of Noah, God destroys the earth's inhabitants with a massive flood. When the waters abate, God offers a rainbow as proof that such an event would never happen again: "Neither will I smite any more every living thing as I have done." -- Genesis 9:12-16

Nevertheless, Jews joined with other peoples to accept the idea of an ending to the world. Persians, for example, predicted a battle between the "sons of light" and the "sons of darkness," a theme that foreshadows Christianity. The Hindu view of cyclical creations may have been merged with the Persian concept to generate the basic doomsday theme in Judaism and, later, Christianity.

Floods provided the main method of destruction: In Greece, Zeus creates the high tide in which only the Titan Prometheus and his son, Deucalion, survived; in Burmese, Indian and other legends, there's always one survivor who sails to safety in some kind of vessel.

In the Babylonian Gilgamesh, the oldest known epic containing this kind of apocalyptic disaster, a great hero seeks out Utnapishtim, the survivor of the great flood that destroyed humanity. In an account written more than 4,000 years ago, Gilgamesh hopes to learn the secret of immortality; he gets that along with a detailed account of a massive flood. Utnapishtim tells of being forewarned, building a great boat and sailing for days until reaching safety while explaining how he achieved immortality. That story is believed by some historians to be the model for the Noah account because of similarities in the description of the boat, use of birds to discover dry land and related aspects. Jews would have heard the tale, which was well known throughout the Middle East and especially in Babylon, site of the Jewish exile after 586 B.C.E.

Immanuel Velikovsky, the late Russian physicist turned historian, once suggested in his controversial book, *Worlds in Collision*, that all the flood accounts were connected to a single event about 3,500 years ago when a comet created watery chaos.

No evidence of such a worldwide flood has ever been found, although residue from a large flood in the Tigris-Euphrates valley uncovered by archeologists this century is thought to be the source of the proto-Noah accounts. Archaeological evidence, however, has demonstrated that settlements above and below the flood are identical. "Inundation in Ur did not lead to the abandonment of the settlement. In fact, it did not lead to an interruption in the occupation." Moreover, evidence of various floods are separated by centuries, indicating there was no one flood of immense portions as described in the Bible. -- Keller, pg. 29

Fortunately, for those who support the concept of total destruction, water has never been the only medium for disaster. The Romans and Greeks believed in a succession of ages, each containing men made of gold, silver, bronze or flesh. In early Greek thinking, the end of the world was a topic for philosophical discussion, not religious debate. Stoicism taught that the end would come with fire and would be reborn in a series of cycles. Famed Greek philosophers Plato and Aristotle thought a series of natural events would initiate a destruction-rebirth cycle. Plato said that there were three ages; the third and present one was perfect and eternal. Both men were idolized in the Middle Ages, so it's not surprising Joachim of Fiore, a celebrated monk asked by the pope to create an apocalyptic calendar, picked up on that cyclical theme. In the late 1100s, he labeled each age thought to have elapsed since Jesus with a different religious theme. He felt the final age, Armageddon, would occur in the mid-1200s.

The Romans, who absorbed a welter of ideas from various cultures, also accepted the concept of a recycled world, with destruction and then the periodic return of the same people and the same world. The poet Virgil, for example, predicted a second voyage of Jason and the Argonauts, a second Trojan War and a second Achilles. Other Romans also imagined a return to the golden age when Saturn supposedly ruled.

The ongoing religious turmoil, wars and philosophical differences during the years that the Romans ruled the Jews led to a widespread conviction that the world was ending. The messiah was to herald that event, known as Armageddon. After all, the concept of a final end is so overwhelming that it needed a divine being, a messiah, to bring it about.

The Essenes, waiting for God to act, relied on the story of the Flood to explain what would happen when Yahweh tired of human iniquity. Only those who followed God's law, as explained in the holy texts, would survive. Christian dogma then linked this horrific scene to Jesus. Those that believed in Him would be saved; those who did not would suffer eternal punishment.

Initially, such a claim would not have garnered much enthusiasm. However, the destruction of the Temple in 70 C.E., an event absolutely cataclysmic in the Jewish world seemed to presage the end of the world. God apparently had fled his house and broken the contract with the Jews. Such an event must be man's fault and presaged the cleansing of the world.

As Jewish sages sought answers in ancient prophetic wisdom, Christian missionaries hurried through the Empire, trying to "save" as many people as possible before the end arrived.

The end-of-the-world concept has been part of Western civilization ever since.

For Jews, the Noah story failed to provide a system of revenge against those who oppressed them. Jewish prophets still envisioned a time when they would again be a holy people following God's laws and when sinners would be eliminated.

The Old Testament prophets had spoken of the coming of the Kingdom of Yahweh, meaning that on the Day of the Lord all existing governments would be destroyed and Yahweh would appear in person as the supreme ruler of the earth. -- Smith, pg. 175

Jewish thinking has been dominated by history and by the belief that God's intentions could be understood through current events. God had made a promise to the Jews: therefore, if they were losing a war or had been conquered, it followed that they must have done something to antagonize God. Once they had repented and returned to God's ways, their leaders reasoned, then God would remove their enemies in a "Day of the Lord."

"The Day of the Lord is prominent in many eschatological texts. This notion belongs to the monarchic tradition complex, representing the dual motif of Yahweh's combat and ensuing victory along with the enthronement of Yahweh as king. For Israel this day was, early on, a cause for rejoicing," one historian said.

That image changed as time frittered away. The Day of the Lord turned into bleak annihilation, characterized in the writings of the early prophets Amos and Zephaniah and later ones like Ezekiel. It's a natural progression. The loss of David's kingdom, tremendous Jewish defeats by the Assyrians and Babylonians, the destruction of the holy First Temple and the resulting exile could "only" have been the result of tremendous failing and could only have been recompensed by tremendous catastrophes.

Other reasons also affected the old end-of-the-world idea.

This change was doubtlessly caused by the breaking down of the tribal barriers and the absorption of the nation in a large empire. With the rise of Alexander the Great's Empire, which extended from Greece to Persia, and later with even more extensive Roman dominion, the Jews found themselves facing a situation where political independence was out of the question. The old hope of national prosperity had to fade, and it was not surprising that they should begin to think that only a cosmic act of God could have the power to break the vast empires oppressing them. -- Wells, pg. 158-159

At first, Cyrus' surprising permission to rebuild Jerusalem seemed to portend a return to the golden age under Davidic rule. It didn't turn out that way. The land remained impoverished; God did not restore Jewish sovereignty. Prophetic hopes turned to bitterness. With such outcries came the only solution -- complete destruction of hated enemies.

Any belief in the concept of the final destruction is directly linked to Jewish writings, in particular the book of Daniel, which was described earlier. Towards the end of Daniel, the text shifts from Hebrew to Aramaic (2:4 to 7:8) and captures the mood of its time. "The Jewish spiritual revival (during the war against the Syrians)... stimulated an outburst of messianic and apocalyptic fervor." -- Schonfield, pg. 31

It was engendered by previous ideas expressed by Jeremiah and Ezekiel. Both had predicted the rebirth of Israel, a rebuilding of the Temple and the return of the holy priests. Yet, despite such hopes, the Jews had remained under foreign control. Zechariah asks why God has not responded (1:12), only to claim the answer is that the Temple had not been rebuilt yet. It soon was. That still didn't change anything.

The author of Daniel decided that God delayed inaugurating his kingdom because the Jewish sins had not abated yet. The writer then reinterpreted the prophetic writings: the 70 years promised by Jeremiah for the return to the holy state of Israel after the Babylonian conquest really meant 70 weeks of years (Dan 9:2, 24). That works out to 490 years — or about 100 years after the lifetime of the author dating from the setting of the book in the Babylonian conquest.

The book also introduced a theory of resurrection (12:2) -- possibly also mentioned by Isaiah in a late apocalyptic addition to an earlier book (26:19). Angels, too, make an appearance, likely borrowed from the Persians, who had winged messengers of the gods. The messengers in the Bible do not have wings. The Greeks and Romans had winged messengers, but their wings were on their shoes.

Resurrection was important psychologically because of the circumstances. Antiochus IV, the Syrian leader, attempted to wipe out Judaism with a series of persecutions, including the deaths of prominent, pious Jews. Mothers who permitted circumcision were hanged with their babies dangling from their necks. Those who refused to renounce Judaism were butchered, exiled or sold into slavery. Under these trying conditions, as historian John Bright noted, "the belief that God would vindicate his justice beyond the grave became an absolute necessity for the majority of Jews." (pg. 439)

Angels seemed an ideal way for God to manifest himself. After all, in the biblical book of Exodus, an angel of death had passed over the houses of the children of Israel during the 10th plague. Daniel supplies names for the important angels (e.g. Michael, Daniel:12:1), replacing the anonymous "messengers" who in Genesis walked slowly up and down Jacob's ladder (Genesis 28:12) or visited Abraham. (Genesis: 18:2) Michael has been understood as "the one like a son of man" (Daniel: 7), taking the place of Baal in the Canaanite myth of a supernatural being who overcomes the beasts of the sea. -- Anchor, Vol. 2, pg. 3

Daniel did far more than simply suggest a new date; the author supplied a name to the being who would inaugurate it — the messiah. For the first time ever, Jews had someone to focus on, an image of a person who would quickly be incarnated.

Those who believed in (Daniel's) interpretation and lived in the reign of Herod the Great (37- 4 B.C.E.) could accept that the Last Times had now begun, and that therefore before very long the coming of the messiah was to be expected. This explains why a strong messianic excitement manifested itself among the Jews from this time onward, and why no one before this had claimed to be the messiah. -- Schonfield, pg. 15

The widespread circulation of Daniel led to a state of "near hysteria ... It was wholly in keeping with the circumstances that a figure like John the Baptist would now appear proclaiming the Kingdom of God was at hand, and calling upon the people to repent and save themselves from the wrath to come."

"The whole area, from Lake of Gennesaret (Sea of Galilee) down to the Dead Sea itself was alive with holy eccentrics," added historian Paul Johnson.

Under the Greco-Roman rule, particularly in the first and second centuries (C.E.), messianic hope became so strong among the Jews that many self-proclaimed messiahs appeared. Jesus, among others, was recognized by his immediate followers as the messiah. -- Nigosian, pg. 142

To augment scripture, Jewish writers also developed separate predictions. Forged Sibylline oracles -- the Sibyl supposedly foresaw the history of Rome and was consulted by Roman authorities in times of trouble -- claimed that a great man would rise from the East as the world disintegrated. The Romans were well aware of the predictions. Roman historian Suetonius wrote, "There had been spread all over the Orient an old and established belief, that it was fated at that for men coming from Judea to rule the world." Josephus, writing for Roman readers, said a man from Judea would soon "become monarch of the whole world."

Josephus saved his life by claiming General Vespasian, who led the Roman army against the Jews starting in 66 C.E., was the predicted "great man." When Vespasian became emperor in 70, he spared the historian's life.

Earlier, Emperor Augustus tried to solve the rising tide of predictions by ordering the destruction of many of the fake oracles. Tiberius, his successor, also purified the Sibylline collection because of a popular prediction that "the end of the empire was at hand."

Those dire forecasts and related prophecies were widespread. Tacitus (55-c.117) wrote a history of Rome that included a section on the Jewish-Roman war of 66 to 70 C.E. He said, "The majority (of Jews) were convinced that the ancient scriptures of their priests alluded to the present as the very time when the Orient would triumph and from Judea would go forth men destined to rule the world." Tacitus was not impressed, saying that Vespasian and his son Titus were the actually prophesied individuals, "but the common people, true to the selfish ambitions of mankind, thought this exalted destiny was reserved for them, and not even their calamities opened their eyes to the truth."

Jews believed the predictions, because a host of writers assured them the ancient prophets were right. For example, the *Psalms of Solomon*, cited in Chapter 1, foresaw the coming Kingdom of God.

Ezra IV, written late in the first century C.E., asks the basic question: "If the world has been created for us, why don't we possess it as an inheritance now?" Many other works duplicated this query and emphasized the growing sense of Jewish frustration at the long-delayed "Last Times."

The idea was not monolithic: some writers built the End of Time around a concept of a Davidic leader who would restore the old kingdom; others preferred a "new and perfect world" that would arise after the destruction of the "present, evil world." -- Anchor, Vol. 11, pg. 597

The founders of Christianity were sure Jesus was the person destined to rule this new Eden. But, given their small numbers and isolated position in a tiny country on the rim of the Roman Empire, how would anyone else find out?

Chapter Thirteen

Paul Gets the Message Out

Our earliest writer about Jesus is best known by the name Paul. He also identified himself as Saul. A native of Tarsus, in what is now Turkey, he claimed to have come to Jerusalem in time to witness the martyrdom of Stephen in the late 30s C.E. That must have been a few years after the death of Jesus. Paul eventually joined the fledgling Nazarene sect, according to his letters, and traveled throughout the Roman Empire, forming small colonies of believers.

We don't know his real name: Paul is a Roman word for "small," a nickname. Born in a Greek-speaking community, he would have had a Greek name, but that has never been discovered.

We do know that he believed that Jesus was sent by God in preparation for the coming end of the world. In his letters, many of which are included in the New Testament, Paul talked about his belief. He is also the first known author to write anything about Jesus. His writings precede the Gospels by many years.

What does Paul tell us about Jesus? Unfortunately, virtually nothing. Paul never cited any sayings associated with Jesus. He described no miracles. Paul's only historic observations were: Jesus was "born of a woman" (Galatians 4:4) and was "descended from David, according to the flesh" (Romans 1:3). He also told us Jesus was Jewish, devoted his ministry to Jews and was crucified.

He didn't even indicate whether Jesus lived 10 years earlier or 100.

Modern Christian historians have claimed that Paul omitted the biographical details because he was writing to people who knew the life of Jesus and had no reason to elaborate. That's simply not plausible. He founded several colonies of believers and was forced to respond when other evangelists went to the same people with a different message. The authentic history of Jesus would have been a very strong asset for him. He offered none.

Paul may not have written even the six or seven biblical epistles now attributed to him. He probably dictated them to a more literate colleague, allowing room for mistakes and faulty copying.

The first great convert to what became Christianity, he began writing no earlier than 39 C.E. Some historians put the date of Paul's first letters as late as 49 C.E. Paul's concern was the expected end of the world initiated by Jesus' death. His goal was to reach as many people as possible so that, when the end came, they could be saved. History was not his touchstone; philosophy was.

Much of what he wrote about himself has come under close scrutiny right along with every other biblical figure. Research into Paul is particularly significant because of his influence on Christian teachings and because we do have authentic material left by him.

Paul described his conversion and subsequent missionary work in his letters. Other details are provided in the book of Acts. The Nazarenes provided some comments on him, too. The different texts provide multiple versions of his life. Some factual errors must have slipped into the current manuscripts as happens when any documents are copied.

Tribal Ties

According to the various accounts, he was born in Tarsus, and he was Jewish and a member of the tribe of Benjamin. His father was a councilman in Tarsus. As a young man, Paul went to Jerusalem to study with a sage, Gamaliel. There, he witnessed the death of Stephen, the first Christian martyr. Paul worked for the High Priest and harassed Christians. He was on his way back from Damascus, home to many Jews, when he was confronted by an image of Jesus. Paul converted to the new faith and began to set up colonies of Christians around the Mediterranean.

Eventually, he had a fight with the leaders of the Nazarenes and was arrested by Roman guards during a melee. Declaring himself a Roman citizen, he demanded a trial in Rome. Shipped there, he survived an arduous journey only to be imprisoned and disappear from history. He is presumed to have died in 64 C.E. during persecutions initiated by the Emperor Nero.

We know Tarsus existed. Tarsus was a major city then, but has long since been buried under the sands of passing time. We also know that members of the city council had to take an oath to the Roman gods, something no Jew could do. Moreover, Paul was not likely to be a member of any tribe. Tribal designations had died out centuries before. That's because the loss of the 10 tribes to the Assyrians meant only Benjamin and Judah survived. Judah was so much larger that Benjamin was simply swallowed up. By the

3rd century B.C.E., Jewish sages no longer refer to tribes. Everyone was a Jew.

So, some historians have argued that Paul was really a God-fearer, raised by his parents to be Jewish. That argument is supported by the Ebionites, who insist Paul was not Jewish or circumcised.

Paul also took inordinate delight in being from Tarsus, "no mean city," he wrote. However, Jews in those days boasted only of being from Jerusalem, the center of their religion.

In Acts, Paul was described as a student in a Jerusalem academy run by Gamaliel, a highly respected figure in the rabbinical commentaries who gets prominent mention in the Mishnah. He was the leader of the Pharisees, partially because he was the grandson of Hillel, the great and most-beloved sage in Jewish history. In his letters, Paul never mentioned Gamaliel, although he claimed to be a Pharisee. The omission is strange. Studying with Gamaliel was a major coupe for any scholar. Moreover, Paul was about 19 at the time. Gamaliel never took anyone as a student who was under 30 or was not fluent in Hebrew, the language of the sacred texts. Paul admitted he did not know Hebrew.

Then, Paul became involved in the stoning of Stephan. The martyr apparently offended the Sanhedrin with comments about Jesus and was immediately killed. The men throwing stones "laid their coats at the feet of a young man named Saul" who "approved of his murder." (Acts 8:1).

Few historians understand this story. The Sanhedrin was an august body. Members did not simply disband to throw stones. In fact, there was a set series of requirements that had to be followed in a capital case. The Gospels describe Jesus going through that procedure. Acts reported that Peter also endured a trial. He was not stoned either.

Moreover, historians cannot agree if the Jews had the power to put anyone to death. Jesus, after all, was executed by Roman authorities.

Moreover, no other early Christian mentions Stephen, whose name means "crown." He was supposedly an early deacon in the church, an institute that didn't exist then or, obviously, have officials.

On the Road to Damascus

Paul moved on to join the High Priest and was "harrying the Church; he entered house after house, seizing men and women, and sending them to prison." (Acts 8:3). He must have been doing that for the High Priest, but that official had no authority outside the Temple. Moreover, he was a Sadducee, while Paul claimed to be a "Pharisee of Pharisees." There is no evidence that the High Priest ever hired a Pharisee to work on his behalf. All extant data shows the parties were bitter enemies.

Paul then "still breathing murderous threats against the disciples of the Lord," went "to the High Priest and applied for letters to the synagogues at Damascus authorizing him to arrest anyone he found, men or women, who followed the new way, and bring them to Jerusalem.'" (Acts: 9) This, too, is troublesome for several reasons. The High Priest had no authority in Damascus. Actually, no Roman did either. Emperor Caligula had granted freedom to the city. It was independent of the Roman Empire.

Paul was akin to an American getting permission from a leading Orthodox rabbi to go to Canada and harass non-Orthodox Jews there. That could not happen.

In Acts 22, Paul recounted his biography to that time:

I am a true-born Jew, a native of Tarsus in Cilicia. I was brought up in this city, and as a pupil of Gamaliel I was thoroughly trained in every point of our ancestral law. I have always been ardent in God's service, as you all are today. And so I began to persecute this movement to the death, arresting its followers, men and women alike, and putting them in chains. For this, I have as witnesses the High Priest and the whole Council of Elders. I was given letters from them to our fellow-Jews at Damascus, and had started out to bring the Christians there to Jerusalem as prisoners for punishment…

Although it's unlikely the author of Acts intended to be ironic, but he managed to do so. Paul, a Pharisee, claimed to be sent to Damascus with the permission of the High Priest and Council of Elders, presumably the Sanhedrin. Meanwhile, according to Acts, the Pharisee members of the Sanhedrin repeatedly countered Sadducee attempts to harass the Nazarenes living in their city. Moreover, Jesus must have been a Pharisee as were all of his followers. All of the comments attributed to Jesus are attested to in surviving Pharisaic literature.

Actually, historians determined that the biblical animosity toward Pharisees occurred after the destruction of the Temple. The Sadducees were destroyed, as were the Zealots and the Essenes. The only major political/religious party to survive belonged to the Pharisees. They accepted the prophetic claims that God had fled his people because they had failed to live up to His commandments. That led to intense scrutiny and imposition of additional rules to ensure the same calamity did not happen again. The early Christian church objected to those restrictions and backdated complaints against the Pharisees into the Gospels.

Paul may have been motivated by attempts to show that Christianity was a purified continuation of Judaism. He considered the Nazarenes as heretics who had deserted Judaism. After his conversion, he changed his view. Now, he believed that Jesus was the Messiah prophesied in the sacred scrolls.

He did not reject the Jewish holy texts, as some of his later followers did. Instead, he felt much of it could be forgotten by the arrival of Jesus. His claim of being a Pharisee might have been his way to link the old ideas of the Jews with his new concept of an updated faith.

Most likely, Paul wanted to establish his credentials as a Jew. By doing so, he enhanced his position during missionary work and was able to reach a wider Jewish audience.

So when Paul declares his Pharisee past, he is not merely proclaiming his own sins – 'See how I have changed, from being a Pharisee persecutor to being a devoted follower of Jesus!' -- he is also proclaiming his credentials -- 'If someone as learned as I can believe that Jesus was the fulfillment of the Torah, who is there fearless enough to disagree?'

Paul said he underwent a conversion on the road from Damascus. Some historians suggest that, since he claimed to suffer from an ailment and was described as falling down in a fit, that he had epilepsy. They think the revelation of Jesus occurred during a seizure. Others considered that it might have been a 'near-death" experience, often characterized by bright lights and the approach of a strange figure.

In reality, Paul's views seem to be drawn more from pagan sources. Perhaps that's because he grew up in a city renowned for its annual spring festival of the risen Herakles. Paul would have seen that as a young man. Judaism has no risen gods; that comes from the Greek and Roman concepts.

Civil Battles

Paul also argued with the early church leaders. Some of that debate was encapsulated in Acts, where Paul wants to reach out to Gentiles, while the Nazarenes preferred to carry Jesus' message only to Jews.

As far as historians can tell from the meager documentation available, Nazarene beliefs paralleled the Pharisees. They worshiped in the Temple, maintained the Sabbath, followed Kosher laws and lived as devout Jews. The exception was that the Nazarenes believed in the resurrection of Jesus, and that Jesus was still the promised Messiah.

They did not believe that Jesus was a divine person, but that, by a miracle from God, he had been brought back to life after his death on the cross, and would soon come back to complete his mission of overthrowing the Romans and setting up the Messianic kingdom. The Nazarenes did not believe that Jesus had abrogated the Jewish religion, or Torah. Having known Jesus personally, they were aware that he had observed the Jewish religious law all his life and had never rebelled against it. His Sabbath cures were not against Pharisee law. The Nazarenes were themselves very observant of Jewish religious law. They practiced circumcision, did not eat the forbidden foods and showed great respect to the Temple. The Nazarenes did not regard themselves as belonging to a new religion; their religion was Judaism. They set up synagogues of their own, but they also attended non-Nazarene synagogues on occasion, and performed the same kind of worship in their own synagogues as was practiced by all observant Jews.

Eventually, they would reject Paul's teachings and spurn him. Some of that was revealed in the Epistles, where Paul complained that missionaries coming after him taught a different message about Jesus. Those missionaries must have come from the Nazarenes, the only other people with any interest in Jesus at the time.

What Motivated Paul?

Looking at the reality of his biography as opposed to what was written, historians have tried to reconstruct what drove Paul to his beliefs. They have developed several possibilities.

As someone outside the Jewish fold, Paul was in a difficult position. He firmly believed that Jesus presaged the coming end. "Paul expected the age to come, which would be introduced by the Parousia (or return) of Jesus, to arrive in the near future... The resurrection of Jesus convinced Paul that the age to come had already begun," *Anchor Bible Dictionary* recorded.

However, the idea was Jewish. Those who would be saved were Jewish. Paul's only choice would be to argue that Jesus came for everyone to alert them about the end of the world, not just Jews. Aware he could never be accepted fully by Jews, Paul found a way to graft Judaism onto pagan concepts of a risen god. He no longer had to follow Jewish law, which he did not know or accept.

He may not have intended to start a new religion, but his approach opened the door to many people who felt stymied by Jewish laws, but wanted to be part of the Chosen People.

Also, Paul fought with James, the head of the Nazarenes. There's some discussion among historians whether James was also the High Priest who was stoned to death around 63 C.E. One historian even argued that James was really the Teacher of Righteousness. He was described as having prayed so much that his knees were covered with calluses.

Paul may have rejected James as the true leader of the church and turned to James' martyred brother, Jesus, in defiance. He argued that Jesus was not chosen to be the messiah until he was on the cross – which would have explained why the Nazarenes, who knew Jesus, were unaware of his significance. In essence, in this argument, the miracles and other events attributed to Jesus were actually performed by James, but were shifted under Paul's influence.

In the long run, it doesn't matter why Paul acted as he did. His efforts to share Jesus' message with the world eventually led to the rise of Christianity. Within a few centuries, Christianity bypassed Judaism and took Abraham's dream in an entirely new direction.

Chapter Fourteen

Christianity Grows Up

In spite of Paul's best efforts – or, maybe, because of them – Jesus became the central figure amid a wide array of religious ideas. Many Jews were drawn to His call for peace and love. Others, God-fearers, appreciated the fact that they did not have to be circumcised to become a member of the "Chosen People." Many pagans were attracted to the morality and ethics exhibited by Jesus' followers. Pagan philosophers noted how members of the early Christian community took care of each other and wished their own religious communities were as loving.

Gnostics Step In

Perhaps the largest group that took an interest in the fledgling faith was the Gnostics, a philosophical and religious movement with roots in pre-Christian times. Gnostics combined elements taken from Asian, Babylonian, Egyptian, Greek and Syrian pagan religions, Babylonian astrology, Judaism and Christianity. They formed their own churches under the name of John, Thomas and other disciples, claiming to have secret knowledge about God, humanity, and the rest of the universe of which the general population was unaware. They also produced documents to support their arguments.

Until the 20th century, most of the Gnostic literature had been suppressed. Still, a surprising amount of material has survived, including the Shepherd of Men, Asclepius, Codex Askewianus, Codex Brucianus, Gospel of Mary, Secret Gospel of John, Odes of Solomon and the Hymn of the Pearl.

Knowledge of Gnosticism jumped dramatically in 1945 after a camel driver from El Qasr in Egypt and his brother found a large clay jar near Nag Hammadi, a village in northern Egypt. They were digging for nitrate-rich earth that they could use for fertilizer. Instead, they uncovered a Gnostic library consisting of 13 volumes. Altogether, there were 51 different works on 1,153 pages. A few were copies of works that were already known; others were duplicated within the library. The rest, 41, were new, previously unknown works, including the Gospel of Thomas, Gospel of Truth, Treatise on the Resurrection, Gospel of Philip, Wisdom of Jesus Christ, Revelation of James, Letter of Peter to Philip and On the Origin of the World.

There were also Coptic versions of Greek texts written during the second and third centuries. Some Gnostic texts were non-Christian; others were originally non-Christian, but had Christian elements added; others were entirely Christian documents.

Finally translated by the late 1970s, the books reveal more about the early history of Christianity than the Dead Sea Scrolls.

Gnostics claimed that Jesus carried a message from heaven that allowed them to acquire "gnosis," or inner knowledge. This gnosis was seen as the inner and esoteric mystical knowledge of ultimate reality, the spark of divinity thought that had been obscured by ignorance.

This knowledge is not considered to be the possession of the masses but of the Gnostics, the Knowers, who are privy to its benefits. While the orthodox 'many' exult in the esoteric religious trappings which stress dogmatic belief and prescribed behavior, the Gnostic 'few' pierce through the surface to the esoteric spiritual knowledge of God.

The writers of the New Testament knew all about the Gnostics. The Carpocratian Gnostics may have been the target of Jude's attack about "... certain men" who "have secretly slipped in among you." The book of Jude, verses 4 to 19, deals mainly with these infiltrators.

Simon Magus, an early opponent of Christianity who was once considered the main rival to Jesus, is thought to have been a Gnostic.

Gnostic ideas appear in the New Testament. In Matthew 4:8-9, for example, Satan took Jesus to a very high mountain and offered him all of the kingdoms of the world if Jesus would only bow down and worship him. The passage matched (and countered) Gnostic belief that the devil owned the world.

Scholars found that in the first century, independent Gnostic sects actually endorsed an array of beliefs, but shared some basic tenets:

• Gnostics believed that they alone understood Christ's message. From earliest times, Messengers of the Light have come forth from the True God in order to assist humans in their quest for knowledge. The most important messengers are Seth (the third son of Adam), Jesus, and the Prophet Mani. The majority of Gnostics always looked to Jesus as the principal savior figure.

Mani, who, by tradition, was martyred some 200 years after Jesus, became the leader of a large religion that, at one time, would number St. Augustus in its ranks. The belief, which looks at the world as good and evil, was a major rival to Christianity in the first centuries after Jesus died.

• Knowledge had a redeeming and liberating function that helped the individual break free of bondage to the world. Jesus is the savior, not because he suffers, but through his life of teaching and establishment of mysteries.

• The Supreme Father God is separated from humans and undetectable. However, that god created a series of supernatural but finite beings called Aeons. One of these was Sophia, a virgin, who in turn gave birth to a defective, inferior Creator-God, also known as the Demiurge ("half maker"). This deity was identified as Yahweh, the Jewish god who was viewed as fundamentally evil, jealous, rigid, lacking in compassion and prone to genocide. The Demiurge "thinks that he is supreme. His pride and incompetence have resulted in the sorry state of the world as we know it, and in the blind and ignorant condition of most of mankind."

• Spirit is good; the body is evil. Gnostics were hostile to the physical world, to matter and the human body. But, they believed that trapped within some people's bodies were the sparks of divinity or seeds of light that were supplied to humanity by Sophia. Elements of that concept show up in the Jewish Kabbalah in the Middle Ages; the sinful body concept would be absorbed into Christianity.

• Persons attain salvation by learning secret knowledge of their divine spark of light or spirit. If so, they can join the Supreme God at death.

• Since the world was created by an inferior god, it was inherently evil. Original sin is not far removed from this view. The snake in the Garden of Eden, then, is not evil, but rather a deliverer who brings knowledge to Adam and Eve.

• Christ's role was to spread knowledge that would free individuals from the Demiurge's control and allow them to return to their spiritual home with the Supreme God at death.

As with early Christians, little is known about Gnostic rituals or accepted scripture. However, we do know that Gnostic groups latched onto Mary Magdalene, often placing her second behind Jesus in importance. Some of that was picked up in the popular novel, *The DaVinci Code*. They also practiced a kind of baptism. A surviving prayer asks that: "In the name of the Father unknown to all, in the Truth, Mother of All, in the One who came down upon Jesus, in the union, redemption and communion of powers."

By the second century, many Christian-Gnostic sects had formed around the eastern end of the Mediterranean and survived into the third century under such leaders as Marcion of Sinope. He wrote a book called *Antitheses*, which got him excommunicated by the Christian leaders of Rome. He believed that the Demiurge arranged Jesus' persecution and crucifixion. As such, Marcion taught, the death of Christ on the cross was only a hallucination, since Jesus did not have a physical body.

Other noted teachers included Valentinus, an Egyptian who founded perhaps the largest and most influential school of Gnosticism; and Carpocrates, who taught that individuals lived many lives before being able to return to God. They supposedly practiced free sexuality, a common canard used by Christians and Jews before them to attack opponents.

Christian leaders belittled Gnostics and their followers as heretics, led by Irenaeus (c. 130 - 200), Clement of Alexandria (c. 145 - 213), Tertullian (c. 160 - 225) and Hippolytus (c. 170 - 236). By the sixth century, they had succeeded in overcoming the Gnostic movement. The only group to have survived into modern times is the Mandaean sect of Iraq and Iran. It has fewer than 15,000 members.

Christians spent years trying to divorce themselves from Gnostic ties. The Gospel writers would have struggled with that concern and made sure the accounts they recorded belied Gnostic beliefs.

How Did Christians Separate from the Jews?

For at least the first five decades after Jesus died, followers continued to worship in synagogues and the Temple. They read the same holy texts and followed the same religious practices. The only exception was Sabbath. The early Christians started their Sabbath on Friday night with the rest of the Jewish population, but extended the holiday through Sunday.

Historians once argued that they chose to move the day of rest to Sunday to separate themselves from the rest of the Jewish population. However, all historical material available shows that Jesus' followers hallowed Sunday prior to the ascension of Christianity. That would imply the day was special to them for religious reasons, possibly because, as the Gospels recorded, Jesus died on a Sunday.

Nevertheless, friction had to arise between mainstream Jews and the followers of Jesus. For starters, Jews firmly believed that any mistake on their part could cause the wrath of God to descend on them, as had happened in the past. No one wanted to go through Babylonian captivity again. Moreover, Roman control of their land implied that God was already unhappy. How would He react to believers among them who now believed in a dead messiah? No prophetic statements had prepared Jews for a messiah who died before achieving the expected goal of ruling over an independent Jewish theocracy.

As beliefs about Jesus solidified, some believers began to argue that Jesus was God incarnate, an idea that Jews rejected. To them, God was a spirit who would not become a man. Finally, around 90 C.E., Jewish religious leaders began to insert into the regular services a prayer that condemned those who teach something contrary to traditional Jewish views.

May there be no hope for apostates. And may you quickly uproot the arrogant kingdom in our day. And may the Christians and heretics instantly perish. May they be erased from the book of life, and may they not be written with the righteous. Blessed are You, Adonai, who humbles the arrogant.

Followers of Jesus could not say that prayer, which was quickly dropped from Jewish services. They responded by forming their own synagogues. In time, they had a separate religion and a new name. Christ is the Greek word for messiah. Greek was the language of the new religion; so, its adherents became known as Christians.

The division also created an incentive to have holy texts. Just as the cherished Jewish manuscripts buttressed Jewish beliefs, Christians needed documents to support their views. Early scrolls, which had served individual communities, now began to spread and be studied with renewed fervor. New texts were written.

The spread of these documents was aided by the fortuitous invention of books. In the past, texts were limited by the length of a scroll. They are bulky and heavy, so writers had to stop at a certain point before the scroll became unwieldy. Books, known technically as "folios," are different. A writer simply added pages, which are then bound together. Books are easily portable, last longer than scrolls and can be of almost unlimited length.

What Happened to the Nazarenes?

The followers of Jesus were increasingly outside mainstream Christianity. They weren't welcomed by the Jews either. By the end of the second century, they either assimilated into Christianity or returned to Judaism.

Other sects suffered similar fates. Followers of John the Baptist, who insisted their founder was greater than Jesus, issued texts and made their claims, but, in the end, were not strong enough to overcome Jesus. The man of peace apparently had some fight in him.

When Christians became the dominant faith in the Roman Empire, they razed pagan temples and took over what had once been sites sacred to other religions. They flattened the followers of Mani, who had once been the god of the Roman Army.

Judaism, too, was brushed aside. Jews banned proselytizing, which had helped build their population to such heights, in fear Christians were spying on them. Jews still do not recruit converts today.

A brief attempt under the Roman Emperor Julian late in the fourth century to revive pagan faiths failed after he was slain in battle early in his reign.

With Julian's death, Abraham's sole survivors were a tiny remnant of Jews and the swelling multitude of Christians now in control of the Empire. To any onlooker, that would have been a strange scenario, considering how hard the Romans fought to suppress the faith.

Say Hello to that Hungry Lion

The rise of Christianity caused problems within the Roman Empire in the first century C.E. Jews in Judea were not popular with the Romans because of the on-going civil war. Christians were worse. At least some Jews fought on the side of Romans in distant wars. They also said prayers for the emperor and did not claim that their God was once a human who was crucified.

The Romans were not impressed nor concerned with claims that the Jewish God had left the Temple. They cared that their emperor, their living god, was accorded his proper respect and received his regular tribute. They were also sophisticated enough to recognize that Jews and Christians represented different sides of the same coin. Both believed in God, but the Christian missionaries were going around like some ancient Chicken Little, insisting that the end of the world was coming.

According to Tacitus, as we read in Chapter 9, Christians suffered persecution under Nero because of the burning of Rome. They reportedly were used as living torches to light the way for the emperor. There have been questions raised about the accuracy of that report. Christians had not been established yet. There may have been a small colony in Rome – Paul's letter to the Romans is in the canon – but its membership must have been small. On the other hand, Tacitus hated Jews because of their attacks on the Romans. He was not fond of Nero either. Perhaps, the famous historian tarred both with the same dark paragraph. No other historian reported the deaths or blamed Christians for the fire that decimated almost half of Rome.

On the other hand, there's no question that Christians really ticked off the Romans. In all, there were 10 major persecutions, culminating early in the fourth century. Christians were fed to beasts, forced to serve in mines until exhaustion killed them, crucified, hung or murdered. Modern historians have found that evidence of such horrific treatment is limited and that Christians exaggerated. However, Eusebius, the church historian, was so depressed by the horrors that he was convinced the world must be ending around 300 C.E. That was the only reason he could think of to justify such brutal suppression.

He identified 10 different persecutions.

1. Nero (Roman emperor, 54–68). Church tradition says that Paul and Peter died at this time in Rome.

2. Domitian (Roman emperor, 81–96).

3. Trajan (Roman emperor, 98–117).

4. Marcus Aurelius, (Roman emperor, 161–180).

5. Septimius Severus (Roman emperor, 193–211).

6. Maximus (Roman emperor, 235–238).

7. Decius (Roman emperor, 249–251

8. Valerian (Roman emperor, 253–260).

9. Aurelian (Roman emperor, 270–275).

10. Diocletian (Roman emperor, 284–305) and **Maximian** (Roman emperor, 285–305) governed together. Diocletian began persecuting Christians in 303. His attacks continued until 313, when Emperor Constantine proclaimed religious freedom. Christianity would not become the sole legal religion of the Empire for decades.

Roman hatred raised enormous problems for Christians who survived the attacks. Many chose to drop the belief while under threat of death, then, when persecution eased, return to the church. Should they be welcomed back? Not everyone thought so. Also, under this intense Roman pressure, Christians began to formulate new concepts of Jesus, creating sects that threatened to undermine the accepted view. One bishop, Arius, proposed that Jesus was an intermediate between God and man. Another suggested that Jesus felt no pain and was only an image of a human. There were many more ideas floating around.

An upstart who rebelled against his emperor, Constantine did not want to alienate a large block of constituents by choosing one view over another. He wasn't Christian, although his mother, Helen, was. Constantine worshiped Sol Invictus, the solar deity, but would convert to Christianity on his deathbed. There was no need to rush because, in the Church view, a person who confessed and accepted Jesus early or late in life was still going to heaven. Constantine, who had a lot to atone for and no desire to retreat from a riotous lifestyle, chose to wait as long as possible.

To try to reach a consensus on Christian ideas, a central concept that everyone could accept, Constantine convened perhaps the most famous church gathering in history. Some 250 to 318 church leaders from countries around the Mediterranean met in Nicaea in 325 C.E. in the first session of its kind.

More than religion was involved. Early Christians inherited the Roman view that the gods were responsible for the stability of the country. If a debate raged, and no one knew who or what was the correct belief, then the country was in grave peril.

The issue of what constituted the true belief was debated widely.

"If you ask a man for change for a piece of silver, he tells you which way the son differs from the father; and if you ask for a loaf of bread, you get a reply that the son is inferior to the father," wrote Gregory, Bishop of Nyssa after visiting Constantinople, the capital of the Roman Empire in the fourth century. "If you ask if your bath is ready, you are solemnly told the son is made out of nothing."

The biggest argument centered around Arius, who argued that Jesus was created by God to serve as an intermediary between man and heaven. He could not have been part of God as proposed by others, the solemn priest said. After all, he asked, was Jesus calling to himself when he cried on the cross, "Father, why has thou forsaken me?"

Arius, who may have been poisoned prior to a later meeting of bishops, lost overwhelmingly (he got two votes) at Nicaea to a belief in a tripartite god: father, son and holy ghost.

The delegates also decided to hold a celebration of Jesus' birthday in December and established when to remember His crucifixion and resurrection. They also approved the Catholic Creed, still dutifully recited by the faithful.

We believe (I believe) in one God, the Father Almighty, maker of heaven and earth, and of all things visible and invisible. And in one Lord Jesus Christ, the only begotten Son of God, and born of the Father before all ages. (God of God) light of light, true God of true God. Begotten not made, consubstantial to the Father, by whom all things were made. Who for us men and for our salvation came down from heaven. And was incarnate of the Holy Ghost and of the Virgin Mary and was made man; was crucified also for us under Pontius Pilate, suffered and was buried; and the third day rose again according to the Scriptures. And ascended into heaven, sits at the right hand of the Father, and shall come again with glory to judge the living and the dead, of whose Kingdom there shall be no end. And (I believe) in the Holy Ghost, the Lord and Giver of life, who proceeds from the Father (and the Son), who together with the Father and the Son is to be adored and glorified, who spoke by the Prophets. And one holy, catholic, and apostolic Church. We confess (I confess) one baptism for the remission of sins. And we look for (I look for) the resurrection of the dead and the life of the world to come. Amen."

The momentous work would continue in future councils ("synods.") Leading bishops met on almost a regular basis through the fourth century. One of them, the bishop of Rome, became the most important, beating out rivals in Constantinople and Alexandra. Being in Rome, the center of the civic empire, helped. So did the accepted belief that apostles Peter and Paul died in Rome. The man in that seat became known as the pope, which is derived from the word for "father" in Latin. He took over the title "Pontifex Maximus," a title used by priests serving Roman pagan gods and often conferred on political leaders like Julius Caesar. As a result, today, the pope is also known as the Pontiff.

Constantine, however, remained the most powerful man in the empire until his death, foreshadowing the conflict between popes and secular leaders through the ages.

As Rome began to totter, the pope slowly assumed the role of ruler of the European world. Titles in the Roman hierarchy were borrowed to create a Christian structure.

There were still disagreements. The Greek half of the church split away over the question of whether Jesus was "like" or "as" God. The two factions still disagree. The Greek Orthodox have their own leader and do not obey the pope. Occasional attempts at reconciliation have failed. The Crusades sacked Constantinople, which didn't help matters. When the Turks threatened to conquer the great city in the 1400s, Greek orthodox leaders and the emperor agreed to merge with the Roman Catholic Church in exchange for immediate aid. That idea was completely ruined by opposition from the masses. When Constantinople was finally overrun in 1453, the western half of Christendom watched silently.

Within a few years, the Church itself, long a monolith that casually crushed any opposition or small sects that arose to challenge its view of the world and Jesus, faced a threat that could not be ignored.

Chapter Fifteen

The Church Faces Protests

Rumblings against the powerful Roman Catholic Church radiated through Europe for centuries. Small cults, designed to purify the faith, rose and fell, or cowered in some distant mountains after soldiers sent by the pope massacred everyone in sight. The Church couldn't maintain a united front, making it vulnerable to reformers. The pope fled Rome for Avignon, France, then returned. At one time, there were three popes. Pope John XXXIII -- this one lived about 600 years before the prelate who took Latin out of the Mass in the 1960s -- was charged with a long list of crimes, including murder and rape. He may have been guilty of most of them.

For a brief period, the Church-led crusades re-conquered the Holy Land. That lasted less than 200 years. Eventually, the Arabs, under Saladin, held off Richard the Lionhearted, and Jerusalem, once again, was under Muslim rule. The Arabs seized reported remnants of the cross that once bore Jesus.

Christians weren't worried: there were enough relics to go around. Many people had grown disgusted with the selling of saintly relics, which led to the multiplication of body parts and endless frauds. The Archbishop of Mainz, for example, supposedly owned "a fair piece of Moses' left horn (based on a biblical mistranslation), a whole pound of the wind that blew for Elijah in the cave of Mt. Horeb and two feathers and an egg of the Holy Ghost." By the mid-1500s, 56 fingers of St. Peter the Dominican dotted European churches, along with 26 heads of St. Julienne, 309 bodies of St. George, 12 heads of St. John the Baptist, 70 veils of the Virgin Mary, not to mention many tears and footprints of Jesus.

Still, the Church endured, humbling kings and dictating daily lives. Then, in 1517, the Church finally met its match. Other theologians had tried and failed to budge the Church, which was swollen with donations and legacies, and was accumulating more wealth by selling passes (called "indulgences") to the living so their souls would spend less time waiting to get into heaven. However, a simple monk, Martin Luther, the least likely of protestors, simply waved a pen, and the whole edifice was shaken.

Luther was upset after John Tetzel, a salesman sent by the Vatican to market indulgences, showed up in Wittenberg where Luther was teaching. The son of a German owner of a copper mine, Luther shouldn't have been anywhere near Tetzel. He was supposed to be a civil servant, not a monk, and had his law degree in hand when, in 1505, a terrific thunderstorm terrified him so much that he vowed that, if he survived, he'd join a monastery. Luther outlasted the gale and promptly left the secular world.

Eventually, he was sent to Wittenberg, an out-of-the-way place, where he could pray and teach without bothering anyone. Even his fellow priests were getting upset with how furiously he sought to beat sin out of his own body.

Instead, in 1517, outraged by what Tetzel was marketing and convinced that the Church had lapsed into heresy, Luther decided to duplicate Abraham and metaphorically smash the idols. This time, using a quill, on Halloween, he wrote down his complaints in 95 theses attacking the pope, indulgences and other church practices, and nailed them to a church door that was commonly used for public announcements. No one noticed because he poured out his anger in Latin. Two years later, he duplicated the effort in German. This time, Luther caused a large enough outcry to be heard in Rome.

His complaints also flew around Europe, aided by the invention of the printing press just 60 years earlier.

Called to answer charges of heresy in 1521, he marched bravely, like Daniel, into the lion's den of angry Cardinals. Expected to apologize and denounce his own writing, Luther reportedly said, "Unless I am convinced by proofs from Scriptures or by plain and clear reasons and arguments, I can and will not retract, for it is neither safe nor wise to do anything against conscience. Here I stand. I can do no other. God help me. Amen."

Instead of being burned for his behavior, Luther was protected by German princes upset that the Church controlled a vast percentage of the Germanic land and siphoned off too much of the local proceeds to please any ruler. With Luther, they had a new religious leader to follow. They rejected Catholicism for Lutheranism, which was very similar, but didn't have a pope. Luther argued that faith alone was necessary for salvation through Jesus. In addition, he noted that the Bible didn't say a word about a pope, his cadre of advisors or a wide variety of other Church particulars. So, he eliminated them from his belief.

Luther's goal was to purify the Church, but, like many reformers before and after him, he ended up creating a new faith that opposed the old one.

Lots of Marching with These Protests

Luther and his German princes soon had plenty of company as countries around Europe picked sides in what became known as the Protestant Reformation. The name comes from the fact the participants were "protesting" against the Roman Catholic Church.

France and Spain stayed with the old belief. The Netherlands and, eventually, England did not. They didn't necessarily become Lutheran either. Luther's bold stance encouraged other theologians to offer their individualized views on God, Jesus and salvation. Some of the new leaders, like John Calvin, Ulrich Zwingli and John Knox, were far more radical than Luther. They attracted followers, too. Soon, the religious conflict sawed western society in half. No magician could unite the Catholic and Protestant portions.

Christians did not see Muslims as their worst enemies any more; their Satan lay within their own ranks. They didn't loath Muslims; they hated each other. As a result, from the 1520s to 1648, the two sides of Christianity fought with undisguised ferocity.

The Church created the Jesuits to teach and invigorated the Inquisition to kill. English sailors reported horror stories of comrades captured by Catholic (mostly Spanish) forces and burned at the stake or sent to galleys as slaves. No cruelty on either side was considered sufficient when trying to protect the sainted Prince of Peace from desecration. The religious conflicts led to the first "modern" war when Charles VIII of France marched at the front of his troops across the Alps toward the conquest of Italy. From that point on, Europe rang with the clash of weapons as Catholics fought Protestants and each other. Popes even led troops into battle.

Central Europe was engulfed from 1618 to 1648 in what was known as the Thirty Years' War, a religious battle of hideous cruelty. It began because Archduke Ferdinand took over the Holy Roman Empire – a misnamed group of mostly Germanic states – with the view of restoring the Catholic faith through his realm. Protestant countries formed a league in self defense; Catholic lands did the same. Bohemian nobles decided in 1618 to revolt against the Empire. They tossed two Catholic envoys and their secretary from a window in the Prague palace. They landed safely on a dung heap 50 feet below, but Catholic leaders decided to avenge the insult.

The toll was incredible: Germany and Austria together lost 8.5 million people; Bohemia's population dropped from 3 million to 800,000. In Bohemia, a German state, 29,000 of the existing 35,000 villages were deserted. Starvation killed many of the noncombatants. The carnage in Bohemia was not an accident: in 1420, Czech Hussites, under the name Ultraquists — a reference to a desire to give both bread and wine to communicants and not just bread as in the Catholic service (*ultraque specie*) – gathered at Mt. Tabor in anticipation of the returning Christ. They were defeated by 1452, but the theology lingered.

Science joined the fray inadvertently. In many ways, the evolving study of light symbolized the sweeping changes. From Holland came the telescope. Through it, Dutch scientist Van Leeuwenhoek revealed far more about the heavens than anyone reading Genesis ever could discover. Among other scholars hard at work in this new realm, Frenchman Rene Descartes provided insight into refraction.

Although such men of genius as Galileo, Harvey, Newton, Bacon and Pascal also lived at this time, science often was the subject of fierce criticism. Religion, caught in the backwash of scientific advances, fought to avoid being drowned. Scholars abruptly shifted the Earth outside the center of the universe. That work, and similar advances, undermined core religious teachings.

When those efforts failed to hold back the scientific tide, science was twisted to support religious views. In 1650, The Rev. James Ussher, archbishop of Armagh, issued his famous study in which he "calculated" that the world was created in 4004 B.C.E. Dr. John Lightfoot, vice-chancellor of the University of Cambridge, added to those findings that life began at 9 a.m., Oct. 23 of that year. Ussher's views became thought of as inspired as the Bible itself.

Caught up in the turmoil between Protestants and Catholics and between science and religion, many people looked to the heavens. They were sure the world was going to end. Predictions rolled from newly coined prophets like silver dollars moving through a stamping machine. The continued delay of the Parousia (the appearance of Jesus) naturally heightened speculation.

The Bible was scoured for clues. Since the canonical book of Revelation mentioned a 1,000-year reign (20:5), chiliasts (from the Greek for "one thousand") had thought the end of the first millennium would initiate the cessation of life. In the 16th century, with the Western World horrified and sickened by the carnage, the concept enjoyed a rebirth of interest beginning in England. Quakerism, for example, owes its beginning to chiliastic thought. They initiated a new wave of new predictions of Armageddon.

The Jehovah Witnesses, Seventh Day Adventists, Church of the Latter Day Saints and several other Christian sects were all founded at least in part on the basis of (obviously inaccurate) forecasts of an immediate end of the world.

While everyone awaited Armageddon, a few would-be messiahs naturally appeared in vain hope of initiating the process.

A group of French priests claimed they would raise Dr. Thomas Emes, an English physician, from the dead on March 25, 1708. The process failed.

In 1785, Jean-Baptiste Ruery, who claimed to be of the line of David, reported that God had told him Jesus was about to start a new age. In the process, the Frenchman would become king of Jerusalem. He did not succeed in his quest. A French cure, motivated by the Revolution, insisted the messiah had been born in August 1792. The French apparently had a yen for such things.

Jacob Frank may have been the most notorious messianic claimant of that era. A Polish-born theologian and son of a rabbi, Frank in the mid-1700s joined a religious sect founded by would-be messiah and Muslim convert Sabbatai Sevi in 1666. Apparently charismatic, Frank worked his way through the ranks of the small cult until he declared that he embodied the elements of the soul that once inhabited Sevi. The basic problem was that Frank argued his followers had to lower themselves to the lowest possible level of human behavior to rid themselves of filth. Sexual freedom drew followers, but offended straight-laced (and appalled) religious leaders. After Frank's death, his daughter, Eva, took up the cause, but, when her beauty faded, so did the number of followers.

Many of these would-be messiahs, inspired by Luther, started their own faiths. Jemima Wilkenson (1752-1820), for example, was the first American messiah and one of the few women in this long line. Williamson was the daughter of a Rhode Island farmer. Very ill at age 20, she apparently died. Before burial, however, she recovered and insisted that she was the reincarnation of Jesus. Her mission was to prepare believers for the end of the world, which, she predicted, would occur within the next few years.

Her revelation attracted wide attention as did her appearance and lifestyle. Tall for a woman with an affection for Scottish kilts and broad masculine hats, Wilkenson could be very persuasive and built up a small congregation of about 250 members, all weaned on strict celibacy and her personal revelations.

She traveled throughout Pennsylvania, Massachusetts, New York, Connecticut and Rhode Island before settling in western New York. Her group, called Universal Friends, lived in a communal environment, befriending Indians and awaiting the predicted Second Coming. It's possible that her presence influenced Joseph Smith, then living in upstate New York and on the verge of founding the Church of the Latter Day Saints.

Wilkenson died in 1820 and was left unburied as her followers awaited the expected resurrection. When decomposition ended that hope, believers began to drift away. The last Universal Friend died in 1874.

Smith, in turn, was hailed with the messianic fervor by followers in the 1820s after reporting the finding of gold tablets containing a new gospel. The text detailed an account of an escape from Israel and beliefs associated with the exiles, including that the American Indians were remnants of the lost 10 tribes of Israel. In time, polygamy was also encouraged. Smith was killed in Illinois while leading his band from New York towards Missouri, where he said the faithful would have to live before the world ended. Eventually, one of his lieutenants, Brigham Young, guided the Latter Day Saints to safety in modern-day Utah. The messianic message and the end-of-the-world prediction remain in the Mormon teachings.

In England, Aleister Crowley (1875 –1947) picked up on that theme. Born in England, Crowley lived a life in a "series of ecstasies, abominations and bizarreries," according to his literary executor. He wrote an array of poetry as well as books of erotica, occult and religion. His most famous work, I-Ching, purports to be a translation of an ancient Chinese book that combines Tao with the life forces of yang and yin. Hating Christianity, Crowley founded his own religion. Akin to the variation on the ideas spouted by Jacob Frank, Crowley's version was predicated on sexual orgies and pagan rites. He was chucked out of France and Italy for his heretical views, one of which was "the only sin is restriction." Excess was the motto, also borrowed, perhaps, from Frank.

Crowley died after World War II following a lifetime of drug abuse, including heroin.

Another fascinating false messiah was Father Divine (1864? - 1965), whose followers called him "God." Born in the mid-1800s, George Baker (both his name and date of birth are uncertain) claimed he came to earth on a puff of smoke about the time of Abraham. He preached peace, communal living, celibacy, honesty and racial equality. The son of a former slave, Divine linked up with existing cults and settled in Harlem, N.Y. There, he opened a community he labeled "Heaven." Eventually, there were more than 70 of them. He died in 1965, worth an estimated $100 million.

The most successful woman messiah was Mary Baker Eddy (1821-1920), who founded Christian Science in the late 1880s. Devoted disciples declared her the messiah and said she would not die, but would return as "the ever-present Christ, the son-daughter of God." A Christian Science book published in the 1990s presented Eddy as "equal to Christ, a divine figure who fulfilled biblical prophecy." Eddy herself denied Virgin Birth, miracles of Christ, atonement and resurrection.

In recent times, David Koresh (1959 - 1993) became one of the most notorious religious leaders. Born Vernon Wayne Howell and a member of the Seventh Day Adventists, he led a group called Branch Davidians. Howell moved his crew into a compound in Waco, Tex., after claiming he was the new messiah. He predicted the end of the world would come in 1993.

The Branch Davidians had actually been founded by Victor Houteff, a Bulgarian immigrant who set up the compound in 1934 to await Christ's return in the near future. He died in 1955, and his wife, Florence, extended the prediction to 1959. Some people left, following Ben Roden, who said he was the reincarnation of King David. Roden died in 1978. His wife, Lois, then became the group's spiritual leader. She died in 1986. In 1987, Howell took over the Branch Davidians by ousting George Roden, the son of George and Lois.

Once in power, Howell promptly changed his name to David Koresh and announced he was the Lamb of God, the risen messiah. He predicted a coming battle between his followers and the forces of Satan. He lived in anonymity for several years until 1992, when his men killed several government agents who came to the compound to check out reports of illegal firearms. The ambush led to the entrance of the FBI, who besieged the compound for more than 70 days that year. Eventually, receiving reports of child abuse among other crimes, they moved in with tanks and tear gas. Koresh apparently set or ordered the compound set on fire, killing 75 adults and children. Seven adults survived.

The resulting uproar created another pretext for would-be messiahs and sociopaths to react against society, and led to the murderous bombing of the federal office building in Oklahoma City in 1995.

One of the more recent claimants, The Rev. Sun Myung Moon (1920 - 2012) proclaimed himself a messiah and founded the Unification Church in the 1950s. The religion is based on Moon's messianic claims with strong ties to Christianity. Starting in Korea, the "Moonies" spread across the world, collecting money and donating all of their worldly goods to the church. Assuming the religious title of reverend, Moon invested in various businesses, including the *Washington Star* newspaper. Moon regularly dictated mass marriages among his followers and eventually was sent to jail in Connecticut for federal income tax invasion. While he was incarcerated, believers gathered outside his prison to pray. The religion split after his death because of philosophical differences between his children.

All these messiahs, all these beliefs, all this turmoil has led to a Christianity today that has more sects than it's possible to count. The sincere efforts made by the Church fathers at Nicaea to develop one coherent view of Jesus and eliminate any others has failed.

Worldwide, Christianity still claims about 2.1 billion members, scattered among its many sects. They include the African Independent Churches, the Aglipayan Church, Amish, Anglican/Episcopalian, Armenian Apostolic, Assembly of God, Baptists, Calvary Chapel, Catholic, Christadelphians, Christian Scientist, Church of the Latter Day Saints, Coptic Christians, Eastern Orthodox, Ethiopian Orthodox, Evangelicals, Iglesia ni Cristo, Jehovah's Witnesses, the Local Church, Lutherans, Methodists, Monophysites, Nestorians, the New Apostolic Church, Pentecostals, Plymouth Brethren, Presbyterian, Seventh-Day Adventist, Shakers, Disciples of Christ; Churches of Christ, the International Church of Christ, Quakers, Uniate churches, United Church of Christ,/Congregationalists, the Unity Church, Universal Church of the Kingdom of God, Vineyard churches and others.

Like their Jewish counterparts, they can be separated into additional categories, ranging from fundamentalist to liberal.

Overall, there are more American Protestants than Catholics – 52 percent to 24 percent, but Protestants are broken into so many smaller units that no one denomination is larger than the Catholic bloc. The largest single religious group in the United States is Catholic, with about 67.2 million members in 2001. Baptists are second with 47,770 million or 16.3 percent of the population.

Here are the top 10 Christian denominations in the United States as of a few years ago.

1. Roman Catholic Church: 67.2 million.

2. Southern Baptist Convention: 47.7 million.

3. United Methodist Church: 8.2 million.

4. Church of Jesus Christ of Latter-day Saints: 5.5 million.

5. Church of God in Christ: 5.4 million.

6. National Baptist Convention USA: 5 million.

7. Evangelical Lutheran Church in America: 4.9 million.

8. National Baptist Convention of America: 3.5 million.

9. Presbyterian Church (U.S.A.): 3.2 million.

10. Assemblies of God: 2.7 million.

All believe in Jesus. Members of each are sure they are saved; they are not so positive about anyone else. Ironically, the fastest growing group is labeled "nones," who are people claiming no religious affiliation. By 2021, they accounted for about 30 percent of Americans.

Chapter Sixteen

Doin' the Vatican Rag

In its 2,000-year history, Christianity has enriched our lives enormously. As Dr. Jaroslav Pelikan, one of this country's foremost religious historians, discovered in his research: If Christianity were removed from Western Civilization, little would be left.

He is right. What would the world be like without music like Handel's Messiah, the artwork like Michelangelo's ceiling of the Sistine Chapel, the warmth of Christmas or the philosophical insights of a Roger Bacon, Thomas Moore or C.S. Lewis? Our seasons revolve around Christian ideas; our lives are infused with Christian icons like Jesus, Mary, Peter, Paul and Judas, who are integral to our lives and literature.

Much of what we take to be Christian, however, was born in another culture and transformed by what became the world's largest religion. This is the same magnetic process that drew pagan concepts into Judaism and allowed them to be altered and updated. Passover, for example, as we saw, started out as a shepherd's holiday and was given a richer context after brushing against Jewish philosophers.

The same process is at work in Christianity. Take Christmas as an example. The holiday celebrates the birth of Jesus, but many aspects of the festive occasion have antecedents reaching back into misty history.

Christmas Debuts

As we saw earlier, Christian leaders at Nicaea voted to create Christmas and Easter. They agreed on dates, but not everyone went along. As a result, Christmas is celebrated on December 25, but, in Hispanic countries, the big day is Jan. 6, the day the traveling magi supposedly arrived in Bethlehem to worship baby Jesus.

The December 25 day was likedly selected for political, not religious, reasons. The bishops and other dignitaries at Nicaea had no idea when Jesus was born. The Bible provides only hints, but does not give a date. Early Christians also did not celebrate any holiday to mark Jesus' birth. The Nicaean delegates had 12 months to choose from. If they based their selection on the story in Luke, they could have chosen August, because that's when shepherds typically are in the field with their flocks in Israel, as the evangelist described. Besides, statistically, more children worldwide are born in August, so their odds would have been slightly higher.

Actually, they opted for December possibly to counter a variety of existing holidays. This is the same process behind the Jewish development of the Sabbath or the Christian attempt to co-opt Halloween from the pagans. In this case, the Romans annually celebrated a huge December event called the Saturnalia, a wild affair in which slaves and masters could switch roles. Everyone took a vacation. Masquerades, cross-dressing and parades entertained the masses. A mock king, called the Lord of Misrule, was crowned. He was voted on by placing a bean into a jar. In time, the bean was baked in a cake, eventually giving rise to fruitcakes. Candles were lit. The Roman god of wine, Bacchus, was honored. His creed featured licentious behavior, which must have added to the merriment and irritated upright Christians.

In addition, the Romans marched around with evergreen boughs and gave gifts.

The holiday marked the beginning of winter and, with it, the death of the sun god. He died on the 22nd and was reborn on the 25th.

Roman philosopher Seneca left this description of the Saturnalia in an essay written in 50 C.E.:

It is now the month of December, when the greatest part of the city is in a bustle. Loose reins are given to public dissipation; everywhere you may hear the sound of great preparations, as if there were some real difference between the days devoted to Saturn and those for transacting business....Were you here, I would willingly confer with you as to the plan of our conduct; whether we should eve in our usual way, or, to avoid singularity, both take a better supper and throw off the toga. -- *the Epistolae*

The same concepts show up in pagan Europe. There, the evergreen tree replaced the human sacrifice. The Yule log of Christmas is a remnant of that ancient ritual. The evergreen, which retained its color and was assumed immortal, became a phallic symbol tied to fertility rituals. To ancient Germans, holly depicted the queen of heaven while white berries on the mistletoe represented drops of semen.

The winter holidays go back even further, to the Egyptians, who set aside 12 days to celebrate at the end of the year. They, too, used greenery – in this case, palm fronds – as symbols of eternal life. Their holiday developed after making changes in their calendar. They originally scheduled only 360 days in a year. The seasons quickly became confusing, so they added five days, creating a massive ceremony in the process.

Another holiday the Christians probably wanted to overshadow was the one celebrating the birthday of Mithra, the Zoroastrian god of truth and light.

The story of the birth, as it appears in Matthew, characterizes how Christianity countered Mithra and drew on other cultures. In his account, you might recall, the Holy Family is in Bethlehem and visited by magi who followed a star from the east.

The magi were astrologers from Persia. The word "magic" is derived from their name. The Bible doesn't actually list names or number of these visitors. Instead, Matthew drew on stories of how young Roman emperors were greeted. Jesus, being a king in his mind, could receive no less a royal treatment.

When the eastern ruler Tiradates, whom Pliny calls a "magus," came to pay homage to Nero, Roman author Dio Cassius records, "He had brought magi with him." Approaching Nero, "he knelt upon the ground, and with arms crossed called him master and did obeisance." That parallels the later report by Matthew that the magi bowed to the ground in homage to Jesus. (Matt. 2:1 1).

Matthew could also have been thinking of what happened to young Augustus Caesar. In his *Life of Augustus*, Roman historian Suetonius wrote that that when young Octavius Caesar was born, "Publius Nigidius Figulus the astrologer, hearing at what hour the child had been delivered, cried out, 'The ruler of the world is now born.' Everyone believes this tale."

In the same section of this work, Suetonius added that when Augustus entered the house of Theogenes the astrologer, the man "rose and flung himself at the feet" of the young man.

The traditional gifts to a young emperor were gold, myrrh and frankincense, the same gifts brought to Jesus.

By the way, the Church had to explain why this impoverished Holy Family didn't suddenly blossom with wealth when they received these gifts. The answer, according to the Church: Joseph and Mary donated the presents to those more needy.

The star that guided the kings has also intrigued historians. Numerous attempts have been made to account for the star. A certain astronomical arrangement – Saturn and Jupiter in conjunction in the constellation of Pisces – was supposed to herald the arrival of the messiah in Jewish mythology. In 1603, German astronomer John Kepler cited that conjunction and calculated that a similar conjunction must have occurred in 7 B.C.E. He speculated that this might have been the true year of Jesus' birth.

Anyone looking at the conjunction in a planetarium will be surprised how faint the combination is. It must be pointed out. It also could not be followed by anyone; it doesn't move fast enough. The same configuration, of course, occurs on a regular basis – about every 2,100 years – without any previous messiahs showing up.

There was no nova (exploding star) in the correct time period either. The closest one was 5 B.C.E.

The most probable source for Matthew's star comes from the religion of Mithra, which centered around a mythical prophet whose symbol was a star. That religion was an early rival to Christianity. Matthew wanted to counter Mithraic claims by having the star point to Jesus instead.

Other Holidays

Easter went through the same process of development. No one celebrated either Christmas or Easter until after the Nicaean Council. The holiday, however, has a very long history. The Babylonians honored the resurrection of their god, Tammuz, who was brought back from the underworld by his mother/wife, Ishtar. The Phoenicians had Adonis and Astarte; the Greeks, Attis and Cybele. As noted earlier, there were plenty of risen gods to choose from.

Spring was a time for rebirth. That's why every religion had a holiday then. The Jews still celebrate Passover, bringing together several existing holidays, infusing it with a new meaning and creating a new one. Eggs remain a constant in many of the spring holidays, because they are a symbol of rebirth. So, the Seder plate at the big Passover meal always includes an egg.

In the Christian world, eggs are there, too, planted by the Easter bunny. Rabbits actually don't lay eggs, but the connection was made through Oester, a German fertility goddess whose name was converted to Easter.

Every deity had a "familiar," an animal that kept him or her company. Witches had black cats. Oester had rabbits.

Historians have long been aware of Easter's connection to older beliefs:

Now the death and resurrection of Attis were officially celebrated at Rome on the 24th and 25th of March, the latter being regarded as the spring equinox, and...according to an ancient and widespread tradition Christ suffered on the 25th of March...the tradition which placed the death of Christ on the 25th of March...is all the more remarkable because astronomical considerations prove that it can have had no historical foundation...When we remember that the festival of St. George in April has replaced the ancient pagan festival of the Parilia; that the festival of St. John the Baptist in June has succeeded to a heathen Midsummer festival of water; that the festival of the Assumption of the Virgin in August has ousted the festival of Diana; that the feast of All Souls [following Halloween] in November is a continuation of an old heathen feast of the dead; and that the Nativity of Christ himself was assigned to the winter solstice in December because that day was deemed the Nativity of the Sun; we can hardly be thought to be rash or unreasonable in conjecturing that the other cardinal festival of the Christian church—the solemnization of Easter—may have been in like manner, and from like motives of edification, adapted to a similar celebration of the Phyrigian god Attis at the vernal equinox...It is a remarkable coincidence...that the Christian and the heathen festivals of the divine death and resurrection should have been solemnized at the same season...It is difficult to regard the coincidence as purely accidental. – Sir James Frazer, *The Golden Bough*, Vol. I, pp. 306-309

Lent

Lent, the 40 days preceding Easter, grew from pagan and Jewish sources. Early Christians had no knowledge of Lent and did not comment on the observance. However, festivals for the risen gods Osiris, Adonis and Tammuz all featured 40-day fasts. Jews associated a 40-day period leading up to God giving them the Torah on Mt. Sinai.

Holy Sites

Vatican

The Roman Catholic Church, like religions before it, carefully selected sites for churches and worship from the many locations already designated by other religions. The Vatican, home to the pope, sits on a pagan gravesite.

When a tomb was found below the building containing, possibly, the bones of St. Peter, the Church declined to let forensic scientists examine the remains partially in fear of embarrassment since so many bones lie under the massive structure.

Jerusalem

The location of Jesus' crucifixion, birth and other key areas mentioned in the Bible are daily visited by dutiful pilgrims who have come to Jerusalem to pray. The sites may be correct, but no one is sure. They were selected by Helen, Constantine's mother, who waited for inspiration to strike as she wandered around David's City. Unfortunately, she was there about 300 years after Jesus died, so many of the important sites were gone. The destruction of Jerusalem in 70 C.E. pretty much jumbled up the place.

We know she was not correct about Golgotha, the place where Jesus was placed on a cross. She chose a site outside Roman control. Since he was crucified by the Romans, that would not have been possible.

Today, visitors cheerfully go to the various, often duplicate, sites in hopes that one of them is correct.

Rituals

Communion

The central Christian ritual, called communion, involves worshipers sipping from a cup of wine and eating a small wafer to symbolize the body and blood of Christ. At one time, the Christian world was convulsed over the question of whether the wine and bread actually transmuted into real flesh and blood after being ingested. That supposition has faded. Now the emphasis is on the metaphorical sense that Jesus was the "blood and body" of life. No cannibalism is involved, an idea that nauseated the Romans and helped fuel their anger against the early Christians.

The origin to Christians derives from the Last Supper, the final meal Jesus ate with his disciples. However, the Nazarenes, the first followers of Jesus, do not describe a ritual like that in their records. Besides, Jesus and his followers were Jewish, and the religion banned blood at a meal. As soon as Jesus offered his companions a cup of wine, saying it contained blood, the room would have cleared out.

Some Christian writers argue that Jesus was creating a new ritual. That's certainly possible, but he would have had no audience to explain it to. Besides, the Gospels do not indicate that he ever gave a rationale for his thinking.

The matter becomes much clearer when we find that Paul described the Last Supper, saying that the Lord told him about the event in a dream. Then, the Bible text basically duplicated Paul's reverie. Paul may have been thinking of a popular and widespread pagan ritual in which blood and wine were eaten in an attempt to come in touch with the divine.

The Last Supper was a Seder, according to three of the Gospel writers, indicating the link to Judaism.

In addition, one such meal was part of the Mithraic religion that Christianity battled for many years. The ritual included a communion-like ritual accompanied with the words quoted earlier: "He who shall not eat of my body nor drink of my blood so that he may be one with me and I with him, shall not be saved."

Wine and bread were pagan symbols for the divine well before Jesus anyway. In 50 B.C.E., the Roman orator Cicero wrote that acquainting a god with corn and the wine was only symbolic. He then asked, "Is anybody so mad as to believe that which he eats is actually a god?"

Baptism

Baptism also draws on Jewish teachings, which encouraged cleanliness. In fact, Jews were mocked by Romans for insisting on ritual cleanings on a daily basis. Romans once had community baths that the vast majority of people used, but not for ritualistic purposes.

Sluices found at Qumran are thought to have fed ritual baths, called *mikvehs*. Today, converts to Judaism and women undergoing purification are required to bathe in a *mikveh*.

Leviticus in the Old Testament lists a variety of laws regarding ritualistic cleansing, which can be seen as primitive baptism: mildew on walls (Lev 14:33-53); purification after childbirth (Lev 12:1-8), acceptance of a healed "leper" back into the community. (Lev 13:1-36, 14:1-32).

Baptismal jars also show up in the story of the Cana wedding where Jesus turned water into wine.

Nearby stood six stone water jars, the kind used by the Jews for ceremonial washing, each holding from twenty to thirty gallons. Jesus said to the servants, "Fill the jars with water" so they filled them to the brim. Then, he told them, "Now draw some out and take it to the master of the banquet." They did so, and the master of the banquet tasted the water that had been turned into wine. -- *John 2:6-9*

The Roman Catholic Church made baptism a sacrament, in accordance with the biblical accounts of the baptism of Jesus and his subsequent baptism of others. The debate whether baptism is for babies or for anyone led to bloody battles in the Middle Ages.

Symbols

Cross

The cross would seem to be original to Christianity, but it is not. The Zealots, the violent sect of Jews, used the cross as a symbol prior to Jesus to commemorate the multitude crucified by the Romans. So many people were nailed to a cross that the land around Jerusalem was denuded of trees. Eventually, the Romans left up the poles and required victims to carry a crossbeam to the site.

The timing of the crucifixion at Passover also features ancient links. Passover occurs at the time of the Vernal Equinox, an event considered important by astrologers during the Roman Empire, who viewed the astrological event as the time of the crossing of two astrological celestial circles. They symbolized the equinox by a cross.

The theme of a divine or semi-divine being sacrificed on a tree, pole or cross, and then being resurrected, is very common in pagan mythology. It appears in the mythology of civilizations stretching from the British Isles (the furthest extent of the Roman Empire) across the Middle East to India. Osiris, the Egyptian god of the underworld, is described with his arms stretched out on a tree like Jesus on the cross. This tree was sometimes shown as a pole with outstretched arms – the same shape as the Christian cross. In the worship of the Greek god Serapis, the cross was a religious symbol. Indeed, the Christian "Latin cross" symbol seems to be based directly on the cross symbol of Osiris and Serapis.

The biblical description of what happened to Jesus fits known history, including scourging and guards around the cross to prevent a rescue. Most everything else could have been based on belief. The Gospel writers had many texts to guide them.

• Isaiah 53:3: "He is despised and rejected of men; a man of sorrows and acquainted with grief; and we hid our faces from him; he was despised and we esteemed him not."

• Psalm 22:16: "For dogs have compassed me; the assembly of the wicked have enclosed me; they pierce my hands and feet."

• Proverbs 31:6: "Give strong drink to him who is ready to perish."

• Psalm 69:21: "They gave me also gall for my meat; and in my thirst they gave me vinegar to drink."

• Isaiah 53:12: "He was numbered with the transgressors."

• Joel: 3:15-16: "The sun and the moon shall be darkened, and the stars shall withdraw their shining. The Lord shall also roar out of Zion, and utter his voice from Jerusalem, and heaven and earth shall shake."

• Zechariah 12:10: "They shall look upon me whom they have pierced, and they shall mourn for him as one mourns for his only son."

Mitre Hat

The pope's unique hat comes from the fish symbol used for Mithra, along with his fisherman's ring. The hat was designed to look like a fish.

Halo

Many Christian religious icons and paintings feature halos, an aura of light hovering over a holy person's head. That image was actually banned in ancient times by the early Church because it was used in pagan artwork. After several centuries, Christian artists could use halos, but they had to be square to distinguish them from pagan versions. Finally, around the 9th century C.E., the Church felt that the pagans had been overcome and permitted artists to incorporate the now-familiar round halos.

Priests

Catholic priests are referred to as "Father." That term came directly from
Jewish sources. Sages were honored with the title, which then was picked
up by the Church.

Indeed, nothing associated with Christianity is original to that religion.
Instead, Christianity embraced a river of Jewish and pagan ideas, rituals and
philosophical concepts, smoothed them, changed them and imbued them
with new life in a faith that has transcended the centuries.

Chapter Seventeen

Under the Crescent Moon

We have devoted many pages to Christianity. That's a reflection not only of the religion's importance in Western civilization, but also because of the difficulty in deciphering its history. Many aspects are debated simply because records have not survived, and those that do exist contradict each other.

Islam, the next monotheistic faith on our list, is much younger. It emerges from the desert with a distinct face and a solid historical base. The mythology which envelops all great leaders cannot completely obscure the founder of this faith. Nor is its history lost in the dark past slowly receding from us.

Islam arose in a part of the world Abraham would have felt comfortable in, yet very alien to Jesus. In lands stretching from England south to the Arabian desert, Christianity towered over the religious landscape, replacing the Roman Empire and controlling life. Around 390, Emperor Theodosius closed the pagan temples and demanded that all Roman citizens worship one God and His son Jesus. For the next 200 years, Christianity tightened its grip on men's lives, even as Goths and Vandals destroyed the Western Roman Empire.

However, in the swirling sands of the Arabian Peninsula, Christianity had only made faint inroads. In the sixth century, the last of Abraham's offspring was about to be born. The entry of Islam continued a pattern begun with the Babylonians more than 2,500 years earlier. In the history of the world, no cultural or linguistic group looms larger than Semitic peoples. Originating from the Arabian Peninsula, Semites are responsible for the first human civilizations, three major world religions, and a set of cultural practices that have been more universal than any introduced by other societies, including the Chinese and Europeans.

Semitic people erupt on the world stage three times: with the growth of Semitic civilizations in Mesopotamia 4,000 years ago; the spread of Christianity and Judaism 2,000 years ago; and, finally, the explosion of Islam 1,500 years ago. This last volcanic burst of Semitic culture would produce a major world religion and social system that still endures.

Judaism and Christianity have changed dramatically over the years; Islam still maintains social standards set down in the beginning of the 7th century.

The Arabian Peninsula is probably the last place one would nominate as a cradle for such influential human cultures: a harsh and demanding place to live, with soaring peaks and flat, hot deserts, much of its wind-swept territory offers little water, shelter from the heat of the day and the deep cold of the night.

Greek historian Herodotus enthusiastically but inaccurately described Arabia as containing frankincense trees surrounded by forms of winged and brightly colored serpents. Actually, the only real color is sandy dunes, grayish camels and white stone buildings.

As a land mass, Arabia is separated from its parent continent, Africa, and from Asia by the Red Sea in the west and the Persian Gulf in the east. Although it is surrounded on three sides by water, there are no good harbors, save for Aden in Yemen. Both the Red Sea and Persian Gulf can be treacherous, something well known to the crews of tankers that regularly carry oil to the West.

Despite the presence of water, much of it is not drinkable. Israelis have set up desalination plants to covert the brackish water into something potable. For most residents, however, the few fresh water springs and desert oases are the only ways to ease the ceaseless thirst.

The Arabian Peninsula can be divided into two distinct climatic and geographical zones. The south along the coast of the Arabian Sea gets regular rain and has an astonishing variety of plant life. This is the Arabia of our mythology, the Arabia of wealth, tropical plants, cities, and spices like frankincense and myrrh. From a very early period, the south of Arabia was heavily populated by sedentary populations who lived in cities and relied on agriculture. Many of these civilizations were very wealthy and powerful, and Semitic peoples in Africa largely owe their origin to these privileged southerners.

In contrast, northern Arabia – that is, all of Arabia north of the southern coast – is one of the most inhospitable places on earth. To the east is a vast desert – one of the largest continuous areas of sand in the world – bordered by arid steppes in the west. The western portion of northern Arabia consists of mountains and flat lands. Across this vast land, there are no rivers to connect peoples together. While the inhabitants of the south have historically lived close together and in constant contact, the residents in the north lived far apart and in relative isolation.

The most forbidding part of northern Arabia is the expanse of sand desert on the eastern side. There is little or no precipitation and so no support for agriculture. The only substantial flora in eastern Arabia is the date palm, a plant magnificently adapted to an arid climate.

This area throughout almost all of human history has been inhabited by nomadic, pastoralist Arabs called Bedouins (which means "desert" in Arabic). The harshness of the environment forced that roving lifestyle. Agriculture was out of the question; instead, the Bedouin moved their herds of goats, sheep, camels and cattle from place to place in search of scarce resources and water. They lived in small, tightly knit, hereditary tribes.

The western coast is slightly less forbidding, and the Arabs who settled there lived in sedentary and larger tribal groups. These Arabs were themselves Bedouin who settled the oases that surround the periphery of the Arabian desert. Because the oases represented a concentration of scarce resources, some tribes won control of these key sites in military battles and regularly fought to maintain their grips.

These two regions, the south and the north, were homes to two entirely separate Semitic peoples: the Sabaeans in the south; Arabs in the north.

Early in their history, the Sabaeans adopted a sedentary way of life in the relatively lush climate of southern Arabia. Eventually, the south came under the control of city-states ruled by priest-kings called mukkarib, whose functions may have been very similar to the earliest kings of Sumer and Akkad. By the time of Jesus, however, these priest-kings had largely given way to a secular monarchy, the malik.

The four most important city-states of the south were Saba' (source of the name Sabaeans), Hadramawt, Qataban, and Ma'in, all located in the southwest of the Arabian Peninsula, the area with the heaviest rainfall in the region. Although the southern lands never formed a political or ethnic unity, the most powerful of all these city-states was Saba', which slowly expanded its political influence to include all the major kingdoms of the south by 300 C.E.

For much of its history, the area around Saba', Hadramawt, Qataban, and Ma'in was a center of incredible wealth legendary all throughout the Fertile Crescent and northern Africa. It provided exotic plants, spices and luxury items that garnered high prices in commerce all throughout the Mediterranean and Asia. Its most lucrative export was an aromatic plant called frankincense, which, in ancient times, grew only in Hadramawt and in the Sabaean colony of Somalia in Africa.

The Sabaeans, however, lived on two major trade routes: one was the ocean-trading route between Africa and India. The harbors of the southwest were centers of commerce with these two continents. Those shores were awash with luxury items, such as spices, imported from these countries. The Sabaeans also got a cut of land tariffs. Their region lay at the southern terminus of land-based trade routes up and down the coast of the Arabian Peninsula. Goods would travel down this land route to be exported to Africa or India, while products from Africa and India would travel north on this land route.

This latter trade route had tremendous consequences for the Arabs in the north and the subsequent history of Islam. Major trading cities grew up along this trade route, and the wealth of the south filtered north into these cities. One of the large cities along that path was Mecca, home of Islam's founder, Muhammad. Mecca had long been a religious center of Arabic culture as its name suggests — one possible derivation of the name, "Mecca," is the word, "makorba," or "temple."

There are three distinct historical periods for pre-Islamic sedentary Arabs. The first period begins with the decline of the Greeks in the Middle East at the same time southern Sabaeans were fading from power. Taking advantage of the weakness, the Arabs penetrate as far north as Petra in Syria and as far south as Najran in what is now Saudi Arabia. As the Arabs began to approach the Mediterranean, they smacked into Rome going in the opposite direction.

The expansion of Roman, and then Byzantine (eastern Romans), and Sabaean power initiated the second period of pre-Islamic Arabia: the period of client-states. During this period, Arab cities found themselves locked into tributary states to three major world powers: the Byzantines in the north, the Persians in the east, and the southern Arabic kingdom of Himyar (the Sabaeans).

At the same time, both Christianity and Judaism were spreading rapidly among the Arabs. Some cities, such as Yathrib, become Judaized cities while a large number become Christian – either Monophysite Christianity of Africa and Syria or the eastern Christianity of Byzantium. Both Judaism and Christianity had very fully penetrated Arabic culture by the beginning of the third period of pre-Islamic history.

This period was concentrated in inner Arabia, particularly in Mecca, as Bedouin culture flourished. The Bedouins not only became a military power in their own right, they also closely allied themselves with the central Arabian cities, such as Yathrib (Medinah) and Mecca. This was the period when classical Arabic, or al-Arabiyya, became the language of Arabic culture and poetry.

This period enjoyed the diffusion of Bedouin values, such as muru'a, or manliness, and the widespread diffusion of Bedouin narratives and poetry.

The most important of these Bedouin achievements, however, was the conquest of Mecca by the tribe of the Quraysh around 500 C.E. The victors turned Mecca into a city-state that was ruled by a council of 10 hereditary chiefs who enjoyed a clear division of power. To aid them were a group of ministers: foreign relations, guardian of the temple, oracles, guardian of offerings to the temple, "one to determine the torts and the damages payable, another in charge of the municipal council or parliament to enforce the decisions of the ministries." Of course, there was a minister to oversee the military.

This organized system helped the Meccans create treaties with such distant empires as Iran, Byzantium and Abyssinia and to work out pacts with the Bedouin tribes who carefully watched the caravan trade routes. The agreements created a lively import-export business through Mecca and gave residents the ability to travel safely. At the same time, foreigners felt comfortable coming to Mecca.

The intermixing cultures inspired poetry and the growth of folk tales. They also opened the eyes of the Arabs, creating new ideas about the treatment of women. As a result, in Mecca, women could own property. They had to consent to a marriage and could divorce their husbands. They could remarry, too.

Life was not perfect for females. Human sacrifice continued. "Burying girls alive did exist in certain classes, but that was rare."

This is the world Muhammad knew. We know his history because many people in his lifetime wrote biographical sketches. As with the Bible, the stories are often intermingled with mythology and hyperbole. Fortunately, Muhammad was also mentioned by non-Arab historians. The resulting confluence of evidence creates a clear, consistent account of an extraordinary life.

As a child, he was introduced to a hodgepodge of religious ideas, including Bedouin polytheism, Judaism, and a little bit of Christianity. The monotheistic religions came initially in the backpacks of Jewish and Christian traders. Then, when the competition heated up, so did the scent of blood.

In 520, armies from the Christianized state of Ethiopia ventured into the Arab lands. They encountered an unusual kind of belief, almost a throwback to Abraham's time when a welter of gods capriciously ruled the people. Arabs throughout the Peninsula worshiped stones and, in many ways, like the Romans, were overwhelmed by religious ideas. They also worshiped three goddesses, al-Lat, al-Uzza, and Manat, daughters of one god, Allah, who originally belonged on a lower run of the Arabic pantheon. He may have been derived from the monotheistic religions of Judaism and Christianity.

Mecca was the center of this religion with its Ka'baa, or "Cube," which served as the temple for the religion. The one remaining symbol of the pre-Islamic days, the Ka'baa contains a black stone, possibly a meteorite, and was once the revered symbol of the moon god, Hubal. At one time, the Ka'baa may have been a temple devoted to the sun, the moon and the five planets. It featured 360 idols, which seems to have an astrological symbolism.

The Ka'baa still exists in Mecca and is visited by thousands of pilgrims each year who now journey far to honor another deity.

"In all of history there is no object of veneration which has been worshiped for a longer time," one historian noted.

Muhammad knew this religion well. The founder of Islam saw the stone many times. His father, Abdullah, had died shortly before his son's birth in 570. His grandfather became Muhammad's caretaker. By custom, the actual rearing was handled by a Bedouin foster-mother, something akin to Moses being raised by a foster princess in an Egyptian palace. This "palace," however, was the desert.

Eventually, Muhammad was returned to his family while barely beyond the toddler stage. His mother, Aminah, took him to his maternal uncles in Medinah to visit the tomb of Abdullah, then died. Muhammad went back to his grandfather, who also died abruptly soon after. Orphaned and alone in a harsh culture, the young boy, only eight, was adopted by his uncle, Abu-Talib, who barely scratched out a living as caretaker of the sacred Ka'baa.

Muhammad wasn't sent to school. He had to work. He was a shepherd, hired out to neighbors. He also participated in caravans that traveled to Syria. At some point, he even opened a small business in Mecca. He could not read or write, but, on his travels, apparently loved to talk with priests and rabbis he met at caravan trading posts. He must have remembered those conversations. The Koran, the Islamic holy text that contains his inspirational thoughts, includes many mentions of Old and New Testament patriarchs and events.

At age 25, he met and married Khadija, a wealthy widow who eventually presented him with six children. At that point in his life, Muhammad seemed unlikely to achieve greatness. Like Abraham before him, his early years were commonplace and of little apparent significance.

Unlike Jesus, of whom there are no extant pictures, Muhammad has been fully described: He was "sturdy and thickset, of medium height, with heavy shoulders and a thick black beard. He was beetle-browed and blessed with long black silken eyelashes, which he painted with kohl. They fell over eyes which were very large and piercing, and often bloodshot. His skin was rosy ... and he had a Roman nose, thin, aristocratic with flaring nostrils. He had dazzling white teeth, but was gap-toothed toward the end of his life."

As a young man, he began to have regular revelations, some apocalyptic in tone:

" ... And when the book of fate is open wide,

And when the heavens are stripped bare

And when Hell is set ablaze,

And when Paradise comes near,

Each soul shall know what it has done!" (Sura lxxxi)

Many of the verses, which Muhammad said were dictated to him by an angel, declare that mankind is doomed unless people follow the ways of God. Like Jewish prophets who arose in earlier times, Muhammad was not sure how to respond to an inner tugging that called on him to proclaim his message.

Some Deep Thinking

He got a push in 605, when the draperies on the outer wall of the Ka'baa caught fire. The building weakened and collapsed in subsequent rains. The Meccans set out to reconstruct the building. Muhammad's shoulders were reportedly injured while carrying transporting stones. The same accounts – and this seems a bit much – say he was given the immense honor of placing the holy stone back into the wall.

Still, the experience seemed to make him more religious. He spent days in a cave, supposedly imitating his saintly grandfather. The tale parallels tales in the Bible where David, Elijah and Jesus all were connected to mysterious caverns and long isolation in prayer..

At age 40, again on a retreat in that cave, Muhammad was visited by an angel who announced that God had chosen him as His messenger to all mankind. "The angel taught him the mode of ablutions, the way of worshipping God and the conduct of prayer."

Muhammad said the divine message was:

With the name of God, the Most Merciful, the All-Merciful.

Read: with the name of thy Lord Who created,

Created man from what clings,

Read: and thy Lord is the Most Bounteous,

Who taught by the pen,

Taught man what he knew not. -- *Koran 96:1-5*

Muhammad shared this revelation with his wife, but hesitated to speak out for another three years. Moses, too, demurred when God called him, insisting he needed a spokesman.

Nevertheless, stories about Muhammad and his heavenly visitor began to circulate. "Skeptics in the city had begun to mock him and cut bitter jokes. They went so far as to say that God had forsaken him."

In response, Muhammad began to talk first to family, then friends. His message was simple: belief in one God, in resurrection of believers and a final judgment before God. He encouraged charity and proper behavior. In this, he was duplicating Jesus and all the Jewish prophets of earlier times.

However, he did something for which later scholars are grateful. Muhammad ordered his revelations to be written down and memorized by converts to his new faith. He called the resulting faith Islam ("submission") which was based on heavenly dictates. People began to join him.

Breaking the Rules

With a surge in membership came the usual reaction of authorities. The official punishment for a heretic was to strip the culprit naked and leave him to die in the desert. They were eager to see how long Muhammad could endure that kind of treatment. He was reportedly tortured. Other Muslims were stretched on burning sands, cauterized with red hot iron and imprisoned with chains on their feet. Finally, Muhammad ordered his followers to flee. Many did. Ironically, Muhammad's most deep-seated enemies included his uncles. One, Abu-Lahab, took over leadership of the tribe.

In time, Muhammad began to envision himself as Paul, who carried the Jewish message of salvation to the gentiles. Muhammad would take that same divine information to the Arabs.

After continued harassment and other related troubles, paralleling biblical accounts of mistreated Jewish prophets and Christian apostles, Muhammad and his few followers finally fled Mecca in 622 and set up a base in the northern community of Yathrib.

That escape, called the hegira, changed history. Muslims began to follow a different cultural path away from Judaism and Christianity. They even have an alternative calendar. Muslims mark July 16, 622 as the beginning of the new era when, after years of struggle, Muhammad was welcomed to Yathrib as king.

Success followed quickly, including a triumphant return to Mecca, battles against the Persians who ruled the Holy Land, and against the Byzantine governor of Egypt. Muhammad even sent a letter to the Byzantine Emperor, ruler of the last remnant of the great Roman empire, asking for surrender (the emperor did not obey), and he made plans to advance the cause of this new and vibrant religion through conquest.

Promises, Promises

His revelations were dictated and collected in the Koran, which Muslims believe to be the preexistent, perfect words of Allah. The Koran testifies of itself that it was given by God through the angel Gabriel to the prophet Muhammad. "This is a revelation from the Lord of the universe. The Honest Spirit (Gabriel) came down with it, to reveal it into your heart that you may be one of the warners, in a perfect Arabic tongue" (Sura 26:192-195). "Say, 'Anyone who opposes Gabriel should know that he has brought down this (the Koran) into your heart, in accordance with God's will, confirming previous scriptures, and providing guidance and good news for the believers.'" (Sura 2:97).

The "previous scriptures" mentioned above are the Hebrew Torah, the Psalms of David, and the Gospels of Jesus Christ (Sura 4:163; 5:44-48). The Koran accepts these books as divinely inspired and even encourages doubters to test its claims by checking those texts. "If you have any doubt regarding what is revealed to you from your Lord, then ask those who read the previous scripture" (Sura 10:94).

However, the Koran thoroughly contradicts the Torah, the Psalms, and the Gospels. For example, the Koran explicitly denies Jesus' crucifixion (Sura 4:157-158) while all four Gospel accounts clearly portray Christ as crucified.

One contradiction in particular has caused a great deal of conflict between Muslims and ethnic Jews. As we saw earlier, Abraham had two sons – Isaac and Ishmael. God promised a child through Sarah, not Hagar (Genesis 17-18), and, in due time, God fulfilled His promise.

And the Lord visited Sarah as He had said, and the Lord did for Sarah as He had spoken. For Sarah conceived and bore Abraham a son in his old age, at the set time of which God had spoken to him. And Abraham called the name of his son who was born to him -- whom Sarah bore to him -- Isaac. -- *Genesis 21:1-3*

Isaac was the child of that promise. He later begot Jacob, the father of the tribes of Israel. Later, in Christian belief, Jesus came into the world through the nation of Israel, fulfilling the covenant that God had made with Abraham.

God also promised to give the land of Canaan (Palestine) to Isaac's descendants, the land which Israel possesses today (Genesis 12:4-7; 13:12-18; 15:1-21; 17:1-22; 21:1-14; 25:19-26; 26:1-6; 35:9-12).

However, the Koran insists that Ishmael was the child of promise (Sura 19:54; compare Sura 37:83-109 with Genesis 22:1-19). So, Muslims believe that God's covenant promises were meant for Ishmael's descendants, not Isaac's. Muhammad descended from Ishmael, giving Muslims claim to the land of God's promise. As a result, since Israel was created as a Jewish state by the United Nations in 1948, there has been unceasing hostility between Israel and her Arab neighbors with major armed conflicts in 1948-49, 1956, 1967, 1973, 1982 and 2006.

Disagreement with Jews started soon after Muhammad and his small band arrived in Yathrib. He thought Jewish residents would welcome him in line with other biblical prophets. Instead, one of their leaders, Ka'b ibn al-Ashraf, aligned himself with the Meccans and promised to help kill Muhammad. The basic problem was that the Jews like their religion, no matter how much pain it caused them, and rejected Muhammad's vision. He also banned alcohol, gambling and games of chance. Jews could have done without the latter two, but wine was a sacred part of their rituals, as with Christians.

Muhammad must have seemed like quite a killjoy.

Meanwhile, he was busy sending out missionaries to spread the word of the new faith. As with the early Christian missionaries, the public wasn't ready to accept his teaching. The Byzantine emperor's daughter adopted Islam, but was promptly lynched by the Christian mob. The leader of Palestine at the time was decapitated and crucified by order of the emperor.

A Muslim ambassador was assassinated in Syria-Palestine. "Instead of punishing the culprit, the emperor Heraclius rushed with his armies to protect him against the punitive expedition sent by the Prophet."

Muhammad was not sitting still, however. He led a 10,000-man army into Mecca and conquered the key city of the region. People flocked to his banner, obeying the age-old view that whoever won must have a stronger god. Muhammad didn't even have to leave any soldiers behind as he returned to Medinah. Mecca was firmly in the Muslim camp.

Nevertheless, Muhammad fought continual wars for 10 years. By 632, Muhammad met 140,000 Muslim pilgrims from around the Mediterranean at the Ka'baa. This led to a famous sermon, akin to Jesus' Sermon on the Mount. Muhammad told them, "Belief in One God without images or symbols, equality of all the Believers without distinction of race or class, the superiority of individuals being based solely on piety; sanctity of life, property and honor; abolition of interest, and of vendettas and private justice; better treatment of women; obligatory inheritance and distribution of the property of deceased persons among near relatives of both sexes, and removal of the possibility of the accumulation of wealth in the hands of the few."

He insisted that the holy Koran and the conduct of the Prophet were to serve as the bases of law and a healthy criterion in every aspect of human life.

Soon after, June 8, 632, the Prophet died. His impact, however, did not fade. Nor has his presence waned in the last 1,400 years.

"Of all the great visionaries who at various times have come to torment an evil world with visions of Paradise," a historian noted, "he was perhaps the most human, the most like ourselves."

Chapter Eighteen

Arabs Take on the World

Muhammad's death unleashed the fury of Arab armies driven by a religious ideal. They swept quickly across the Middle East, pausing only at the gates of the Byzantine stronghold of Constantinople, leaped the Mediterranean into Spain and were only stopped from conquering Europe by the Frankish army at Tours in 732. The Arabs call the battle site "the pavement of martyrs."

As Arab armies marauded, the religion began to splinter. The process echoed what happened after the death of Jesus. Muhammad had named no successor. Jesus had none either. Eventually, newly risen Church leaders settled on the view of Jesus that still dominates Roman Catholic thinking. In contrast, Islam was broken in two and never healed. It's as if the Protestant Reformation occurred while the Church was forming. The Shiites wanted someone from Muhammad's family to continue in leadership, while the Sunnis prefered the most capable individual available. The two have also developed different holidays and ways of following the Prophet's directions.

The two went their separate ways from the moment Muhammad died. Many members of the faith nominated Ali, Muhammad's son-in-law, cousin and first convert, to step into Muhammad's leadership role, a position known as the Caliph ("successor"). Instead, he waited patiently as Abu Bakr (632-634), Umar (634-644) and Uthman (644-656) all became Caliphs. One set of Muslims argued that Muhammad created a dynasty, so his descendents should be the only leaders. They referred to themselves as *ahl al bayt* or "people of the house."

When Ali finally became Caliph after Uthman was assassinated, he found himself locked in a struggle with Aisha, wife of the Prophet and daughter of Abu Bakr. Aisha accused Ali of laggardly pursuing the Uthman's assassins. After a fierce battle between the two sides, Ali won and forced Aisha into retirement.

However, Ali then had to fight Mu'awiya Ummayad, Uthman's cousin and governor of Damascus. Ummayad also declined to back Ali unless the assassins were apprehended. Once again, soldiers on opposing forces clashed.

At the Battle of Suffin, Mu'awiya's soldiers cleverly stuck verses of the Koran onto the ends of their spears. Ali's pious troops refused to fight them. Backed into a corner, Ali worked out a compromise with Mu'awiya. His gesture, while politically expedient, undermined his popular support, and he was killed by one of his own men in 661.

Mu'awiya promptly seized the title of Caliph. Ali's elder son Hassan, wanted to do the same thing. His existence threatened Mu'awiva's budding dynasty, but not for long. In a pattern familiar from Roman history, Hassan died within a year, allegedly poisoned. Ali's younger son, Hussein, did not protest openly, but bided his time. He was sure that the caliphate would return to him when Mu'awiya died. Instead, Mu'awiya's son, Yazid, claimed the throne when his father passed away in 680.

Hussan then recruited an army, but proved no match for his rival. He and his troops were annihilated in the Battle of Karbala. Hussein's infant son, Ali, survived. Shiites ("party of Ali") rallied around him, while Sunnis ("custom" or "tradition") went with the strongest man, Yazid. The two political/religious parties have never reconciled.

To complicate matters, Muhammad's line ended in 873 when the last Shiite leader, Al-Askari, who had no brothers, disappeared within days of inheriting the leadership mantel at the age of four. The Shiites refused to accept that he was gone, and insisted the toddler was merely in hiding and would return.

The man who became the head of the Shiites took on pope-like qualities. The entire sect adopted essentially the Roman Catholic Church structure. The Ayatollah Khomeini, a Shiite who led the Iranian revolution against the Shah, was accorded massive support because of that.

The Shiites believe their imams have inherited some of Muhammad's brilliance. They also glorify Ali, and focus on martyrdom and suffering. Their position outside the mainstream has drawn other beleaguered people living in Iran and India.

Sunnis, on the other hand, belong to multiple sects. They have no clergy.

Sunnis and Shiites agree on the core fundamentals of Islam and recognize each others as Muslims. However, many Sunnis believe that Shiites "seem to take the fundamentals of Islam very much for granted, shunting them into the background and dwelling on the martyrdoms of Ali and Hussein. This is best illustrated at Ashura, a Muslim holiday when, each evening, over a period of 10 days, the Shiites commemorate the Battle of Karbala. A wailing imam whips up the congregation into a frenzy of tears and chest beating.

The two sects have different calls to prayer and follow different rituals. To the horror of Sunnis, Shiites combine prayers, sometimes only saying them three times a day instead of the prescribed five. Shiites may say different prayers, too, drawing on verses written by Ali and Fatima, which Sunnis consider the worst options. Shiites also permit muttah – a fixed-term, temporary marriage – which is banned by the Sunnis although it was permitted when Muhammad was alive.

The groups have worked together occasionally, but the recent war in Iraq exacerbated by their differences. Sectarian attacks are commonplace, even desecrating favorite mosques. The same battle is being played out in Pakistan.

The disparity in size doesn't help. Census figures show that Shiite Muslims dominate Iran. They control the population in Yemen and Azerbaijan, and represent about half the population of Iraq. Sizeable Shiite communities exist in Bahrain, the east coast of Saudi Arabia and in Lebanon. The well-known guerilla organization, Hezbollah, now heading the Palestine Liberation Organization, follows the Shiite beliefs.

Overall, worldwide, Shiites constitute 10 to 15 percent of the Muslim population.

They also have a messianic aspect to their faith. That crept into Islam less than 60 years after Muhammad died. Ali and his descendents were being bumped off by opponents. Some of the Shiites began to think that one child had survived. Naturally, as the story circulated, the heir was reported hidden by Allah, or by courageous Shiite supporters. The boy became known as the Madhi and was gradually promoted to messianic status.

The belief crystallized into the idea that a Mahdi would return and "implement the divine kingdom on earth."

The combustible combination of Islam and Jewish mysticism soon generated a cauldron full of would-be messiahs. In 645, one claimant, unidentified by name, assaulted several Muslim strongholds before being caught and, ironically, crucified.

One in the eighth century took the name Abu Isa (father of Jesus) and raised an army of 10,000 zealots. The ragtag host decided to take Palestine by force and confronted Caliph Abd al-Malik and his battle-hardened soldiers. The resulting massacre abruptly ended Abu Isa's brief career. His followers, however, said he did not die, but "slipped into a hole in a mountain."

By then, the Arabs were lords over a vast empire. When their religious fervor cooled, the Arabs settled down to rule their lands, with interludes of peace broken by occasional bouts of civil war, changes in dynasties and tiffs with the Greeks still holding onto Byzantium and to the tarnished Roman Empire name.

They contributed a stream of great scholars and scientists to the world, including mathematician Al-Khwarizmi; physicist Alhazen, whose works were translated into Latin about 1,000 years ago; physician Avicenna, who traveled throughout Europe and whose textbook was required in European universities; Alburundi, a geographer who, among other feats, worked out latitude and longitude; and Averroes, a philosopher who translated Aristotle for his people.

Arab power, however, did not last long. In 1273, a group of Turkish tribesmen under Ertughrul came to the aid of the sultan in a battle against Mongols, the invaders from China. In 1288, Ertughrul died and was succeeded by his son, Osman – in the West known as Ottoman. The Crusades had brought Christian armies into Jerusalem in the 1100s. For two centuries, they watched as Arabs battled with each other. They knew they were no match for a united Arab front.

They were right. Within the next 200 years, the Ottoman Turks had seized the Arab empire. "They won every battle they fought, and fought continuously."

Their approach was simple: they started with cattle raids and then bought land. Neighboring farmers paid tribute, then converted to Islam to avoid the payment. They built their capital in Adrianople, on the European side of the straits, across from Byzantium. After recovering from fresh attacks by the Mongols under Tamerlane (Timur the Lame) in the early Middle Ages, the Turks resumed their conquests.

In 1453, Byzantium fell and, with it, all of Asia Minor now belonged to the Ottomans. By 1517, they controlled Egypt, Palestine, Syria and Iraq. Attacks on Europe followed, eventually, in 1683, leading to an unsuccessful siege of Vienna. That failure in the Austrian snows – essentially a stalemate – ended Turkish hopes for power outside Asia Minor.

Their focus became the Middle East where conflicts within Abraham's siblings continued unabated. Jews were "forced to wear special badges and costumes. Conversion to Judaism was strictly forbidden by Muslims and Christians alike." Muslims did not force Jews or Christians to join Islam. Jews paid taxes to live in Muslim lands, but were often prosperous. In 1492, as Jews fled Catholic Spain, they were welcomed in Islamic Turkey. In 1562, Sultan Sulieman the Magnificent invited Jews to rebuild Tiberias.

Still, there were problems. Leaders in Baghdad and Cairo encouraged anti-Jewish acts. As Sulieman signed the agreement on Tiberias, other Arabs were claiming that a predicted messiah would arise in Tiberias and mean the end of Islam.

Such implacable hatred led to conflicts. In 1648, Arabs accused the Jews of starting an epidemic – the same claim that accompanied the Black Death in Christian lands centuries earlier and led to murders of innocent Jews. That followed on the heels of a threat by Mohammed Pasha to expel or execute Jews if a drought were not broken in three days. The rains fortuitously arrived on time. Faced with more Arab claims and related threats, many Jews simply fled Jerusalem.

Still, in many ways, Jews directed their animosity not toward the earthly Arabic government, but at Christianity. No Muslim government, after all, allowed the kind of mistreatment of Jews encouraged by Christian rulers in Europe. Jews weren't even angry with the Greek Orthodox Church, the main Christian representative in the Levant. Their ire was reserved for the Roman Catholic Church, which kept anti-Semitism burning through this era. A 1960s Stanford University study found the Church – and western Christianity in general – responsible for the continuation of anti-Jewish sentiment among parishioners. Later, Pope John Paul II apologized for the Church's past behavior and tried to construct stronger links to the Jewish community.

The Muslims shared in the animosity. They faced off against Christians, mainly ignoring the land-less and powerless Jews. After all, there was always the danger the Christians would try to recapture the Holy Land, as they had once before. They even consider the United States' excursion into Iraq in 1992 as a continuation of crusades, which ended almost 800 years ago.

But, the Ottoman Empire was weak for centuries: "(It was) not even a nation, but a host of peoples, an imperial family, and a system."

The Turks began to falter by 1566 after 10 successive capable sultans ruled. "The effectiveness of the entire structure depended on the sultan. After the first 10 generations, the sultans mostly were weaklings, drunkards, debauchees, men of little experience or political understanding."

While the Thirty Years' War raged in Europe, preventing attacks on their decaying fronts, the Ottomans suffered internal anarchy, riotous troops and several coups. In time, the country became known as the "sick man of Europe."

The cure came at the end of World War I. Arab hegemony was dead. The Turks were pushed back behind their current border.

The Holy Land may have been promised to Abraham, but, in the 20th century, it inherited only bloodshed, hatred and continuing murderous attacks by Arabs, Christians and Jews alike.

The problems accelerated in the late 1800s as Jews increasingly bought up and settled what had been Bedouin grazing lands. The nomads had little use for property rights and thought they were swindling buyers by selling the acreage. Something similar happened in this country as gleeful Indians sold land to European settlers only to realize later that ownership meant far more than tradition.

At the same time, geopolitics entered the fray. The English and French had won World War I with American help. They saw the Middle East as virgin territory that any imperialistic country could exploit. The French wanted control of half the land, principally Syria and Lebanon. The English settled for Palestine.

Unfortunately for the cause of peace, not every British subject agreed with the division of spoils. T.E. Lawrence, an English linguist who helped translate Turkish codes, had become a hero by riding with the Arabs, organizing them, overcoming feuds and leading them in guerilla battles against the Turks. To get their cooperation, he had promised them independence. At the same time, the English wanted Jewish aid in the area. Lord Balfour, representing England, had already issued a declaration promising the Jews an independent state.

It was impossible for both sides to resolve this disagreement. The Jews felt they had been promised a refuge; the Arabs felt they had been promised control of their own land. About 90 percent of Palestine was Arabic.

Meanwhile, Jews kept flooding into the land. The Jewish population in Palestine jumped from about 50,000 by the beginning of 1900 to approximately 300,000 before World War II.

Trying to maintain control, Palestinians staged a general strike in April 1936 to protest Jewish migration, which they saw as a threat to their rights.

The British countered with a plan to divide Palestine into three distinct units: a Jewish one in the north, another state for the Arabs in the south, and a third section to remain under the British administration in the Jerusalem- Tel Aviv corridor. Both sides hated the concept. The British gave up and tried to hold back Jewish immigration.

Since diplomacy wouldn't work, all sides chose the familiar method of extermination. Both Jews and Arabs attacked their English overlords and each other in a deadly game of murder and revenge.

The situation took on mote urgency during World War II as Jews desperately sought escape from the Nazis. No country opened their doors to refugees, adding to the pressure to resolve the problem after the war ended. Surviving Jews moved from concentration camps to refugee camps, and looked toward Palestine as their only hope. Arabs, on the other hand, feared being overrun and displaced. Religious animosities only added to the distrust and disdain.

Finally, in 1947, the English gave up and submitted the whole *mishigas* (mess) to the newly-established United Nations in the aftermath of World War II. The move followed the successful bombing of the King David Hotel, home to the British headquarters, by Jewish militants. As discussed earlier, the United Nations then voted to split the land into Jewish and Arab halves. At that time, 749,000 Arabs and 9,250 Jews lived in the territory where the proposed Arab state would be set up, while 497,000 Arabs and 498,000 Jews lived in the part which was to become the Jewish state.

When the plan was approved, leaders of the newly created Israel declared statehood in April 1948. Then, Jews and Arabs promptly went to war. More than half of the Palestinians in the Jewish sector abandoned their homes and headed towards the West Bank and Gaza Strip, where they lived as refugees. The West Bank of the Jordan River fell under the jurisdiction of the Hashemite kingdom of Transjordan; the Gaza Strip fell under the Egyptian administration.

The winter of 1949, the first winter of exile for more than seven hundred fifty thousand Palestinians, was cold and hard. Families huddled in caves, abandoned huts, or makeshift tents. Many of the starving were only miles away from their own vegetable gardens and orchards in occupied Palestine - - the new state of Israel. At the end of 1949 the United Nations finally acted. It set up the United Nations Relief and Works Administration (UNRWA) to take over 60 refugee camps from voluntary agencies. It managed to keep people alive, but only barely. -- *Our Roots Are Still Alive* (The Peoples Press Palestine)

That view was countered by Jewish leaders who argued that the Arabs were not forced to flee and could have remained as Israeli citizens. They also point out that Arab countries should have accepted their countrymen. Instead, even today, those camps have become hotbeds of radicals, terrorists and would-be avengers, determined to kill the Israelis. That vow, part of the Palestine Liberation Organization's constitution, has always been a stumbling block to any real peace negotiations.

The battle continues. The Israelis have developed a top fighting force and are renowned for their prowess. They have extracted hostages from Uganda in a daring raid and bombed nuclear facilities in Iraq. Their secret police, Mossad, is feared worldwide.

At the same time, Arabs have maintained a constant state of war against the Jewish state. Egypt and Jordan did sign peace agreements with Israel, but rising conservative forces, using the Koran as their evidence, threaten to undermine western-oriented regimes and replace them with more aggressive, anti-Israeli rules. Iran is a prime example: there, the western-leaning shah was ousted by Islamic religious leaders who imposed their beliefs on the population and continue to foment war.

Seeing the United States as the main supporter of Israel, Arabs have also directed their attacks against distant, symbolic targets, like the World Trade Center in New York City.

Ironically, the Koran, like the Bible, does not sanction such behavior.

"The Koran is saying to humans, this is the final guidance from your Creator, for the specific purpose of worshiping him and creating a civil society where you can live in peace with one another," according to Muslim scholar Imam Sulayman S. Nyang of Howard University in Washington, D.C. He was interviewed as part of a National Geographic Society report.

"Muslims around the world rely on the Koran for guidance," Nyang said. "Devout followers heed the call to prayer five times each day and recite passages from the holy book. Muslims believe that the Koran is God's unfiltered message – teaching them how to lead a good life and become a better, more moral person."

For most Muslims, the callous and indiscriminate taking of human life via terrorists' acts violates Allah's wishes, he said. It defies the Koran's central message and undermines the peace that Islam promises to deliver to all people.

"You do not kill innocent people, you do not cheat, you do not lie, you do not destroy any property of other human beings," added Imam Abdullah Khouj, an Islamic scholar and director of the Islamic Center, in Washington, D.C. "Human life in Islam is extremely sacred. We're not talking about just Muslim [life], but human life in general."

Which is exactly what the Jewish and Christian sacred texts say, too.

Chapter Nineteen

Splitsville Under the Stars

Muhammad bequeathed his followers an array of revelations to guide them through life. Just as the Bible contains multiple commandments, rules and directions – some of which can be adduced from examples, others that are spelled out – the Koran provides similar guidelines.

Central to Islamic belief is the absolute power of God. Islam is strictly monotheistic, believing that there is only one God, omnipotent and merciful, and that associating any human being or image with God is an unforgivable sin. That, of course, parallels the Second Commandment against graven images. This rule explains the Muslim rejection of Christianity, since Islam does not acknowledge the divinity of Jesus. It also clarifies why Islamic armies were so brutal when confronting Arabic tribes that worshiped idols.

Muslims believe that Muhammad was the last of a series of prophets that God sent to earth. While respecting the teachings of all earlier prophets, such as Moses, Jesus and Elijah, Muslims believe that Allah sent his final message to Muhammad in order to correct the corruption of the previous revelations. They revere the Prophet as the embodiment of the perfect believer, accept his actions and words as a model of ideal conduct. Unlike Jesus, whom Christians believe was God's son, Muhammad was a mortal with extraordinary qualities. Today, many Muslims insist that pictures of Muhammad are improper and against their faith. However, at one time, they created many images, although none became holy icons as in some Christian sects.

Both Christians and Muslims accept the existence of a devil, but Islamic theology maintains that God is the most important figure. As a result, Satan ("adversary") is not nearly as significant in Islam as he is in Christianity. The devil also has no role to play in Judaism although he plays a prominent position in the canonical book of Job.

Also, unlike Christianity, Muslims do not accept the concept of original sin. They believe that God pardoned Adam's sin in order for human beings to begin life without sin. Muslims who have sinned in their lives and who sincerely repent and submit to God can be forgiven for their transgressions.

Muslims share with Jews and Christians a belief in a Judgment Day, when the world will end and the dead will rise to be judged.

Here is a closer look at the many elements of this faith.

Allah

The name of God is not something to be trifled with. Jews were so adamant that God's name, Yahweh, was not to be spoken except by the High Priest and only on the holiest day of the year, that sages ruled the only heresy was saying the holy name aloud. The prohibition against using God's name in vain is in the 10 Commandments. The control of the use of that name was so complete that historians today have no idea how the four letters were actually pronounced.

In the Bible, Yahweh speaks to several people, including Adam, Abraham and Moses. In Islam, Allah speaks to Muhammad. The idea that any deity could select someone to speak for him to the people was not uncommon. Zoroaster also claimed that Ahura Mazda – another Babylonian god – spoke to him and insisted that he spread that god's message.

Both Yahweh and Ahura Mazda were worshiped before becoming associated with a particular religion. Archeologists found three different variations of Yahweh in Canaanite inscriptions-- Yahh, Ya/El and Yah. The deity was shown in association "with radiance, as from the sun, and a radiant serpent." That iconic snake might have survived without Josiah's reforms

Allah, the name Muhammad identified with his God, also has a long history that precedes the religion. After all, Muhammad's father's name was Abdullah, which means "servant" of Allah.

Prior to Muhammad, then, Allah was already worshiped by the pagan Arabs in a pantheon of deities. Allah was even worshiped in the Ka'baa at Mecca before Muhammad was born. Muhammad proclaimed a god the Meccans were already familiar with and was never accused of preaching a different Allah than the one they already followed.

The verses of the Koran make it clear that the very name Allah existed in the Jahiliyya or pre-Islamic Arabia. Certain pagan tribes believed in a god whom they called 'Allah' and whom they believed to be the creator of heaven and earth and holder of the highest rank in the hierarchy of the gods. It is well known that the Quraish as well as other tribes believed in

Allah, whom they designated as the 'Lord of the House' (i.e., of the Ka'baa)...It is therefore clear that the Koranic conception of Allah is not entirely new. -- *Faruq Sheriff, A Guide to the Contents of the Qur'an*

The name Allah shows up in Sabean, Minoan and particularly Libyanite inscriptions. Historians report the name occurs in two South Arabian inscriptions: a Minoan one found at al-'Ula; the other, a Sabean, but abounds in the form HLH in the Libyanite inscriptions of the fifth century B.C.E. Libya, which evidently got the god from Syria, was the first center of the worship of this deity in Arabia. The name occurs as Hallah in the Safa inscriptions five centuries before Islam and also in a pre-Islamic Christian-Arabic inscription found in umm-al-Jimal, Syria, and ascribed to the sixth century.

The name also is found as part of proper names, like the el in Daniel or Jacobel. The feminine form of Allah, Allat, is found commonly among the names on inscriptions from North Arabia.

The name itself may derive from two Arabic words that translate "the God." The word, however, is Aramaic and derives from a descriptive term used in pagan faiths to identify their superior deity. It translates as "top god." As a result, the name is comparative to the Jewish "elohim," which means gods, or the Greek "theos," which also means gods. The revealed name for elohim is "Yahweh." The revealed name for theos is Jesus.

In reality, Muslims never were given a revealed name for the top god, but, over time, the word Allah took on that connotation.

Arabs would have heard the term "Allah" used when traveling Christian and Jews came through Arabia and discussed religion. To the visitors, the word Allah would have simply been a generic designation for their God. For Arabs, however, the same word would have had a meaning rooted in their own culture.

In the pre-Muhammad days, Allah had company, what the Koran disdainfully labels "associates:" Ailat ("goddess") may have stood for one aspect of Venus, the morning star; Uzza, (the all-powerful) who also shared traits with Venus; and Manat, the goddess of fate, who held the shears which cut the thread of life and who was worshiped in a shrine on the sea-shore.

In addition to the black stone in the Ka'baa, there were as many as 360 idols, the kind of idols Abraham would have been familiar with.

Interestingly, there was no idol of Allah, perhaps reflecting his superior status.

Yahweh, too, had companions, based on stone images of his consorts found by archeologists.

The Arabs, like the Jews, eliminated any such connotations with other deities, even changing accepted hymns to reflect the new ideology. The Old Testament has psalms copied from the Egyptians that once praised the sun god, Aten, but now praise Yahweh. In Islam, the processional chant of the pagans of the Age of Barbarism was, "Here I am, O Allah, here I am; You have no partner except such a partner as You have; You possess him and all that is his." The Muslim version reads now: "Here I am, O Allah, here I am; You have no partner; the praise and the grace are Yours, and the empire; You have no partner." -- *F.E. Peters, The Hajj*

At first, Allah was only the god of contracts who watched over travelers. As he became more important in the years prior to Islam, he assumed other tasks. He became the moon god, a role familiar to Abraham. He also evolved into the god of sky and rain, a key necessity of life in the desert. With Muhammad, he becomes God of the world, of all believers, the one and only who admits of no associates or consorts in the worship of Him. This conforms with Jewish and Christian monotheistic views.

The Prophet's mission was not only to proclaim God's existence, but to deny the existence of all lesser deities. The Koran regularly refers to Muhammad's adversaries in Mecca, swearing by God, invoking Him, and recognizing His sovereignty as Creator. The conflict that arose came from the fact the people of Mecca did not understand or allow that God alone should be worshiped. They insisted that, if God had willed it, they would have refrained from believing in other deities (Surah vi. 148), "clearly implying that God approved of their concurrent idolatry." -- *Kenneth Cragg, The Call of The Minaret*

Muhammad's success changed that thinking forever.

Pillars of the Faith

Judaism stands on the Torah. Christianity has the New Testament to support its beliefs. In addition to the Koran, Islam has *arkan ud-Din,* "pillars of the faith," five religious duties expected of every pious Muslim.

The five pillars are cited throughout the Koran on an individual basis, but Muhammad listed them together when he was asked to define Islam. After his death, Islamic leaders designated these pillars as "anchoring points" within the Muslim community. Believers who obeyed the five pillars are thought to receive rewards both in this life and in the afterlife.

All Muslim sects endorse this unusual pentagon. The Shiites have increased the total by adding "the jihad, payment of the imam's tax, encouragement of good deeds and prevention of evil."

First Pillar

Creed (*Shahada*): The statement of Shahada in Arabic is: "Ashhadu al-la ilaha illa-llah wa ashhadu anna Muhammadar rasulu-llah." In English, that equates:: "I bear witness that there is no God but Allah and I bear witness that Muhammad is His Messenger." This declaration of the faith must be uttered publicly at least once in a Muslim's lifetime, although most Muslims recite it daily.

Converts can join the Muslim community simply by reciting the shahada in complete sincerity. The vow is also echoed in the regular call to prayer, included in the daily ritual prayer and recited in the moments before death.

The shahada is serves as the source of Islamic beliefs in angels, the Koran, the Bible, the prophets and a Day of Judgment.

Second Pillar

Prayer (*Salate*): The Muslim holy day is Friday, when congregations gather just past noon in a *masjid*, or mosque in English, the Muslim place of worship. The three holiest places of worship in the Islamic world are the Mosque of the Ka'baa in Mecca, the Mosque of the Prophet Muhammad in Medina, and the Masjid Aqsa, adjacent to the Dome of the Rock in Jerusalem. In them, an imam, or religious leader, gives a sermon and leads the congregation in prayer.

Muslims do not need to be in a mosque in order to pray, however. As is true for devout Christians and Jews, they may do it anywhere – a house, office, school, or even outside. All they have to do is face the Ka'baa in Mecca. Jews turn toward Jerusalem. The Muslims did that, too, initially, but when the Jews of Medinah rejected Muhammad's call, he shifted the direction of prayers away from David's City.

Prayers must be performed five times daily – at dawn, noon, mid-afternoon, sunset, and nightfall. The prayers always contain verses from the Koran and must be said in Arabic. Muslims believe that prayer provides a direct link between the worshiper and God.

The Friday service matches the Jews, who also have a singular prayer – the *Shema* – which characterizes their faith. The Catholic Creed would have the same effect, but not all Christian sects have such statements. Jews also are not obligated to worship in a synagogue or temple, whereas attendance of a Catholic mass used to be mandatory.

Third Pillar

Purifying Tax *(zakat)*: Muslims believe that all things belong to God, and that humans only hold wealth in trust for Him. For that reason, they think wealth should be distributed throughout the community of believers, or *umma*, through a purifying tax. The usual payment is 2.5 per cent of a person's assets. That means everything: grains; fruit; camels; cattle; sheep and goats; gold and silver; and movable goods.

The money is distributed to the poor, debtors, volunteers in jihad, pilgrims, and the collectors of the tax. At one time, slaves seeking to buy their freedom got a handout. There's even a website where Muslims can use a calculator to figure out how much *zakat* they should donate.

Additional charity work is also encouraged.

The Koran explicitly requires *zakat* (9:60) and often places it alongside prayer when discussing a Muslim's duties. ("Perform the prayer and give the alms." 2:43, 110, 277) For those who believe in taking their wealth with them, the Koran minces no words: the fires of hell will heat up the coins, and the greedy will be branded with it (9:34-35).

The *zakat* is designed to be sure the wealthy help the poor, a practice that boosted Christianity in the eyes of pagans during its early years. Jews, too, are mandated in the Bible to assist those in need. In the canonical Book of Ruth, for example, Boaz, a wealthy farmer, meets his new wife by following biblical injunctions to leave some crops in the field for the needy. Ruth was gleaning the residue when Boaz saw her. Ruth's greatest descendant was King David.

The Islamic state used to enforce *zahar*, but, today, it's individual choice unless a country, like Saudi Arabia, demands strict adherence to religious law (shari'a).

The Shiites emphasize this pillar by requiring an additional one-fifth tax (khums) that must be paid to the hidden Imam for the benefit of orphans, the poor, travelers, and the imams.

Zahar is similar to voluntary tithing in both Judaism and Christianity. In the Church of the Latter Day Saints, tithing is a religious requirement.

Fourth Pillar

Fasting *(sawm)*: During the month of Ramadan, the ninth month in the Islamic calendar, Muslims fast between dawn and dusk. They must abstain from food, liquid, and intimate contact during those hours of the day, in order to commemorate the Muslim belief that Ramadan was the month in which the Koran descended from the highest heaven to the lowest, from which it was then revealed to Muhammad in pieces over 22 years. Fasting is seen as a method of self-purification, by cutting oneself off from worldly comforts.

The sick, elderly, travelers, and nursing or pregnant women are permitted to break the fast during Ramadan, provided they make up for it during an equal number of days later in the year. Children begin the ritual at puberty.

The end of Ramadan is celebrated by the *Eid al-Fitr*, one of the major festivals on the Muslim calendar.

Jewish and Christian calendars are also dotted with fasts, but none longer than a day.

Fifth Pillar

Pilgrimage *(Hajj)*: All Muslims are required to make one pilgrimage to Mecca in their lifetimes, provided they are physically and financially able to do so. The Hajj begins in the 12th month of the Islamic lunar calendar which means, like Ramadan, it does not correspond to a specific month in the solar calendar. Modern transportation methods, particularly the airplane, have made it possible for many more Muslims to make the Hajj today than 1,400 years ago.

Like Ramadan, the end of the Hajj is also celebrated with a festival, the *Eid al-Adha*, which is celebrated by all Muslims, whether or not they made the pilgrimage. This festival and the *Eid al-Fitr* at the end of Ramadan comprise the highlights of the Islamic year.

Pilgrimages are encouraged in both Judaism and Christianity, but none are mandatory.

Sects

Both Judaism and Christianity have divided into multiple sects and have been that way for centuries. Islam is no different. The biggest sects, the Sunni and Shiites, have been discussed previously.

The four Sunni schools of law (*madhahib*) – the Hanafi, the Maliki, the Shafi'i and the Hanbali – are sometimes mistakenly thought of as different sects, but are not. The schools refer to four great Islamic scholars, who may have taught slightly different ideas, but were actually students of one another.

The Shiites have one major school of thought known as the Jafaryia or the "Twelvers," and a few minor schools of thought, as the "Seveners" or the "Fivers." These names all refer to the number of imams they recognize after the death of Muhammad. The term Shiite is usually meant to be synonymous with the Jafaryia/Twelvers.

Shiite and Sunni communities are splintered into thousands of smaller sub-sects and cults with an incredible diversity of beliefs.

Islamic Sects

Sufis

They represent a mystical tradition in Islam., seeking an alternative way of approaching the faith through a direct experience of God. Prominent throughout Islamic history, more than half of the male Muslim population was attached to a Sufi order (tariqa) in the 19th century.

To the Sunnis, Sufism is considered to be an integral part of Islam.

"Whirling dervishes," a group known to spin in religious ecstasy until collapsing, are Sufi.

Jews who became attracted to the Kabbalah, a mystical book introduced around the 1100s C.E., share the same interest as the Sufi in reaching out to the divine through spiritual means. So did the ancient Gnostics.

Wahhabis

They are strict traditionalists, an approach popular on the Arabian Peninsula, but have little support elsewhere.

Ismailis

An offshoot of the Shiites, they accept the Aga Khan, an honorary title dating back more than 1,000 years as their spiritual leader and refuse to join other Muslims in prayer. Today's Aga Khan is a Harvard-educated businessman living in Switzerland. The Ismailis left the fold not long after Muhammad's death by accepting one son of the sixth imam, Ishmail, as their titular head while other Shiites accepted a different son.

Ismailis gave birth to their own sub-sects, including one of the most famous heresies in Islam, the Nizaris. The Crusaders had another name for them, the Assassins. Formed in the 1200s, they were Shiites who worked murderously to protect the interests of Ali's descendants. They fought with the Knights Templar, the power behind the Jerusalem throne under a leader called the "Old Man of the Mountains."

Kurds

Residents of Kurdistan, these people can be found in communities throughout the Middle East. Ethnically related to Iranians, the Kurds have found conquerors of all stripes, including Sumerians, Assyrians, Persians, Mongols, Crusaders and Turks. Eventually, in the 10th century, the Kurds accepted Islam.

Kahrijites

In Arabic, their name means "to go out." They earned that title by leaving Islam almost as soon as the religion was founded. They simply disagreed with some of the teachings.

Ahmadiyya

A messianic arm of Islam, this sect was founded by Mirza Ghulam Ahmad (c. 1839-1908) in India. He claimed to be everything from the biblical messiah to Muhammad, Jesus and the Hindu god Krishna. After his death and the death of a successor, the sect divided in two. One recognizes Ahmad as a prophet; another sees him as only a reformer. Today, about 170 million Ahmadiyya Muslims reside mainly in Pakistan.

Ahmadiyya Islam is also associated with several Sufi orders, most notably the Al-Badawi order of Egypt, named for an Islamic saint who died in 1276.

The multiple sects naturally have created friction within Islam. In reality, as one historian noted, "Every single person practicing Islam in the world today is a heretic in the eyes of at least one other such person."

However, unlike Christian churches, mosques are not denominational. Traditional Friday prayer services are largely similar in every sect, and Muslims of any background are welcome to attend services at any mosque.

Gender Equality

Women have gotten short shrift in all three monotheistic religions. In Judaism, women are responsible for taking care of the house and family. The important task of handling religion is left to the men. In Orthodox services, men and women are seated in separate areas, so the males will not be distracted from their sacred duties. In Christianity, women are often shunted aside. Early theology insisted that women do not possess souls and are inherently evil, because of Eve's original sin of getting Adam to munch on a forbidden apple.

"Believing women descended from the sinful Eve colored Christian ideas of women's character for centuries – as untrustworthy, morally inferior, wicked beings – with menstruation, pregnancy, and childbirth believed to be punishment for all women after Eve."

The Koran paints a different picture. Men and women are created equally. Neither gender is superior. Both can go to heaven. Adam and Eve both were responsible for losing Eden, but, since both repented, both were forgiven. Women are here, the Koran says, to give birth, but also to perform good deeds, just like the men.

As such, women are not possessions of men. They can choose their own husbands, keep their own names, build capital, divorce if necessary and keep property.

The Koran also requires men and women to dress modestly. For women, that has translated into the *Hijab*, which women use to cover their heads and body except for eyes and hands. Others limit it just to hair.

Muhammad's farsighted guidelines, however, ran smack into the real world and, today, are rarely followed. Women are often kept away from schools and live circumscribed lives unlike anything the Prophet seems to have recommended.

Holidays

Several holidays have already been listed. Ramadan is the best known Islamic holiday perhaps because of the novelty of a lengthy fast. The holiday, which celebrates the Koran, got wide attention in this country when Muslim athletes tried to compete in athletic games after not eating all day.

Muslims use the last 10 days of the holiday for devotions and good deeds in an effort to draw closer to God. "The night on which the first verses of the Koran were revealed to the Prophet, known as the Night of Power (*Lailat ul-Qadr*), is generally taken to be the 27th night of the month. The Koran states that this night is better than a thousand months. Therefore, many Muslims spend the entire night in prayer."

The holiday comes with special foods, prayers and readings from the Koran, the same as the Jewish Passover.

The 27th day of Ramadan is set aside as Lailat-ul-Qadr, the day the Archangel Gabriel introduced the first words of the Koran to Muhammad. Muhammad reportedly stayed awake all night. Some Muslims duplicate that feat, praying for forgiveness of any sin. In a way, the holiday also resembles the Jewish Yom Kippur, when devout Jews gather in synagogues, fast and ask God to pardon their sins.

Other important holidays include:

Hijrat

This holiday commemorates Muhammad's exit from Mecca to the city of Yathrib (Medinah) in 622. This event, called the Hegira, marks the start of the Muslim calendar. As noted earlier, Islamic years are numbered starting from the Hegira.

Ashura

This holiday, cited earlier, recalls the martyrdom of Imam Hussain, the grandson of Muhammad in 663. The Shiites consider this day extremely important, since they still bemoan Hussain's death.

In addition, the day is also linked to an old holiday once followed by Jews in Medinah. They would fast to remember their salvation from the Pharaoh in Egypt. Muslims multiplied the reasons behind the occasion by saying, on this day, Noah's Ark also came to rest on Mt. Ararat, Abraham was born and the Ka'baa was built.

Eid Milad-un-Nabi

The Muslim Christmas without the commercial whoop-de-doo, it is celebrated on the 12th day of the month Rabee-ul-Awwal and commemorates the birth of Muhammad. The day is not totally joyous because Muslims also mark his death at the same time.

As with Christmas, this holiday was not celebrated in earlier times and has not attained universal status in all Muslim countries.

Eid-ul-Adha

The Festival of Sacrifice recalls the biblical account of Abraham being asked to sacrifice his son Isaac. A sheep or cow gets it in the neck on this day, and much of the meat is donated to the poor. In some Muslim countries, this is a public holiday.

Laylat Al-Baraa

Borrowing from the Jewish Yom Kippur, on this "the night of repentance," forgiveness is granted to those who repent.

Muslims, like Jews, follow a lunar calendar. That's much shorter than a solar calendar. So holidays move around every year.

Leaders

The Muslims, like the Jews, have no set hierarchy. There's no pope, archbishop, monsignor or Cardinal among them. Orthodox Jews do have a head rabbi in Jerusalem, but he has little authority. The divisive question of "who is a Jew," which has convulsed Jewish philosophers for centuries, went to the Israeli Supreme Court for a ruling, not some religious body.

Muslims recognize several ranks of religious authorities.

Caliph

This is the anglicized Arabic word for "successor" and refers to the men who followed Muhammad. The term has fallen into disuse, but meant someone who was a "prince" of the community, but not necessarily a prophet.

Imam

Meaning "leader," an imam is an accepted religious leader, but whose authority may be limited to a single community or be widespread.

Ayatollah

From the Persian, "sign of God," this term is given to a Shiite scholar who has gained expertise in Islamic fields of jurisprudence, ethics, philosophy and mysticism, and usually teaches in schools of Islamic sciences. Ayatollahs who achieve widespread recognition can issue a legal ruling that gains instant acceptance.

Symbols

Islam does not have many symbols, unlike the Jewish star or the cross. The crescent moon, which appears on the flags of various countries, such as Turkey and Pakistan, is really not a religious icon, but was the insignia of the Ottoman Empire. So was the single star, which is often joined with the moon. Westerners saw them so often in Middle Eastern countries, they simply assumed the crescent moon and star were symbols of Islam.

Among the Muslims, only the Shiites have a symbol, a sword. They associate it with Ali, who was killed in battle.

On the other hand, colors have long been part of Islamic symbolism. They were associated with various dynasties as battle standards. Four colors – white for the Ummayads; black for the Abbasids; green for the Fatimids – have become traditional in Islamic countries along with red.

Green has accorded particularly high status because it was reportedly Muhammad's favorite color. He was supposed to have worn a green cloak and turban, and fought under a green banner. The Koran (Surah 18:31) gives some credence to that claim, saying that the "inhabitants of paradise will wear green garments of fine silk."

Priests

Islam has no priests or seminaries for training priests, imams or ayatollahs. People achieve that status through community recognition based on religious knowledge and/or scholarship.

All of them are expected to know the Koran, the last great holy text given the world by an offspring of Abraham.

Conclusion

This survey of the three major Western monotheistic religions has demonstrated how dependent they are on each other. Jerome recognized that in the fourth century. Ordered to translate the holy Christian books in the fourth century, he actually turned to the Jewish Bible and translated it first. Christian ideas of a messiah, he realized, were meaningless without the earlier texts.

Islam, too, requires knowledge of the Bible to understand. Muhammad's entire belief rests on the frail back of Ishmael, who is little more than a name in Genesis.

Despite the clear links, members of the three faiths continue to fuss and fight with deadly intent around the world. Yet, as we saw, beliefs are very similar, all built around a love for each other and a belief in a single God. They all talk of peace and long for the day when all mankind will accept the inspired words of God's prophets.

The similarities far outweigh the differences.

Perhaps in the coming years, as communication tightens the binds that unite all of us, adherents will begin to focus on what all three religions share and what tremendous impact they have had together on culture, morality and ethics. Then, in the words of Isaiah, a prophet honored in three religions and whose prediction is recorded in a book revered by the same three religions:

In the last days, the mountain of the house of the Lord will be the most important of the mountains. It will be raised above the hills. All the nations will come to it. Many people will come and say, 'Come, let us go up to the mountain of the Lord, to the house of the God of Jacob. Then He will teach us about His ways, that we may walk in His paths. For the Law will go out from Zion, and the Word of the Lord from Jerusalem.' He will judge between the nations, and will decide for many people. And they will beat their swords into plows, and their spears into knives for cutting vines. Nation will not lift up sword against nation, and they will not learn about war anymore.

Communication

In order for people to share ideas, they have to communicate. Initially, specially trained writers, called scribes, developed pictures to represent ideas. Egyptian hieroglyphics are the best known, but Chinese letters today still consist of stylized pictures.

However, commerce needed some form of communication that was easier to read and share. Phoenician traders developed the first known alphabet, where symbols represented sounds. We are still indebted to them today.

	'aleph, the ox, began as the image of an ox's head. It represents a glottal stop before a vowel. The Greeks, needing vowel symbols, used it for **alpha** (A). The Romans used it as **A**.	
	Beth, the house, may have derived from a more rectangular Egyptian alphabetic glyph of a reed shelter (but which stood for the sound h). The Greeks called it **beta** (B), and it was passed on to the Romans as **B**.	
	Gimel, the camel, may have originally been the image of a boomerang-like throwing stick. The Greeks called it **gamma** (Γ). The Etruscans -- who had no g sound -- used it for the k sound, and passed it on to the Romans as **C**. They in turn added a short bar to it to make it do double duty as **G**.	
	Daleth, the door, may have originally been a fish. The Greeks turned it into **delta** (Δ), and passed it on to the Romans as **D**.	

He may have meant window, but originally represented a man, facing us with raised arms, calling out or praying. The Greeks used it for the vowel **epsilon** (E, "simple E"). The Romans used it as **E**.

Waw, the hook, may originally have represented a mace. The Greeks used one version of waw which looked like our F, which they called digamma, for the number 6. This was used by the Etruscans for v, and they passed it on to the Romans as **F**. The Greeks had a second version -- **upsilon** (Υ) -- which they moved to the back of their alphabet. The Romans used a version of upsilon for **V**, which later would be written **U** as well, then adopted the Greek form as **Y**. In 7th century England, the **W** -- "double-u" -- was created.

Zayin may have meant sword or some other kind of weapon. The Greeks used it for **zeta** (Z). The Romans only adopted it later as **Z**, and put it at the end of their alphabet.

H.eth, the fence, was a "deep throat" (pharyngeal) consonant. The Greeks used it for the vowel **eta** (H), but the Romans used it for **H**.

Teth may have originally represented a spindle. The Greeks used it for **theta** (Θ), but the Romans, who did not have the th sound, dropped it.

Yodh, the hand, began as a representation of the entire arm. The Greeks used a highly simplified version of it for **iota** (I). The Romans used it as **I**, and later added a

	variation for **J**.	
	Kaph, the hollow or palm of the hand, was adopted by the Greeks for **kappa** (K) and passed it on to the Romans as **K**.	
	Lamedh began as a picture of an ox stick or goad. The Greeks used it for **lambda** (Λ). The Romans turned it into **L**.	
	Mem, the water, became the Greek **mu** (M). The Romans kept it as **M**.	
	Nun, the fish, was originally a snake or eel. The Greeks used it for **nu** (N), and the Romans for **N**.	
	Samekh, which also meant fish, is of uncertain origin. It may have originally represented a tent peg or some kind of support. It bears a strong resemblance to an Egyptian pillar seen in many sacred carvings. The Greeks used it for **xi** (Ξ) and a simplified variation of it for **chi** (X). The Romans kept only the variation as **X**.	
	'ayin, the eye, was another "deep throat" consonant. The Greeks used it for **omicron** (O, "little O"). They developed a variation of it for **omega** (Ω, "big O"), and put it at the end of their alphabet. The Romans kept the original for **O**.	

٦	**Pe**, the mouth, may have originally been a symbol for a corner. The Greeks used it for **pi** (Π). The Romans closed up one side and turned it into **P**.	⌐
ᴨ	**Sade**, a sound between s and sh, is of uncertain origin. It may have originally been a symbol for a plant, but later looks more like a fish hook. The Greeks did not use it, although an odd variation does show up as sampi (ϡ), a symbol for 900. The Romans had no need for it.	ϡ
φ	**Qoph**, the monkey, may have originally represented a knot. It was used for a sound similar to k but further back in the mouth. The Greeks only used it for the number 90 (Ϙ), but the Etruscans and Romans kept it for **Q**.	φ
⊲	**Resh**, the head, was used by the Greeks for **rho** (P). The Romans added a line to differentiate it from their P and made it **R**.	⌐
W	**Shin**, the tooth, may have originally represented a bow. Although it was first pronounced sh, the Greeks used it sideways for **sigma** (Σ). The Romans rounded it to make **S**.	ᴗ
X	**Taw**, the mark, was used by the Greeks for **tau** (T). The Romans used it for **T**.	X

Bibliography

Anchor Bible Dictionary, Doubleday (New York), 1992.

Angus, S.A., The Mystery Religions, Dover Publications (New York), 1975; replicate of 1928 edition

Armstrong, Karen, A History of God, Alfred A. Knopf (New York), 1993

Asimov, Isaac, Asimov's Guide to the Bible, The Old Testament, Avon Books (New York), 1971

Atkins, G. Glenn and Braden, Charles, Procession of the Gods, Harper & Brothers (New York), 1936

Baigent, Michael, Richard Leigh, Henry Lincoln, The Messianic Legacy, Dell (New York), 1986

Baring-Gould, Sabine, Curious Myths of the Middle Ages, edited by Edward Hardy, Barnes & Noble Books (New York), 1994

Barnes, Harry Elmer, An Intellectual and Cultural History of the Western World, Dover Publications (New York), 1965

Beltz, Walter, God and The Gods, Pelican Books (New York), 1973

Bobrick, Benson, Wide as the Waters, Simon & Schuster (New York), 2001

Boorstin, Daniel J., The Discovers, Random House (New York), 1983

Bossy, John, Christianity in the West 1400-1700, Oxford University Press (New York), 1985

Bowersock, G.W., Hellenism in Late Antiquity, University of Michigan Press (Lansing, MI), 1990

Brandon, S.G.F., The Trial of Jesus of Nazareth, Scarborough House Briarcliff Manor (New York), 1979

Bright, John, History of Israel, SCM (London, England), 1962

Brinton, Crane et. al, editors, A History of Civilization, Vol. 1, Prentice Hall Inc. (Englewood Cliffs, N.J.), 1967

Brown, Schuyler, The Origins of Christianity, Oxford University Press (New York), 1984

Bryan, Mike, Chapter and verse, Random House (New York), 1991

Burleigh, Michael, Earthly Powers, Harper-Collins (New York), 2005

Burns, Edward McNall, Western Civilizations, W.W. Norton & Co. (New York), 1958

Carcopino, Jerome, Daily Life in Ancient Rome, Yale University Press (New Haven, CT), 1968

Carey, John, Ed., Eyewitness to History, Harvard University Press (Cambridge, MA), 1987

Carpenter, Humphrey, Jesus, Hill and Wang (New York), 1980

Carroll, James, Constantine's Sword, Houghton Mifflin Co. (Boston), 2001

Chadwick, Henry, The Early Church, Pelican Books (New York), 1983

Cheetham, Nicholas, Keepers of the Keys, Charles Scribner's Sons (New York), 1983

Clark, Kenneth, Civilization, Harper & Row (New York), 1969

Cohn, Haim, The Trial and Death of Jesus, Harper & Row (New York), 1967

Crossan, John Dominic, The Historical Jesus, HarperSan Francisco (San Francisco, CA), 1992

--- Who Killed Jesus? HarperSanFrancisco (San Francisco, CA), 1995

Cumont, Franz, The Mysteries of Mithra, Dover Publications (New York), 1956

Dartmouth Bible, Houghton Mifflin Co. (Boston, MA) 1961

Dickens, A.G., Reformation and Society in Sixteenth-Century Europe, Harcourt, Brace & World Inc. (New York) 1966

Dimont, Max, Jews, God and History, Simon and Schuster (New York), 1962

--- The Indestructible Jews, New American Library (New York), 1973

Eban, Abba, My People, Vol. 1, Behrman House Inc. (New York), 1978.

Ehrman, Bart. D., Jesus, Apocalyptic Prophet of the New Millennium, Oxford University Press (New York), 1999

-- The Lost Gospel of Judas Iscariot, Oxford University Press (New York), 2006

Eisenman, Robert and Michael Wise, The Dead Sea Scrolls Uncovered, Barnes & Noble (New York), 1994

Eisenman, Robert, James, 1996

Encyclopedia Judaeica, Keter Publishing House (Jerusalem), 1972

Erdoes, Richard, AD 1000, Barnes & Noble Books (New York), 1995

Eusebius, The History of the Church, trans. G.A. Williamson, Penguin Books (New York), 1981

Ferrell, Lori Anne, The Bible and the People, Yale Press (New Haven), 2008

Finkelstein, Israel and Neil Asher Silberman, David and Solomon, Free Press (New York), 2006

Fox, Robin Lane, Pagans and Christians. Alfred A. Knopf Inc. (New York), 1987

---The Classical World, Basic Books, (New York), 2006

Franck, Adolphe, The Kabbalah, Bell Publishing (New York), 1940

Friedrich, Otto, The End of the World: A History, Coward, McCann & Geogheghan (New York), 1982

Garrison, Omar V., The Encyclopedia of Prophecy, Citadel Press, (Secaucus, NJ), 1978

Gibbon Edward, The Decline and Fall of The Roman Empire, The Modern Library, (New York)

Glover, T.R., The Ancient World, Penguin Books (Baltimore, MD), 1964

Grant, Michael, Jesus: An Historian's Review of the Gospels, Charles Scribner's Sons (New York), 1977.

Grayzel, Solomon, A History of the Jews, Jewish Publication Society of America (New York), 1967

Greenstone, Julius, The Messiah Idea in Jewish History, Jewish Publication Society (Philadelphia, PA), 1907

Guban, Susan, Judas: A Biography, Norton & Sons (New York), 2009

Guignebert, Charles, Jesus, University Books (New York), 1956

Heidel, Alexander, The Gilgamesh Epic and Old Testament Parallels, Chicago Press (Chicago, IL) 1963

Herodotus, The Histories, Trans. Aubrey de Selincourt, Penguin Books (New York), 1980

James, E.O, The Ancient Gods, G.P. Putnam's Sons (New York), 1960

Jenkins, Philip, Mystics and Messiahs, Oxford University Press (New York), 2000

Jewish Encyclopedia: www.jewishencyclopedia.com, 2002

Johnson, Paul, A History of Christianity, Atheneum (New York), 1979

Josephus, Flavius, Collected Works, translated by William Whiston, Baker Book House (Grand Rapids, MI), 1982

Kaufmann, Yehezkel, The Religion of Israel, Trans. Moshe Greenberg, University of Chicago Press (Chicago, IL) 1956

Kavanaugh., Fr. James, A Modern Priest looks at His Outdated Church, Trident Press (New York), 1967

Keller, Wilhelm, The Bible As History, second edition, Bantam Books (New York), 1982

Kirsch, Jonathan, A History of the End of the World, Harper-Collins (San Francisco), 2006

Klingaman, William, The First Century, HarperCollins Publishers (New York), 1990

Langmuir, Gavin. I, History, Religions and Institutions, University of California Press (Los Angeles), 1990

Legge, Francis, Forerunners and Rivals of Christianity, University Books (Hyde Park, NY), 1964

Longford, Elizabeth, ed., The Oxford Book of Royal Anecdotes, Oxford University Press (Oxford, England), 1989

Maccoby, Hyam, The Mythmaker: Paul and the Invention of Christianity, Harper & Row (San Francisco, CA), 1987

--- Judas Iscariot and the Myth of Jewish Evil, The Free Press (New York), 1992

Matthews, Roy T. and F. DeWitt Plat, The Western Humanities, Mayfield Publishing (Mountain View, CA), 1992

McCall, Andrew, The Medieval Underworld, Barnes & Noble (New York), 1993

Meagher, John C., The Trueing of Christianity, Doubleday (New York), 1990

Miller, J. Maxwell and John H. Hayes, A History of Ancient Israel and Judah, Westminster Press (Philadelphia, PA), 1986

Moynihan, Brian, The Faith, Random House (New York), 2002

Nigosian, S.A., World Faiths, St. Martins Press (New York), 1990

Noth, Martin, The History of Israel, trans. Dr. P.R. Ackroyd, Harper & Row (New York), 1960

Oden Robert A. Jr., The Bible Without Theology, Harper & Row (San Francisco, CA), 1987

O'Grady, Jean, Early Christian Heresies, Barnes & Noble (New York), 1985

Pagels, Elaine, The Origin of Satan, Random House (New York), 1995

Parrinder, Geoffrey ed., World Religions, Facts on File (New York), 1984

Pelikan, Jaroslave, Whose Bible Is It? Penguin Group (New York), 2005

Perera, Victor, "Burning Questions," New Yorker Magazine, Nov. 6, 1995

Pfeifer, Charles F., The Dead Sea Scrolls and the Bible, Weathervane Books (New York), 1969

Potok, Chaim, Wanderings, Fawcett Crest Books (New York), 1978

Redhead, Briand and Frances Gumley, The Good Book, Gerald Duckworth & Co. Ltd. (London, England), 1987

Reiss, Tom, The Orientalist, Random House (New York), 2005

Robertson, J.M., Pagan Christs, Dorset Press (New York), 1987

Romer, John, Testament, The Bible and History, Henry Holt & Co. (New York), 1988

Scholem, Gershom, Sabbatai Sevi: The Mystical Messiah, Translated by Rabbi J. Zwi Werblowsky. Princeton University Press (Princeton, NJ), 1973

Schonfield, Hugh, The Passover Plot, Bantam Books Inc. (New York), 1967

--- Those Incredible Christians, Element Books Ltd. (Dorset, England), 1985

Schurer, Emil, Jewish People in the Time of Jesus, ed. Nathan Glatzer, Schocken Books (New York), 1961

Suetonius, The Twelve Caesars, trans. Robert Graves, Penguin Books (New York), 1978

Sheler, Jeffrey, Is the Bible True? HarperSan Francisco, 1999

Shermer, Michael & Grobman, Alex, Denying History, University of California Press (Los Angeles), 2000

Shorto, Russell, Gospel Truth, Riverhead Books (New York), 1997

Swah, Eva, Eve of Destruction, Lowell House (Los Angeles), 1995

Smith, Homer W., Man and His Gods, Grosset & Dunlap (New York), 1957

Smith, Huston, The Religions of Man, Harper & Row (New York), 1965

Smith, Morton, Jesus the Magician, Barnes & Noble (New York), 1993

The Holy Scriptures, Jewish Publication Society of America (New York), 1964

Wallechinsky, David and Amy Wallace, The Book of Lists, Little, Brown and Co. (New York), 1993

Walsh, Michael, The Triumph of the Meek, Harper & Row (San Francisco, CA), 1999

Weber, Eugen, Apocalypses, Harvard University Press (Cambridge, MA), 1999

Wells, G.A., Who Was Jesus?, Open Court Publishing Co., (La Salle, IL), 1989

Werblowsky, R. J. Zwi and Geoffrey Wigoden, The Encyclopedia of the Jewish Religion, Holt, Rinehart & Winston Inc. (New York), 1965.

Wilson, A.N., God's Funeral, W.W. Norton & Co. (New York), 1999

Wilson, Ian, Jesus: The Evidence, Harper & Row (San Francisco, CA), 1984

Wroe, Ann, Pontius Pilate, Random House (New York), 1999

About the Author

A native of Maine who grew up in Northeast Ohio, William Paul Lazarus began studying religious history as a child and has never stopped. By age 13, he was teaching Sunday School. After moving to Florida in 1986, he branched out to teaching in his home and at various institutions, including Daytona Beach Community College and Stetson University. A professional journalist with a career in media and long-time college writing instructor, he regularly speaks at churches and synagogues around Florida, and had a successful radio show on WROD (1340 AM) in Daytona Beach. His book on religious history, *Comparative Religion for Dummies*, was published by Wiley Press in 2008. Other books include *Joy to the World: The Lore and Tradition of Christmas Carols* (2020); and *Messiah* (2021)

He and his wife live in Ormond Beach, Florida.

His name is real, despite the biblical connotations. His grandfather had a long Russian last name and did not like it, so, while in college, unilaterally changed it to Lazarus, a name he thought was shorter and easier to pronounce.

www.ingramcontent.com/pod-product-compliance
Lightning Source LLC
Chambersburg PA
CBHW071324120626
46546CB00002B/427